50% OFF
TExES Science of Teaching Reading (293) Prep Course!

By Mometrix

Dear Customer,

We consider it an honor and a privilege that you chose our TExES Science of Teaching Reading Study Guide. As a way of showing our appreciation and to help us better serve you, we are offering **50% off our online TExES 293 Prep Course**. Many TExES 293 courses are needlessly expensive and don't deliver enough value. With our course, you get access to the best TExES Science of Teaching Reading prep material, and **you only pay half price**.

We have structured our online course to perfectly complement your printed study guide. The TExES 293 Prep Course contains **in-depth lessons** that cover all the most important topics, **40+ video reviews** that explain difficult concepts, over **350 practice questions** to ensure you feel prepared, and more than **300+ digital flashcards**, so you can study while you're on the go.

Online TExES Science of Teaching Reading (293) Prep Course

Topics Included:

- Reading Pedagogy
  - Curriculum and Instruction
  - Diverse Learners and Specific Needs
- Reading Development: Foundational Skills
  - Grammar and Comprehension
  - Fluency Acquisition
- Reading Development: Comprehension
  - Vocabulary Development and Word Analysis
  - Context Clues and Affixes

Course Features:

- TExES Science of Teaching Reading Study Guide
  - Get content that complements our best-selling study guide.
- Full-Length Practice Tests
  - With over 350 practice questions, you can test yourself again and again.
- Mobile Friendly
  - If you need to study on the go, the course is easily accessible from your mobile device.
- TExES 293 Flashcards
  - Our course includes a flashcard mode with over 300 content cards to help you study.

To receive this discount, visit us at mometrix.com/university/texesstr/ or simply scan this QR code with your smartphone. At the checkout page, enter the discount code: **texstr50off**

If you have any questions or concerns, please contact us at support@mometrix.com.

FREE Study Skills Videos/DVD Offer

Dear Customer,

Thank you for your purchase from Mometrix! We consider it an honor and a privilege that you have purchased our product and we want to ensure your satisfaction.

As part of our ongoing effort to meet the needs of test takers, we have developed a set of Study Skills Videos that we would like to give you for <u>FREE</u>. These videos cover our *best practices* for getting ready for your exam, from how to use our study materials to how to best prepare for the day of the test.

All that we ask is that you email us with feedback that would describe your experience so far with our product. Good, bad, or indifferent, we want to know what you think!

To get your FREE Study Skills Videos, you can use the **QR code** below, or send us an **email** at <u>studyvideos@mometrix.com</u> with *FREE VIDEOS* in the subject line and the following information in the body of the email:

- The name of the product you purchased.
- Your product rating on a scale of 1-5, with 5 being the highest rating.
- Your feedback. It can be long, short, or anything in between. We just want to know your impressions and experience so far with our product. (Good feedback might include how our study material met your needs and ways we might be able to make it even better. You could highlight features that you found helpful or features that you think we should add.)

If you have any questions or concerns, please don't hesitate to contact me directly.

Thanks again!

Sincerely,

Jay Willis
Vice President
<u>jay.willis@mometrix.com</u>
1-800-673-8175

TExES

Science of Teaching Reading (293) Secrets Study Guide

**TExES Exam Review
and Practice Test for the
Texas Examinations
of Educator Standards**

Written and edited by Mometrix Test Prep

Printed in the United States of America

This paper meets the requirements of ANSI/NISO Z39.48-1992 (Permanence of Paper).

Mometrix offers volume discount pricing to institutions. For more information or a price quote, please contact our sales department at sales@mometrix.com or 888-248-1219.

Mometrix Media LLC is not affiliated with or endorsed by any official testing organization. All organizational and test names are trademarks of their respective owners.

Paperback
ISBN 13: 978-1-5167-1514-5
ISBN 10: 1-5167-1514-4

DEAR FUTURE EXAM SUCCESS STORY

First of all, **THANK YOU** for purchasing Mometrix study materials!

Second, congratulations! You are one of the few determined test-takers who are committed to doing whatever it takes to excel on your exam. **You have come to the right place.** We developed these study materials with one goal in mind: to deliver you the information you need in a format that's concise and easy to use.

In addition to optimizing your guide for the content of the test, we've outlined our recommended steps for breaking down the preparation process into small, attainable goals so you can make sure you stay on track.

We've also analyzed the entire test-taking process, identifying the most common pitfalls and showing how you can overcome them and be ready for any curveball the test throws you.

Standardized testing is one of the biggest obstacles on your road to success, which only increases the importance of doing well in the high-pressure, high-stakes environment of test day. Your results on this test could have a significant impact on your future, and this guide provides the information and practical advice to help you achieve your full potential on test day.

Your success is our success

We would love to hear from you! If you would like to share the story of your exam success or if you have any questions or comments in regard to our products, please contact us at **800-673-8175** or **support@mometrix.com**.

Thanks again for your business and we wish you continued success!

Sincerely,
The Mometrix Test Preparation Team

Need more help? Check out our flashcards at:
http://mometrixflashcards.com/TExES

TABLE OF CONTENTS

Introduction

Thank you for purchasing this resource! You have made the choice to prepare yourself for a test that could have a huge impact on your future, and this guide is designed to help you be fully ready for test day. Obviously, it's important to have a solid understanding of the test material, but you also need to be prepared for the unique environment and stressors of the test, so that you can perform to the best of your abilities.

For this purpose, the first section that appears in this guide is the **Secret Keys**. We've devoted countless hours to meticulously researching what works and what doesn't, and we've boiled down our findings to the five most impactful steps you can take to improve your performance on the test. We start at the beginning with study planning and move through the preparation process, all the way to the testing strategies that will help you get the most out of what you know when you're finally sitting in front of the test.

We recommend that you start preparing for your test as far in advance as possible. However, if you've bought this guide as a last-minute study resource and only have a few days before your test, we recommend that you skip over the first two Secret Keys since they address a long-term study plan.

If you struggle with **test anxiety**, we strongly encourage you to check out our recommendations for how you can overcome it. Test anxiety is a formidable foe, but it can be beaten, and we want to make sure you have the tools you need to defeat it.

Review Video Directory

As you work your way through this guide, you will see numerous review video links interspersed with the written content. If you would like to access all of these review videos in one place, click on the video directory link found on the bonus page: **mometrix.com/bonus948/texesscitread**

1

Secret Key #1 – Plan Big, Study Small

There's a lot riding on your performance. If you want to ace this test, you're going to need to keep your skills sharp and the material fresh in your mind. You need a plan that lets you review everything you need to know while still fitting in your schedule. We'll break this strategy down into three categories.

Information Organization

Start with the information you already have: the official test outline. From this, you can make a complete list of all the concepts you need to cover before the test. Organize these concepts into groups that can be studied together, and create a list of any related vocabulary you need to learn so you can brush up on any difficult terms. You'll want to keep this vocabulary list handy once you actually start studying since you may need to add to it along the way.

Time Management

Once you have your set of study concepts, decide how to spread them out over the time you have left before the test. Break your study plan into small, clear goals so you have a manageable task for each day and know exactly what you're doing. Then just focus on one small step at a time. When you manage your time this way, you don't need to spend hours at a time studying. Studying a small block of content for a short period each day helps you retain information better and avoid stressing over how much you have left to do. You can relax knowing that you have a plan to cover everything in time. In order for this strategy to be effective though, you have to start studying early and stick to your schedule. Avoid the exhaustion and futility that comes from last-minute cramming!

Study Environment

The environment you study in has a big impact on your learning. Studying in a coffee shop, while probably more enjoyable, is not likely to be as fruitful as studying in a quiet room. It's important to keep distractions to a minimum. You're only planning to study for a short block of time, so make the most of it. Don't pause to check your phone or get up to find a snack. It's also important to **avoid multitasking**. Research has consistently shown that multitasking will make your studying dramatically less effective. Your study area should also be comfortable and well-lit so you don't have the distraction of straining your eyes or sitting on an uncomfortable chair.

 The time of day you study is also important. You want to be rested and alert. Don't wait until just before bedtime. Study when you'll be most likely to comprehend and remember. Even better, if you know what time of day your test will be, set that time aside for study. That way your brain will be used to working on that subject at that specific time and you'll have a better chance of recalling information.

Finally, it can be helpful to team up with others who are studying for the same test. Your actual studying should be done in as isolated an environment as possible, but the work of organizing the information and setting up the study plan can be divided up. In between study sessions, you can discuss with your teammates the concepts that you're all studying and quiz each other on the details. Just be sure that your teammates are as serious about the test as you are. If you find that your study time is being replaced with social time, you might need to find a new team.

2

Secret Key #2 – Make Your Studying Count

You're devoting a lot of time and effort to preparing for this test, so you want to be absolutely certain it will pay off. This means doing more than just reading the content and hoping you can remember it on test day. It's important to make every minute of study count. There are two main areas you can focus on to make your studying count.

Retention

It doesn't matter how much time you study if you can't remember the material. You need to make sure you are retaining the concepts. To check your retention of the information you're learning, try recalling it at later times with minimal prompting. Try carrying around flashcards and glance at one or two from time to time or ask a friend who's also studying for the test to quiz you.

To enhance your retention, look for ways to put the information into practice so that you can apply it rather than simply recalling it. If you're using the information in practical ways, it will be much easier to remember. Similarly, it helps to solidify a concept in your mind if you're not only reading it to yourself but also explaining it to someone else. Ask a friend to let you teach them about a concept you're a little shaky on (or speak aloud to an imaginary audience if necessary). As you try to summarize, define, give examples, and answer your friend's questions, you'll understand the concepts better and they will stay with you longer. Finally, step back for a big picture view and ask yourself how each piece of information fits with the whole subject. When you link the different concepts together and see them working together as a whole, it's easier to remember the individual components.

Finally, practice showing your work on any multi-step problems, even if you're just studying. Writing out each step you take to solve a problem will help solidify the process in your mind, and you'll be more likely to remember it during the test.

Modality

Modality simply refers to the means or method by which you study. Choosing a study modality that fits your own individual learning style is crucial. No two people learn best in exactly the same way, so it's important to know your strengths and use them to your advantage.

For example, if you learn best by visualization, focus on visualizing a concept in your mind and draw an image or a diagram. Try color-coding your notes, illustrating them, or creating symbols that will trigger your mind to recall a learned concept. If you learn best by hearing or discussing information, find a study partner who learns the same way or read aloud to yourself. Think about how to put the information in your own words. Imagine that you are giving a lecture on the topic and record yourself so you can listen to it later.

For any learning style, flashcards can be helpful. Organize the information so you can take advantage of spare moments to review. Underline key words or phrases. Use different colors for different categories. Mnemonic devices (such as creating a short list in which every item starts with the same letter) can also help with retention. Find what works best for you and use it to store the information in your mind most effectively and easily.

3

Secret Key #3 – Practice the Right Way

Your success on test day depends not only on how many hours you put into preparing, but also on whether you prepared the right way. It's good to check along the way to see if your studying is paying off. One of the most effective ways to do this is by taking practice tests to evaluate your progress. Practice tests are useful because they show exactly where you need to improve. Every time you take a practice test, pay special attention to these three groups of questions:

- The questions you got wrong
- The questions you had to guess on, even if you guessed right
- The questions you found difficult or slow to work through

This will show you exactly what your weak areas are, and where you need to devote more study time. Ask yourself why each of these questions gave you trouble. Was it because you didn't understand the material? Was it because you didn't remember the vocabulary? Do you need more repetitions on this type of question to build speed and confidence? Dig into those questions and figure out how you can strengthen your weak areas as you go back to review the material.

 Additionally, many practice tests have a section explaining the answer choices. It can be tempting to read the explanation and think that you now have a good understanding of the concept. However, an explanation likely only covers part of the question's broader context. Even if the explanation makes perfect sense, **go back and investigate** every concept related to the question until you're positive you have a thorough understanding.

As you go along, keep in mind that the practice test is just that: practice. Memorizing these questions and answers will not be very helpful on the actual test because it is unlikely to have any of the same exact questions. If you only know the right answers to the sample questions, you won't be prepared for the real thing. **Study the concepts** until you understand them fully, and then you'll be able to answer any question that shows up on the test.

It's important to wait on the practice tests until you're ready. If you take a test on your first day of study, you may be overwhelmed by the amount of material covered and how much you need to learn. Work up to it gradually.

On test day, you'll need to be prepared for answering questions, managing your time, and using the test-taking strategies you've learned. It's a lot to balance, like a mental marathon that will have a big impact on your future. Like training for a marathon, you'll need to start slowly and work your way up. When test day arrives, you'll be ready.

Start with the strategies you've read in the first two Secret Keys—plan your course and study in the way that works best for you. If you have time, consider using multiple study resources to get different approaches to the same concepts. It can be helpful to see difficult concepts from more than one angle. Then find a good source for practice tests. Many times, the test website will suggest potential study resources or provide sample tests.

Practice Test Strategy

If you're able to find at least three practice tests, we recommend this strategy:

UNTIMED AND OPEN-BOOK PRACTICE

Take the first test with no time constraints and with your notes and study guide handy. Take your time and focus on applying the strategies you've learned.

TIMED AND OPEN-BOOK PRACTICE

Take the second practice test open-book as well, but set a timer and practice pacing yourself to finish in time.

TIMED AND CLOSED-BOOK PRACTICE

Take any other practice tests as if it were test day. Set a timer and put away your study materials. Sit at a table or desk in a quiet room, imagine yourself at the testing center, and answer questions as quickly and accurately as possible.

Keep repeating timed and closed-book tests on a regular basis until you run out of practice tests or it's time for the actual test. Your mind will be ready for the schedule and stress of test day, and you'll be able to focus on recalling the material you've learned.

Secret Key #4 – Pace Yourself

Once you're fully prepared for the material on the test, your biggest challenge on test day will be managing your time. Just knowing that the clock is ticking can make you panic even if you have plenty of time left. Work on pacing yourself so you can build confidence against the time constraints of the exam. Pacing is a difficult skill to master, especially in a high-pressure environment, so **practice is vital**.

Set time expectations for your pace based on how much time is available. For example, if a section has 60 questions and the time limit is 30 minutes, you know you have to average 30 seconds or less per question in order to answer them all. Although 30 seconds is the hard limit, set 25 seconds per question as your goal, so you reserve extra time to spend on harder questions. When you budget extra time for the harder questions, you no longer have any reason to stress when those questions take longer to answer.

Don't let this time expectation distract you from working through the test at a calm, steady pace, but keep it in mind so you don't spend too much time on any one question. Recognize that taking extra time on one question you don't understand may keep you from answering two that you do understand later in the test. If your time limit for a question is up and you're still not sure of the answer, mark it and move on, and come back to it later if the time and the test format allow. If the testing format doesn't allow you to return to earlier questions, just make an educated guess; then put it out of your mind and move on.

On the easier questions, be careful not to rush. It may seem wise to hurry through them so you have more time for the challenging ones, but it's not worth missing one if you know the concept and just didn't take the time to read the question fully. Work efficiently but make sure you understand the question and have looked at all of the answer choices, since more than one may seem right at first.

Even if you're paying attention to the time, you may find yourself a little behind at some point. You should speed up to get back on track, but do so wisely. Don't panic; just take a few seconds less on each question until you're caught up. Don't guess without thinking, but do look through the answer choices and eliminate any you know are wrong. If you can get down to two choices, it is often worthwhile to guess from those. Once you've chosen an answer, move on and don't dwell on any that you skipped or had to hurry through. If a question was taking too long, chances are it was one of the harder ones, so you weren't as likely to get it right anyway.

On the other hand, if you find yourself getting ahead of schedule, it may be beneficial to slow down a little. The more quickly you work, the more likely you are to make a careless mistake that will affect your score. You've budgeted time for each question, so don't be afraid to spend that time. Practice an efficient but careful pace to get the most out of the time you have.

6

Secret Key #5 – Have a Plan for Guessing

When you're taking the test, you may find yourself stuck on a question. Some of the answer choices seem better than others, but you don't see the one answer choice that is obviously correct. What do you do?

The scenario described above is very common, yet most test takers have not effectively prepared for it. Developing and practicing a plan for guessing may be one of the single most effective uses of your time as you get ready for the exam.

In developing your plan for guessing, there are three questions to address:

- When should you start the guessing process?
- How should you narrow down the choices?
- Which answer should you choose?

When to Start the Guessing Process

Unless your plan for guessing is to select C every time (which, despite its merits, is not what we recommend), you need to leave yourself enough time to apply your answer elimination strategies. Since you have a limited amount of time for each question, that means that if you're going to give yourself the best shot at guessing correctly, you have to decide quickly whether or not you will guess.

Of course, the best-case scenario is that you don't have to guess at all, so first, see if you can answer the question based on your knowledge of the subject and basic reasoning skills. Focus on the key words in the question and try to jog your memory of related topics. Give yourself a chance to bring the knowledge to mind, but once you realize that you don't have (or you can't access) the knowledge you need to answer the question, it's time to start the guessing process.

It's almost always better to start the guessing process too early than too late. It only takes a few seconds to remember something and answer the question from knowledge. Carefully eliminating wrong answer choices takes longer. Plus, going through the process of eliminating answer choices can actually help jog your memory.

Summary: Start the guessing process as soon as you decide that you can't answer the question based on your knowledge.

7

How to Narrow Down the Choices

The next chapter in this book (**Test-Taking Strategies**) includes a wide range of strategies for how to approach questions and how to look for answer choices to eliminate. You will definitely want to read those carefully, practice them, and figure out which ones work best for you. Here though, we're going to address a mindset rather than a particular strategy.

Your odds of guessing an answer correctly depend on how many options you are choosing from.

Number of options left	5	4	3	2	1
Odds of guessing correctly	20%	25%	33%	50%	100%

You can see from this chart just how valuable it is to be able to eliminate incorrect answers and make an educated guess, but there are two things that many test takers do that cause them to miss out on the benefits of guessing:

- Accidentally eliminating the correct answer
- Selecting an answer based on an impression

We'll look at the first one here, and the second one in the next section.

To avoid accidentally eliminating the correct answer, we recommend a thought exercise called **the $5 challenge**. In this challenge, you only eliminate an answer choice from contention if you are willing to bet $5 on it being wrong. Why $5? Five dollars is a small but not insignificant amount of money. It's an amount you could afford to lose but wouldn't want to throw away. And while losing

$5 once might not hurt too much, doing it twenty times will set you back $100. In the same way, each small decision you make—eliminating a choice here, guessing on a question there—won't by itself impact your score very much, but when you put them all together, they can make a big difference. By holding each answer choice elimination decision to a higher standard, you can reduce the risk of accidentally eliminating the correct answer.

The $5 challenge can also be applied in a positive sense: If you are willing to bet $5 that an answer choice *is* correct, go ahead and mark it as correct.

Summary: Only eliminate an answer choice if you are willing to bet $5 that it is wrong.

8

Which Answer to Choose

You're taking the test. You've run into a hard question and decided you'll have to guess. You've eliminated all the answer choices you're willing to bet $5 on. Now you have to pick an answer. Why do we even need to talk about this? Why can't you just pick whichever one you feel like when the time comes?

The answer to these questions is that if you don't come into the test with a plan, you'll rely on your impression to select an answer choice, and if you do that, you risk falling into a trap. The test writers know that everyone who takes their test will be guessing on some of the questions, so they intentionally write wrong answer choices to seem plausible. You still have to pick an answer though, and if the wrong answer choices are designed to look right, how can you ever be sure that you're not falling for their trap? The best solution we've found to this dilemma is to take the decision out of your hands entirely. Here is the process we recommend:

Once you've eliminated any choices that you are confident (willing to bet $5) are wrong, select the first remaining choice as your answer.

Whether you choose to select the first remaining choice, the second, or the last, the important thing is that you use some preselected standard. Using this approach guarantees that you will not be enticed into selecting an answer choice that looks right, because you are not basing your decision on how the answer choices look.

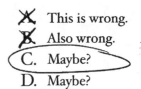

This is not meant to make you question your knowledge. Instead, it is to help you recognize the difference between your knowledge and your impressions. There's a huge difference between thinking an answer is right because of what you know, and thinking an answer is right because it looks or sounds like it should be right.

Summary: To ensure that your selection is appropriately random, make a predetermined selection from among all answer choices you have not eliminated.

Test-Taking Strategies

This section contains a list of test-taking strategies that you may find helpful as you work through the test. By taking what you know and applying logical thought, you can maximize your chances of answering any question correctly!

It is very important to realize that every question is different and every person is different: no single strategy will work on every question, and no single strategy will work for every person. That's why we've included all of them here, so you can try them out and determine which ones work best for different types of questions and which ones work best for you.

Question Strategies

⊘ READ CAREFULLY

Read the question and the answer choices carefully. Don't miss the question because you misread the terms. You have plenty of time to read each question thoroughly and make sure you understand what is being asked. Yet a happy medium must be attained, so don't waste too much time. You must read carefully and efficiently.

⊘ CONTEXTUAL CLUES

Look for contextual clues. If the question includes a word you are not familiar with, look at the immediate context for some indication of what the word might mean. Contextual clues can often give you all the information you need to decipher the meaning of an unfamiliar word. Even if you can't determine the meaning, you may be able to narrow down the possibilities enough to make a solid guess at the answer to the question.

⊘ PREFIXES

If you're having trouble with a word in the question or answer choices, try dissecting it. Take advantage of every clue that the word might include. Prefixes can be a huge help. Usually, they allow you to determine a basic meaning. *Pre-* means before, *post-* means after, *pro-* is positive, *de-* is negative. From prefixes, you can get an idea of the general meaning of the word and try to put it into context.

⊘ HEDGE WORDS

Watch out for critical hedge words, such as *likely, may, can, sometimes, often, almost, mostly, usually, generally, rarely,* and *sometimes.* Question writers insert these hedge phrases to cover every possibility. Often an answer choice will be wrong simply because it leaves no room for exception. Be on guard for answer choices that have definitive words such as *exactly* and *always.*

⊘ SWITCHBACK WORDS

Stay alert for *switchbacks.* These are the words and phrases frequently used to alert you to shifts in thought. The most common switchback words are *but, although,* and *however.* Others include *nevertheless, on the other hand, even though, while, in spite of, despite,* and *regardless of.* Switchback words are important to catch because they can change the direction of the question or an answer choice.

⌀ Face Value

When in doubt, use common sense. Accept the situation in the problem at face value. Don't read too much into it. These problems will not require you to make wild assumptions. If you have to go beyond creativity and warp time or space in order to have an answer choice fit the question, then you should move on and consider the other answer choices. These are normal problems rooted in reality. The applicable relationship or explanation may not be readily apparent, but it is there for you to figure out. Use your common sense to interpret anything that isn't clear.

Answer Choice Strategies

⌀ Answer Selection

The most thorough way to pick an answer choice is to identify and eliminate wrong answers until only one is left, then confirm it is the correct answer. Sometimes an answer choice may immediately seem right, but be careful. The test writers will usually put more than one reasonable answer choice on each question, so take a second to read all of them and make sure that the other choices are not equally obvious. As long as you have time left, it is better to read every answer choice than to pick the first one that looks right without checking the others.

⌀ Answer Choice Families

An answer choice family consists of two (in rare cases, three) answer choices that are very similar in construction and cannot all be true at the same time. If you see two answer choices that are direct opposites or parallels, one of them is usually the correct answer. For instance, if one answer choice says that quantity x increases and another either says that quantity x decreases (opposite) or says that quantity y increases (parallel), then those answer choices would fall into the same family. An answer choice that doesn't match the construction of the answer choice family is more likely to be incorrect. Most questions will not have answer choice families, but when they do appear, you should be prepared to recognize them.

⌀ Eliminate Answers

Eliminate answer choices as soon as you realize they are wrong, but make sure you consider all possibilities. If you are eliminating answer choices and realize that the last one you are left with is also wrong, don't panic. Start over and consider each choice again. There may be something you missed the first time that you will realize on the second pass.

⌀ Avoid Fact Traps

Don't be distracted by an answer choice that is factually true but doesn't answer the question. You are looking for the choice that answers the question. Stay focused on what the question is asking for so you don't accidentally pick an answer that is true but incorrect. Always go back to the question and make sure the answer choice you've selected actually answers the question and is not merely a true statement.

⌀ Extreme Statements

In general, you should avoid answers that put forth extreme actions as standard practice or proclaim controversial ideas as established fact. An answer choice that states the "process should be used in certain situations, if..." is much more likely to be correct than one that states the "process should be discontinued completely." The first is a calm rational statement and doesn't even make a definitive, uncompromising stance, using a hedge word *if* to provide wiggle room, whereas the second choice is far more extreme.

⊘ Benchmark

As you read through the answer choices and you come across one that seems to answer the question well, mentally select that answer choice. This is not your final answer, but it's the one that will help you evaluate the other answer choices. The one that you selected is your benchmark or standard for judging each of the other answer choices. Every other answer choice must be compared to your benchmark. That choice is correct until proven otherwise by another answer choice beating it. If you find a better answer, then that one becomes your new benchmark. Once you've decided that no other choice answers the question as well as your benchmark, you have your final answer.

⊘ Predict the Answer

Before you even start looking at the answer choices, it is often best to try to predict the answer. When you come up with the answer on your own, it is easier to avoid distractions and traps because you will know exactly what to look for. The right answer choice is unlikely to be word-for-word what you came up with, but it should be a close match. Even if you are confident that you have the right answer, you should still take the time to read each option before moving on.

General Strategies

⊘ Tough Questions

If you are stumped on a problem or it appears too hard or too difficult, don't waste time. Move on! Remember though, if you can quickly check for obviously incorrect answer choices, your chances of guessing correctly are greatly improved. Before you completely give up, at least try to knock out a couple of possible answers. Eliminate what you can and then guess at the remaining answer choices before moving on.

⊘ Check Your Work

Since you will probably not know every term listed and the answer to every question, it is important that you get credit for the ones that you do know. Don't miss any questions through careless mistakes. If at all possible, try to take a second to look back over your answer selection and make sure you've selected the correct answer choice and haven't made a costly careless mistake (such as marking an answer choice that you didn't mean to mark). This quick double check should more than pay for itself in caught mistakes for the time it costs.

⊘ Pace Yourself

It's easy to be overwhelmed when you're looking at a page full of questions; your mind is confused and full of random thoughts, and the clock is ticking down faster than you would like. Calm down and maintain the pace that you have set for yourself. Especially as you get down to the last few minutes of the test, don't let the small numbers on the clock make you panic. As long as you are on track by monitoring your pace, you are guaranteed to have time for each question.

⊘ Don't Rush

It is very easy to make errors when you are in a hurry. Maintaining a fast pace in answering questions is pointless if it makes you miss questions that you would have gotten right otherwise. Test writers like to include distracting information and wrong answers that seem right. Taking a little extra time to avoid careless mistakes can make all the difference in your test score. Find a pace that allows you to be confident in the answers that you select.

12

⊘ Keep Moving

Panicking will not help you pass the test, so do your best to stay calm and keep moving. Taking deep breaths and going through the answer elimination steps you practiced can help to break through a stress barrier and keep your pace.

Final Notes

The combination of a solid foundation of content knowledge and the confidence that comes from practicing your plan for applying that knowledge is the key to maximizing your performance on test day. As your foundation of content knowledge is built up and strengthened, you'll find that the strategies included in this chapter become more and more effective in helping you quickly sift through the distractions and traps of the test to isolate the correct answer.

Now that you're preparing to move forward into the test content chapters of this book, be sure to keep your goal in mind. As you read, think about how you will be able to apply this information on the test. If you've already seen sample questions for the test and you have an idea of the question format and style, try to come up with questions of your own that you can answer based on what you're reading. This will give you valuable practice applying your knowledge in the same ways you can expect to on test day.

Good luck and good studying!

Reading Pedagogy

Transform passive reading into active learning! After immersing yourself in this chapter, put your comprehension to the test by taking a quiz. The insights you gained will stay with you longer this way. Scan the QR code to go directly to the chapter quiz interface for this study guide. If you're using a computer, simply visit the bonus page at **mometrix.com/bonus948/texesscitread** and click the Chapter Quizzes link.

Factors that Impact Student Learning

HOME AND COMMUNITY FACTORS THAT IMPACT STUDENT LEARNING

Students are exposed to multiple social and cultural factors from their homes and communities that significantly impact learning, so it is imperative that the teacher is conscious of these factors to effectively adapt instruction and assessment to enhance students' learning. Students are often held to different academic and behavioral expectations by their parents, depending on their social and cultural background, that affect self-motivation, engagement, and academic performance. When adapting instruction and assessment, teachers must ensure that all students are held to high expectations while providing individual students with the necessary supports for success. Teachers must also consider the availability of community resources that offer support and enhance learning, as this differs among social and cultural groups. Students from low sociocultural backgrounds may lack quality resources such as libraries, tutoring, or after-school activities, so teachers must adapt to include time outside of instruction for completing assignments, additional support, and use of school resources. Community problems pose obstacles that hinder students' motivation, self-concept, and attitude toward learning. It is important that teachers establish a safe, welcoming, and engaging classroom while providing the necessary academic and behavioral supports to foster equity and promote a growth mindset.

SELF-DIRECTED LEARNING

In a **self-directed learning** environment, students are given a sense of agency that enhances self-motivation, feelings of ownership and responsibility for their own learning. By choosing what and how they learn based on their individual interests, learning styles, and preferences, students have the ability to explore and inquire freely, thus increasing their natural curiosity and motivation to do so. In choosing their own learning, students determine their own learning goals, thus creating a sense of ownership and self-responsibility. This sentiment is also increased when students can tailor their learning according to their own needs and challenge themselves based upon their skills and abilities. Furthermore, when students achieve self-decided goals, they develop a sense of ownership over their learning. In order to foster a self-guided environment in which students are fully engaged in their own learning, teachers must adopt a facilitator role in instruction and offer support when necessary. Instruction and assessment must allow multiple opportunities for student choice in how learning is determined and demonstrated. By providing opportunities for self-evaluation and reflection, teachers further facilitate self-motivation, ownership, and responsibility over students' own learning through encouraging them to make personal connections, reflect on accomplishments, and seek areas for self-improvement.

TEACHER ROLES IN STUDENT LEARNING

The teacher's role is multifaceted in nature, and teachers must often adopt multiple roles within a single lesson to effectively facilitate learning and accommodate individual students' needs. The role of the **lecturer**, **model**, and **facilitator** are applicable to different learning situations and have varying impacts on learning. As the lecturer, the teacher delivers direct instruction to students. This role is most appropriate when introducing a new concept, providing instructions for an upcoming activity, or reviewing material. In addition, teachers can effectively communicate new skills, ideas, and thought processes through modeling to students, as this is a highly influential method of instruction. When teachers serve as facilitators, they guide students in learning while offering support, scaffolding, and assistance when necessary. This role is effective in active and open-ended learning situations in which students are encouraged to explore, practice, and engage in creative problem solving. Through this method, teachers allow students to adopt a self-directed approach that encourages ownership over their own learning, thus creating an engaging, empowering learning experience.

IMPACT OF STUDENT ROLES ON LEARNING

Students adopt multiple roles in the learning process, and teachers must be cognizant of individual learning styles and specific learning situations to determine which role is most applicable and effective for enhancing learning. As **active learners**, students participate and interact throughout the learning process. In this role, students are encouraged to implement higher-order thinking skills through exploration, inquiry, and problem solving, thus creating an engaging learning environment that promotes the retainment of information. This role is particularly effective in learning situations in which students are practicing new skills, testing hypotheses, and exploring new concepts. The opportunity to actively participate in learning allows them to better internalize new information and formulate creative solutions to problems. Active learning also occurs in effectively designed collaborative learning situations. As **group participants**, students can build upon one another's skills, abilities, and experiences to solve problems, explore new information, and understand new perspectives to enhance the overall learning experience. When students are learning new skills, behaviors, or thought processes, they often adopt the role of the observer. Modeling is an influential instructional strategy, and in **observing** the teacher or another more experienced individual, students learn to utilize and implement new information in learning situations.

GARDNER'S THEORY OF MULTIPLE INTELLIGENCES

When determining instruction, activities, and assessment, teachers must consider and incorporate students' various approaches to learning. Every student learns differently and has unique needs, and thus, teachers must ensure that auditory, visual, kinesthetic, and tactile learning styles are addressed in all areas of curriculum to maximize students' learning potential. Through incorporating multiple modalities using Howard Gardner's **theory of multiple intelligences** as a framework, teachers can design content and activities that deliver instruction in a variety of ways simultaneously (visual-spatial, linguistic, musical, naturalistic, interpersonal, intrapersonal, logical-mathematical, bodily-kinesthetic). Through this approach, student understanding is reinforced, and each student is provided the opportunity to learn in the way that best suits their individual needs. By differentiating instruction with these modalities, teachers can incorporate several strategies simultaneously when teaching a concept, such as independent practice, cooperative learning, music, art, problem solving, and movement. Opportunities for student choice in learning further allows the integration of multiple modalities in instruction, as it lets students decide the method of learning that is best tailored to their individual learning style and needs.

Howard Gardner's Theory of Multiple Intelligences

Visual/Spatial	Prefers visual representations, able to visualize with the mind's eye, excels in activities that incorporate drawing, building, creative expression, and manipulatives.
Logical-Mathematical	Prefers activities that require order, analysis, and problem-solving using logical reasoning. Excels in solving math equations, conducting science experiments, puzzles, and analyzing data.
Verbal-Linguistic	Prefers learning through reading, writing, speaking, and listening. Often skilled in acquiring foreign languages. Excels in activities that incorporate discussion, debate, oral presentations, and written assignments.
Bodily-Kinesthetic	Prefers hands-on learning experiences that involve movement and physical interaction with the learning environment. Excels in activities that involve sports, dance, building, and hands-on projects.
Interpersonal	Prefers learning opportunities that involve communicating and collaborating with others. Excels in partner, small group, and whole-group learning activities.
Intrapersonal	Prefers to learn and work independently. Usually possesses a strong sense of self-awareness. Excels in activities that allow for independent, self-paced learning and self-reflection.
Musical	Learns best when music is incorporated into instruction. Prefers using songs, mnemonic devices and rhythms to learn concepts and retain information.
Naturalistic	Learns best when opportunities to connect with nature are incorporated into instruction. Prefers activities such as nature walks, identifying and classifying elements of nature, and working outside.

MULTIPLE LITERACIES

Multiple literacies are part of modern learning and business. To be successful, people must effectively process and share different types of information using **multiple media forms**. Therefore, teachers must devote instructional time to teaching students the skills they need to succeed in this technology-rich environment.

Teaching multiple literacies requires a mixture of explicit instruction, guided practice, and opportunities for application. For example, teachers need to teach students to find supporting details in digital texts. They may explicitly teach this skill during mini-lessons by modeling how they highlight key phrases. Teachers may then ask students to highlight key phrases in digital texts independently while they observe and provide feedback. Students may then be given multiple opportunities to apply this skill throughout the year to complete projects and assignments.

Teachers should also provide opportunities for students to interact with texts of all types and communicate using different media. They can offer choices in projects and assignments as long as instructional objectives are met. This method allows students to pursue their own interests and leads to increased engagement and ownership over learning.

CHARACTERISTICS OF AUDITORY LEARNERS

Auditory learners easily gather and process information through listening. For example, they may determine main ideas from lectures, assess subtle details from speakers' tones during conversations, and follow oral directions to complete multistep tasks. Auditory learners often enjoy speaking as well, and they may frequently participate in class discussions and conversations.

Teachers can implement many instructional strategies to support auditory learners. They can incorporate read-alouds, discussions, and lectures into classroom activities. They can provide audio versions of textbooks and storybooks. They can also record lectures so students can listen to them later to prepare for assignments and assessments. Teachers can allow students to interview others to gather information, and they can introduce songs, chants, and rhymes to assist with memorization. When designing projects and assessments, teachers can allow students to complete oral reports or presentations. Additionally, they can allow students to think through problems out loud and offer verbal feedback. Directions can also be given orally.

CHARACTERISTICS OF VISUAL LEARNERS

Visual learners easily gather and process information by observing. They may learn by seeing written words, photographs, models, or any other visual representations of information. For example, they may locate words signaling the main ideas of written texts, summarize events detailed in illustrations, or complete new tasks after seeing the steps modeled.

Teachers can implement many instructional strategies to support visual learners. They can encourage visual learners to take notes when reading new texts or learning new concepts. Notes can consist of words, pictures, or combinations of both. Teachers can also provide written directions to complete tasks, or they can visually model the steps. Additionally, teachers can use photos, realistic objects, diagrams, and other visual materials when introducing new concepts to learners. They can provide graphic organizers to help learners visualize the connections among concepts. When reading aloud, teachers can also share and discuss the illustrations. When teachers are designing projects and assessments, they can allow students to present their learning through multimedia presentations, models, or other visual means.

CHARACTERISTICS OF KINESTHETIC LEARNERS

Kinesthetic learners learn best by doing. They benefit from watching people model how to do things and being given opportunities to do things themselves. They also benefit from opportunities to be active within the classroom.

Teachers can implement many instructional strategies to support kinesthetic learners. They can consider active ways for students to learn and practice new concepts. For example, first grade students can trace sight words in chalk and hop along the letters, helping them memorize the spellings. Students of all ages can complete science experiments that allow them to mix, measure, and complete other scientific tasks. During math lessons on comparing and ordering numbers, students can form human number lines and discuss the processes they used.

Classroom arrangements and routines are also important for kinesthetic learners. Teachers can consider flexible seating arrangements and opportunities to move throughout the classroom to accommodate these students' needs.

CHARACTERISTICS OF TACTILE LEARNERS

Tactile learning is sometimes viewed as a synonym of kinesthetic learning, but there are some key differences. Kinesthetic learning refers to active learning by doing, and **tactile learning** refers to learning through **physical touch**. Tactile learners benefit from frequent opportunities to feel and manipulate items during instruction.

Teachers can implement many instructional strategies to support tactile learners. For example, early childhood students can trace letter cards made of different textures. Students can be given opportunities to spell words in rice, sand, or other textured materials. Manipulating letter tiles can also be used during word work activities. When completing science activities, students can feel objects and describe their textures. During math activities, students can use manipulatives to explore concepts and solve problems. When teachers are designing projects and assessments, they can also allow students to present their learning using models constructed from types of artistic materials.

USING INSTRUCTIONAL STRATEGIES THAT ADDRESS ALL LEARNING MODALITIES

Teachers should consider all learning modalities and accommodate auditory, visual, kinesthetic, and tactile learners within the classroom. This is important for several reasons, including the possibility that each student may display preferences for multiple modalities. Additionally, students can benefit from having information presented in multiple ways. For example, students may learn how to complete new tasks by watching their teachers model the steps. However, if given opportunities to practice the steps themselves, students may be better able to remember and apply them in the future.

Teachers need to consider the specifics of each concept they are teaching when determining which **modalities** to address during instruction. For example, it is difficult to teach letter formation using only oral directions. Students benefit from seeing the process teachers use to form each letter and from having opportunities to practice forming the letters independently. When teaching rhyming, auditory instruction is important. All modalities play a role in learning.

Classrooms are also made up of **diverse students** who prefer different modalities. To meet the needs of all learners, teachers can offer instructional choices and present information in multiple ways. For example, teachers can offer print and auditory versions of texts. Directions can be provided in written form and spoken verbally. Teachers can also offer project choices that allow students to present their learning in oral, written, or visual form.

Assessment Methodology

ASSESSMENT METHODS

Effective teaching requires multiple methods of assessment to evaluate student comprehension and instructional effectiveness. Assessments are typically categorized as diagnostic, formative, summative, and benchmark, and are applicable at varying stages of instruction. **Diagnostic** assessments are administered before instruction and indicate students' prior knowledge and areas of misunderstanding to determine the path of instruction. **Formative** assessments occur continuously to measure student engagement, comprehension, and instructional effectiveness. These assessments indicate instructional strategies that require adjustment to meet students' needs in facilitating successful learning, and include such strategies as checking for understanding, observations, total participation activities, and exit tickets. **Summative** assessments are given at the end of a lesson or unit to evaluate student progress in reaching learning targets and identify areas of misconception for reteaching. Such assessments can be given in the form of exams and quizzes, or project-based activities in which students demonstrate their learning through hands-on, personalized methods. Additionally, portfolios serve as valuable summative assessments in allowing students to demonstrate their progress over time and provide insight regarding individual achievement. **Benchmark** assessments occur less frequently and encompass large portions of curriculum. These assessments are intended to evaluate the progress of groups of students in achieving state and district academic standards.

ASSESSMENT TYPES

- **Diagnostic:** These assessments can either be formal or informal and are intended to provide teachers with information regarding students' level of understanding prior to beginning a unit of instruction. Examples include pretests, KWL charts, anticipation guides, and brainstorming activities. Digital resources, such as online polls, surveys, and quizzes are also valuable resources for gathering diagnostic feedback.
- **Formative:** These assessments occur throughout instruction to provide the teacher with feedback regarding student understanding. Examples include warm-up and closure activities, checking frequently for understanding, student reflection activities, and providing students with color-coded cards to indicate their level of understanding. Short quizzes and total participation activities, such as four corners, are also valuable formative assessments. Numerous digital resources, including polls, surveys, and review games, are also beneficial in providing teachers with formative feedback to indicate instructional effectiveness.
- **Summative:** Summative assessments are intended to indicate students' level of mastery and progress toward reaching academic learning standards. These assessments may take the form of written or digital exams and include multiple choice, short answer, or long answer questions. Examples also include projects, final essays, presentations, or portfolios to demonstrate student progress over time.
- **Benchmark:** Benchmark assessments measure students' progress in achieving academic standards. These assessments are typically standardized to ensure uniformity, objectivity, and accuracy. Benchmark assessments are typically given as a written multiple choice or short answer exam, or as a digital exam in which students answer questions on the computer.

> **Review Video: Formative and Summative Assessments**
> Visit mometrix.com/academy and enter code: 804991

DETERMINING APPROPRIATE ASSESSMENT STRATEGIES

As varying assessment methods provide different information regarding student performance and achievement, the teacher must consider the most applicable and effective assessment strategy in each stage of instruction. This includes determining the **desired outcomes** of assessment, as well as the information the teacher intends to ascertain and how they will apply the results to further instruction. **Age** and **grade level** appropriateness must be considered when selecting which assessment strategies will enable students to successfully demonstrate their learning. Additionally, the teacher must be cognizant of students' individual differences and learning needs to determine which assessment model is most **accommodating** and reflective of their progress. It is also important that the teacher consider the practicality of assessment strategies, as well as methods they will use to implement the assessment for maximized feedback regarding individual and whole-class progress in achieving learning goals.

ASSESSMENTS THAT REFLECT REAL-WORLD APPLICATIONS

Assessments that reflect **real-world applications** enhance relevancy and students' ability to establish personal connections to learning that deepen understanding. Implementing such assessments provides authenticity and enhances engagement by defining a clear and practical purpose for learning. These assessments often allow for hands-on opportunities for demonstrating learning and can be adjusted to accommodate students' varying learning styles and needs while measuring individual progress. However, assessments that focus on real-world applications can be subjective, thus making it difficult to extract concrete data and quantify student progress to guide future instructional decisions. In addition, teachers may have difficulty analyzing assessment results on a large scale and comparing student performance with other schools and districts, as individual assessments may vary.

DIAGNOSTIC TESTS

Diagnostic tests are integral to planning and delivering effective instruction. These tests are typically administered prior to beginning a unit or lesson and provide valuable feedback for guiding and planning instruction. Diagnostic tests provide **preliminary information** regarding students' level of understanding and prior knowledge. This serves as a baseline for instructional planning that connects and builds upon students' background knowledge and experiences to enhance success in learning. Diagnostic tests allow the teacher to identify and clarify areas of student misconception prior to engaging in instruction to ensure continued comprehension and avoid the need for remediation. They indicate areas of student strength and need, as well as individual instructional aids that may need to be incorporated into lessons to support student achievement. In addition, these tests enable the teacher to determine which instructional strategies, activities, groupings, and materials will be most valuable in maximizing engagement and learning. Diagnostic tests can be **formal** or **informal**, and include such formats as pre-tests, pre-reading activities, surveys, vocabulary inventories, and graphic organizers such as KWL charts to assess student understanding prior to engaging in learning. Diagnostic tests are generally not graded as there is little expectation that all students in a class possess the same baseline of proficiency at the start of a unit.

FORMATIVE ASSESSMENTS

Formative assessments are any assessments that take place in the **middle of a unit of instruction**. The goals of formative assessments are to help teachers understand where a student is in their progress toward **mastering** the current unit's content and to provide the students with **ongoing feedback** throughout the unit. The advantage of relying heavily on formative assessments in instruction is that it allows the teacher to continuously **check for comprehension** and adjust instruction as needed to ensure that the whole class is adequately prepared to proceed at the end of the unit. To understand formative assessments well, teachers need to understand that any interaction that can provide information about the student's comprehension is a type of formative assessment which can be used to inform future instruction.

Formative assessments are often a mixture of formal and informal assessments. **Formal formative assessments** often include classwork, homework, and quizzes. Examples of **informal formative assessments** include simple comprehension checks during instruction, class-wide discussions of the current topic, and exit slips, which are written questions posed by teachers at the end of class, which helps the teacher quickly review which students are struggling with the concepts.

SUMMATIVE ASSESSMENTS

Summative assessment refers to an evaluation at the end of a discrete unit of instruction, such as the end of a course, end of a unit, or end of a semester. Classic examples of summative assessments include end of course assessments, final exams, or even qualifying standardized tests such as the SAT or ACT. Most summative assessments are created to measure student mastery of particular **academic standards**. Whereas formative assessment generally informs current instruction, summative assessments are used to objectively demonstrate that each individual has achieved adequate mastery of the standards in question. If a student has not met the benchmark, they may need extra instruction or may need to repeat the course.

These assessments usually take the form of **tests** or formal portfolios with rubrics and clearly defined goals. Whatever form a summative takes, they are almost always high-stakes, heavily-weighted, and they should always be formally graded. These types of assessments often feature a narrower range of question types, such as multiple choice, short answer, and essay questions to help with systematic grading. Examples of summative assessments include state tests, end-of-unit or chapter tests, end-of-semester exams, and assessments that formally measure student mastery of topics against a established benchmarks.

Project-based assessments are beneficial in evaluating achievement, as they incorporate several elements of instruction and highlight real-world applications of learning. This allows students to demonstrate understanding through a hands-on, individualized approach that reinforces connections to learning and increases retainment. **Portfolios** of student work over time serve as a valuable method for assessing individual progress toward reaching learning targets. Summative assessments provide insight regarding overall instructional effectiveness and are necessary for guiding future instruction in subsequent years but are not usually used to modify current instruction.

> **Review Video: Assessment Reliability and Validity**
> Visit mometrix.com/academy and enter code: 424680

BENCHMARK ASSESSMENTS

Benchmark assessments are intended to quantify, evaluate, and compare individual and groups of students' achievement of school-wide, district, and state **academic standards.** They are typically administered in specific intervals throughout the school year and encompass entire or large units of curriculum to determine student mastery and readiness for academic advancement. Benchmark assessments provide data that enable the teacher to determine students' progress toward reaching academic goals to guide current and continued instruction. This data can be utilized by the school and individual teachers to create learning goals and objectives aligned with academic standards, as well as plan instructional strategies, activities, and assessments to support students in achieving them. In addition, benchmark assessments provide feedback regarding understanding and the potential need for remediation to allow the teacher to instill necessary supports in future instruction that prepare students for success in achieving learning targets.

ALIGNMENT OF ASSESSMENTS WITH INSTRUCTIONAL GOALS AND OBJECTIVES

To effectively monitor student progress, assessments must align with **instructional goals** and **objectives**. This allows the teacher to determine whether students are advancing at an appropriate pace to achieve state and district academic standards. When assessments are aligned with specific learning targets, the teacher ensures that students are learning relevant material to establish a foundation of knowledge necessary for growth and academic achievement. To achieve this, the teacher must determine which instructional goals and objectives their students must achieve and derive instruction, content, and activities from these specifications. Instruction must reflect and reinforce learning targets, and the teacher must select the most effective strategies for addressing students' needs as they work to achieve them. Assessments must be reflective of content instruction to ensure they are aligned with learning goals and objectives, as well as to enable the teacher to evaluate student progress in mastering them. The teacher must clearly communicate learning goals and objectives throughout all stages of instruction to provide students with clarity on expectations. This establishes a clear purpose and focus for learning that enhances relevancy and strengthens connections to support student achievement.

CLEARLY COMMUNICATING ASSESSMENT CRITERIA AND STANDARDS

Students must be clear on the purpose of learning throughout all stages of instruction to enhance understanding and facilitate success. When assessment **criteria** and **standards** are clearly communicated, the purpose of learning is established, and students are able to effectively connect instructional activities to learning goals and criteria for assessment. Communicating assessment criteria and standards provides students with clarity on tasks and learning goals they are expected to accomplish as they prepare themselves for assessment. This allows for more **focused instruction** and engagement in learning, as it enhances relevancy and student motivation. Utilizing appropriate forms of **rubrics** is an effective strategy in specifying assessment criteria and standards, as it informs students about learning goals they are working toward, the quality of work they are expected to achieve, and skills they must master to succeed on the assessment. Rubrics indicate to students exactly how they will be evaluated, thus supporting their understanding and focus as they engage in learning to promote academic success.

RUBRICS FOR COMMUNICATING STANDARDS

The following are varying styles of rubrics that can be used to communicate criteria and standards:

- **Analytic:** Analytic rubrics break down criteria for an assignment into several categories and provide an explanation of the varying levels of performance in each one. This style of rubric is beneficial for detailing the characteristics of quality work, as well as providing students with feedback regarding specific components of their performance. Analytic rubrics are most effective when used for summative assessments, such as long-term projects or essays.
- **Holistic:** Holistic rubrics evaluate the quality of the student's assignment as a whole, rather than scoring individual components. Students' score is determined based upon their performance across multiple performance indicators. This style of rubric is beneficial for providing a comprehensive evaluation but limits the amount of feedback that students receive regarding their performance in specific areas.
- **Single-Point:** Single point rubrics outline criteria for assignments into several categories. Rather than providing a numeric score to each category, however, the teacher provides written feedback regarding the students' strengths and ways in which they can improve their performance. This style of rubric is beneficial in providing student-centered feedback that focuses on their overall progress.
- **Checklist:** Checklists typically outline a set of criteria that is scored using a binary approach based upon completion of each component. This style increases the efficiency of grading assignments and is often easy for students to comprehend but does not provide detailed feedback. This method of grading should generally be reserved for shorter assignments.

COMMUNICATING HIGH ACADEMIC EXPECTATIONS IN ASSESSMENTS

The attitudes and behaviors exhibited by the teacher are highly influential on students' attitudes toward learning. Teachers demonstrate belief in students' abilities to be successful in learning when they communicate **high academic expectations**. This promotes students' **self-concept** and establishes a **growth mindset** to create confident, empowered learners that are motivated to achieve. High expectations for assessments and reaching academic standards communicates to students the quality of work that is expected of them and encourages them to overcome obstacles as they engage in learning. When communicating expectations for student achievement, it is important that the teacher is aware of students' individual learning needs to provide the necessary support that establishes equitable opportunities for success in meeting assessment criteria and standards. Setting high expectations through assessment criteria and standards while supporting students in their learning enhances overall achievement and establishes a foundation for continuous academic success.

EFFECTIVE COMMUNICATION AND IMPACT ON STUDENT LEARNING

Communicating high academic expectations enhances students' self-concept and increases personal motivation for success in learning. To maximize student achievement, it is important that the teacher set high academic expectations that are **clearly** communicated through **age-appropriate** terms and consistently reinforced. Expectations must be reflected through learning goals and objectives, and **visible** at all times to ensure student awareness. The teacher must be **specific** in communicating what they want students to accomplish and clearly detail necessary steps for achievement while assuming the role of facilitator to guide learning and provide support. Providing constructive **feedback** throughout instruction is integral in reminding students of academic expectations and ensuring they are making adequate progress toward reaching learning goals. When high academic expectations are communicated and reinforced, students are empowered with a sense of confidence and self-responsibility for their own learning that promotes their desire to learn. This ultimately enhances achievement and equips them with the tools necessary for future academic success.

ANALYZING AND INTERPRETING ASSESSMENT DATA

Teachers can utilize multiple techniques to effectively analyze and interpret assessment data. This typically involves creating charts and graphs outlining different data subsets. They can list each learning standard that was assessed, determine how many students overall demonstrated proficiency on the standard, and identify individual students who did not demonstrate proficiency on each standard. This information can be used to differentiate instruction. Additionally, they can track individual student performance and progress on each standard over time.

Teachers can take note of overall patterns and trends in assessment data. For example, they can determine if any subgroups of students did not meet expectations. They can consider whether the data confirms or challenges any existing beliefs, implications this may have on instructional planning and what, if any, conclusions can be drawn from this data.

Analyzing and interpreting assessment data may raise new questions for educators, so they can also determine if additional data collection is needed.

USING ASSESSMENT DATA TO DIFFERENTIATE INSTRUCTION FOR INDIVIDUAL LEARNERS

By analyzing and interpreting assessment data, teachers can determine if there are any specific learning standards that need to be retaught to their entire classes. This may be necessary if the data shows that all students struggled in these specific areas. Teachers may consider reteaching these standards using different methods if the initial methods were unsuccessful.

Teachers can also form groups of students who did not demonstrate proficiency on the same learning standards. Targeted instruction can be planned for these groups to help them make progress in these areas. Interventions can also be planned for individual students who did not show proficiency in certain areas. If interventions have already been in place and have not led to increased learning outcomes, the interventions may be redesigned. If interventions have been in place and assessment data now shows proficiency, the interventions may be discontinued.

If assessment data shows that certain students have met or exceeded expectations in certain areas, enrichment activities can be planned to challenge these students and meet their learning needs.

ALIGNING ASSESSMENTS WITH INSTRUCTIONAL GOALS AND OBJECTIVES

Assessments that are congruent to instructional goals and objectives provide a **clear purpose** for learning that enhances student understanding and motivation. When learning targets are reflected in assessments, instructional activities and materials become more **relevant**, as they are derived from these specifications. Such clarity in purpose allows for more focus and productivity as students engage in instruction and fosters connections that strengthen overall understanding for maximized success in learning. Aligning assessments with instructional goals and objectives ensures that students are learning material that is relevant to the curriculum and academic standards to ensure **preparedness** as they advance in their academic careers. In addition, it enables the teacher to evaluate and monitor student progress to determine whether they are progressing at an ideal pace for achieving academic standards. With this information, the teacher can effectively modify instruction as necessary to support students' needs in reaching desired learning outcomes.

NORM-REFERENCED TESTS

On **norm-referenced tests**, students' performances are compared to the performances of sample groups of similar students. Norm-referenced tests identify students who score above and below the average. To ensure reliability, the tests must be given in a standardized manner to all students.

Norm-referenced tests usually cover a broad range of skills, such as the entire grade-level curriculum for a subject. They typically contain a few questions per skill. Whereas scores in component areas of the tests may be calculated, usually overall test scores are reported. Scores are often reported using percentile ranks, which indicate what percentage of test takers scored lower than the student being assessed. For example, a student's score in the 75th percentile means the student scored better than 75% of other test takers. Other times, scores may be reported using grade-level equivalency.

One advantage of norm-referenced tests is their objectivity. They also allow educators to compare large groups of students at once. This may be helpful for making decisions regarding class placements and groupings. A disadvantage of norm-referenced tests is that they only indicate how well students perform in comparison to one another. They do not indicate whether or not students have mastered certain skills.

CRITERION-REFERENCED TESTS

Criterion-referenced tests measure how well students perform on certain skills or standards. The goal of these tests is to indicate whether or not students have mastered certain skills and which skills require additional instruction. Scores are typically reported using the percentage of questions answered correctly or students' performance levels. Performance levels are outlined using terms such as below expectations, met expectations, and exceeded expectations.

One advantage of criterion-referenced tests is they provide teachers with useful information to guide instruction. They can identify which specific skills students have mastered and which skills need additional practice. Teachers can use this information to plan whole-class, small-group, and individualized instruction. Analyzing results of criterion-referenced tests over time can also help teachers track student progress on certain skills. A disadvantage of criterion-referenced tests is they do not allow educators to compare students' performances to samples of their peers.

WAYS THAT STANDARDIZED TEST RESULTS ARE REPORTED

- **Raw scores** are sometimes reported and indicate how many questions students answered correctly on a test. By themselves, they do not provide much useful information. They do not indicate how students performed in comparison to other students or to grade-level expectations.

- **Grade-level equivalents** are also sometimes reported. A grade-level equivalent score of 3.4 indicates that a student performed as well as an average third grader in the fourth month of school. It can indicate whether a student is performing above or below grade-level expectations, but it does not indicate that the student should be moved to a different grade level.
- **Standard scores** are used to compare students' performances on tests to standardized samples of their peers. Standard deviation refers to the amount that a set of scores differs from the mean score on a test.
- **Percentile ranks** are used on criterion-referenced tests to indicate what percentage of test takers scored lower than the student whose score is being reported.
- **Cutoff scores** refer to predetermined scores students must obtain in order to be considered proficient in certain areas. Scores below the cutoff level indicate improvement is needed and may result in interventions or instructional changes.

FORMAL AND INFORMAL ASSESSMENTS

Assessments are any method a teacher uses to gather information about student comprehension of curriculum, including improvised questions for the class and highly-structured tests. **Formal assessments** are assessments that have **clearly defined standards and methodology**, and which are applied consistently to all students. Formal tests should be objective and the test itself should be scrutinized for validity and reliability since it tends to carry higher weight for the student. Summative assessments, such as end-of-unit tests, lend themselves to being formal tests because it is necessary that a teacher test the comprehension of all students in a consistent and thorough way.

Although formal assessments can provide useful data about student performance and progress, they can be costly and time-consuming to implement. Administering formal assessments often interrupts classroom instruction, and may cause testing anxiety.

Informal assessments are assessments that do not adhere to formal objectives and they do not have to be administered consistently to all students. As a result, they do not have to be scored or recorded as a grade and generally act as a **subjective measure** of class comprehension. Informal assessments can be as simple as asking a whole class to raise their hand if they are ready to proceed to the next step or asking a particular question of an individual student.

Informal assessments do not provide objective data for analysis, but they can be implemented quickly and inexpensively. Informal assessments can also be incorporated into regular classroom instruction and activities, making them more authentic and less stressful for students.

USING VARIOUS ASSESSMENTS

The goal of **assessment** in education is to gather data that, when evaluated, can be used to further student learning and achievement. **Standardized tests** are helpful for placement purposes and to reflect student progress toward goals set by a school district or state. If a textbook is chosen to align with district learning standards, the textbook assessments can provide teachers with convenient, small-scale, regular checks of student knowledge against the target standard.

In order be effective, teachers must know where their students are in the learning process. Teachers use a multitude of **formal and informal assessment methods** to do this. Posing differentiated discussion questions is an example of an informal assessment method that allows teachers to gauge individual student progress rather than their standing in relation to a universal benchmark.

Effective teachers employ a variety of assessments, as different formats assess different skills, promote different learning experiences, and appeal to different learners. A portfolio is an example of an assessment that gauges student progress in multiple skills and through multiple media. Teachers can use authentic or performance-based assessments to stimulate student interest and provide visible connections between language-learning and the real world.

ASSESSMENT RELIABILITY

Assessment reliability refers to how well an assessment is constructed and is made up of a variety of measures. An assessment is generally considered **reliable** if it yields similar results across multiple administrations of the assessment. A test should perform similarly with different test administrators, graders, and test-takers and perform consistently over multiple iterations. Factors that affect reliability include the day-to-day wellbeing of the student (students can sometimes underperform), the physical environment of the test, the way it is administered, and the subjectivity of the scorer (with written-response assessments).

Perhaps the most important threat to assessment reliability is the nature of the **exam questions** themselves. An assessment question is designed to test student knowledge of a certain construct. A question is reliable in this sense if students who understand the content answer the question correctly. Statisticians look for patterns in student marks, both within the single test and over multiple tests, as a way of measuring reliability. Teachers should watch out for circumstances in which a student or students answer correctly a series of questions about a given concept (demonstrating their understanding) but then answer a related question incorrectly. The latter question may be an unreliable indicator of concept knowledge.

MEASURES OF ASSESSMENT RELIABILITY

- **Test-retest reliability** refers to an assessment's consistency of results with the same test-taker over multiple retests. If one student shows inconsistent results over time, the test is not considered to have test-retest reliability.
- **Intertester reliability** refers to an assessment's consistency of results between multiple test-takers at the same level. Students at similar levels of proficiency should show similar results.
- **Interrater reliability** refers to an assessment's consistency of results between different administrators of the test. This plays an especially critical role in tests with interactive or subjective responses, such as Likert-scales, cloze tests, and short answer tests. Different raters of the same test need to have a consistent means of evaluating the test-takers' performance. Clear rubrics can help keep two or more raters consistent in scoring.
- **Intra-rater reliability** refers to an assessment's consistency of results with one rater over time. One test rater should be able to score different students objectively to rate subjective test formats fairly.
- **Parallel-forms reliability** refers to an assessment's consistency between multiple different forms. For instance, end-of-course assessments may have many distinctive test forms, with different questions or question orders. If the different forms of a test do not provide the same results, it is said to be lacking in parallel-forms reliability.
- **Internal consistency reliability** refers to the consistency of results of similar questions on a particular assessment. If there are two or more questions targeted at the same standard and at the same level, they should show the same results across each question.

ASSESSMENT VALIDITY

Assessment validity is a measure of the relevancy that an assessment has to the skill or ability being evaluated, and the degree to which students' performance is representative of their mastery of the topic of assessment. In other words, a teacher should ask how well an assessment's results correlate to what it is looking to assess. Assessments should be evaluated for validity on both the **individual question** level and as a **test overall**. This can be especially helpful in refining tests for future classes. The overall validity of an assessment is determined by several types of validity measures.

An assessment is considered **valid** if it measures what it is intended to measure. One common error that can reduce the validity of a test (or a question on a test) occurs if the instructions are written at a reading level the students can't understand. In this case, it is not valid to take the student's failed answer as a true indication of his or her knowledge of the subject. Factors internal to the student might also affect exam validity: anxiety and a lack of self-esteem often lower assessments results, reducing their validity of a measure of student knowledge.

An assessment has content validity if it includes all the **relevant aspects** of the subject being tested—if it is comprehensive, in other words. An assessment has **predictive validity** if a score on the test is an accurate predictor of future success in the same domain. For example, SAT exams purport to have validity in predicting student success in a college. An assessment has construct validity if it accurately measures student knowledge of the subject being tested.

MEASURES OF ASSESSMENT VALIDITY

- **Face validity** refers to the initial impression of whether an assessment seems to be fit for the task. As this method is subjective to interpretation and unquantifiable, it should not be used singularly as a measurement of validity.
- **Construct validity** asks if an assessment actually assesses what it is intended to assess. Some topics are more straightforward, such as assessing if a student can perform two-digit multiplication. This can be directly tested, which gives the assessment a strong content validity. Other measures, such as a person's overall happiness, must be measured indirectly. If an assessment asserted that a person is generally happy if they smile frequently, it would be fair to question the construct validity of that assessment because smiling is unlikely to be a consistent measure of all peoples' general happiness.
- **Content validity** indicates whether the assessment is comprehensive of all aspects of the content being assessed. If a test leaves out an important topic, then the teacher will not have a full picture as a result of the assessment.
- **Criterion validity** refers to whether the results of an assessment can be used to **predict** a related value, known as **criterion**. An example of this is the hypothesis that IQ tests would predict a person's success later in life, but many critics believe that IQ tests are not valid predictors of success because intelligence is not the only predictor of success in life. IQ tests have shown validity toward predicting academic success, however. The measure of an assessment's criterion validity depends on how closely related the criterion is.
- **Discriminant validity** refers to how well an assessment tests only that which it is intended to test and successfully discriminates one piece of information from another. For instance, a student who is exceptional in mathematics should not be able to put that information into use on a science test and gain an unfair advantage. If they are able to score well due to their mathematics knowledge, the science test did not adequately discriminate science knowledge from mathematics knowledge.
- **Convergent validity** is related to discriminant validity, but takes into account that two measures may be distinct, but can be correlated. For instance, a personality test should distinguish self-esteem from extraversion so that they can be measured independently, but if an assessment has convergent validity, it should show a correlation between related measures.

PRACTICALITY

An assessment is **practical** if it uses an appropriate amount of human and budgetary resources. A practical exam doesn't take very long to design or score, nor does it take students very long to complete in relation to other learning objectives and priorities. Teachers often need to balance a desire to construct comprehensive or content-valid tests with a need for practicality: lengthy exams consume large amounts of instruction time and may return unreliable results if students become tired and lose focus.

ASSESSMENT BIAS

An assessment is considered biased if it disadvantages a certain group of students, such as students of a certain gender, race, cultural background, or socioeconomic class. A **content bias** exists when the subject matter of a question or assessment is familiar to one group and not another—for example, a reading comprehension passage which discusses an event in American history would be biased against students new to the country. An **attitudinal bias** exists when a teacher has a pre-conceived idea about the likely success of an assessment of a particular individual or group. A **method bias** arises when the format of an assessment is unfamiliar to a given group of students. **Language bias** occurs when an assessment utilizes idioms, collocations, or cultural references unfamiliar to a group of students. Finally, **translation bias** may arise when educators attempt to translate content-area assessments into a student's native language—rough or hurried translations often result in a loss of nuance important for accurate assessment.

AUTHENTIC ASSESSMENTS

An authentic assessment is an assessment designed to closely resemble something that a student does, or will do, in the real world. Thus, for example, students will never encounter a multiple-choice test requiring them to choose the right tense of a verb, but they will encounter context in which they have to write a narration of an event that has antecedents and consequents spread out in time—for example, their version of what caused a traffic accident. The latter is an example of a potential **authentic assessment**.

Well-designed authentic assessments require a student to exercise **advanced cognitive skills** (e.g., solving problems, integrating information, performing deductions), integrate **background knowledge**, and confront **ambiguity**. Research has demonstrated that mere language proficiency is not predictive of future language success—learning how to utilize knowledge in a complex context is an essential additional skill.

The terms "authentic" and "performance-based" assessments are often used interchangeably. However, a performance-based assessment doesn't necessarily have to be grounded in a possible authentic experience.

PERFORMANCE-BASED ASSESSMENTS

A performance-based assessment is one in which students demonstrate their learning by performing a **task** rather than by answering questions in a traditional test format. Proponents of **performance-based assessments** argue that they lead students to use **high-level cognitive skills** as they focus on how to put their knowledge to use and plan a sequence of stages in an activity or presentation. They also allow students more opportunities to individualize their presentations or responses based on preferred learning styles. Research suggests that students welcome the chance to put their knowledge to use in real-world scenarios.

Advocates of performance-based assessments suggest that they avoid many of the problems of language or cultural bias present in traditional assessments, and thus they allow more accurate assessment of how well students learned the underlying concepts. In discussions regarding English as a second language, they argue that performance assessments come closer to replicating what should be the true goal of language learning—the effective use of language in real contexts—than do more traditional exams. Critics point out that performance assessments are difficult and time-consuming for teachers to construct and for students to perform. Finally, performative assessments are difficult to grade in the absence of a well-constructed and detailed rubric.

TECHNOLOGY-BASED ASSESSMENTS

Technology-based assessments provide teachers with multiple resources for evaluating student progress to guide instruction. They are applicable in most formal and informal instructional settings and can be utilized as formative and summative assessments. Technology-based assessments simplify and enhance the efficiency of determining comprehension and instructional effectiveness, as they quickly present the teacher with information regarding student progress. This data enables the teacher to make necessary adjustments to facilitate student learning and growth. Implementing this assessment format simplifies the process of aligning them to school and district academic standards. This establishes objectivity and uniformity for comparing results and progress among students, as well as ensures that all students are held to the same academic expectations. While technology-based assessments are beneficial, there are some shortcomings to consider. This format may not be entirely effective for all learning styles in demonstrating understanding, as individualization in technology-based assessment can be limited. These assessments may not illustrate individual students' growth over time, but rather their mastery of an academic standard, thus hindering the ability to evaluate overall achievement. As technology-based evaluation limits hands-on opportunities, the real-world application and relevancy of the assessment may be unapparent to students.

ADVANTAGES AND DISADVANTAGES OF TECHNOLOGY-BASED ASSESSMENTS

Technology-based assessments can have many advantages. They can be given to large numbers of students at once, limited only by the amounts of technological equipment schools possess. Many types of technology-based assessments are instantly scored, and feedback is quickly provided. Students are sometimes able to view their results and feedback at the conclusion of their testing sessions. Data can be quickly compiled and reported in easy-to-understand formats. Technology-based assessments can also often track student progress over time.

Technology-based assessments can have some disadvantages as well. Glitches and system errors can interfere with the assessment process or score reporting. Students must also have the necessary prerequisite technological skills to take the assessments, or the results may not measure the content they are designed to measure. For example, if students take timed computer-based writing tests, they should have proficient typing skills. Otherwise, they may perform poorly on the tests despite strong writing abilities. Other prerequisite skills include knowing how to use a keyboard and mouse and understanding how to locate necessary information on the screen.

PORTFOLIO ASSESSMENTS

A **portfolio** is a collection of student work in multiple forms and media gathered over time. Teachers may assess the portfolio both for evidence of progress over time or in its end state as a demonstration of the achievement of certain proficiency levels.

One advantage of **portfolio assessments** is their breadth—unlike traditional assessments which focus on one or two language skills, portfolios may contain work in multiple forms—writing samples, pictures, and graphs designed for content courses, video and audio clips, student reflections, teacher observations, and student exams. A second advantage is that they allow a student to develop work in authentic contexts, including in other classrooms and at home.

In order for portfolios to function as an objective assessment tool, teachers should negotiate with students in advance of what genres of work will be included and outline a grading rubric that makes clear what will be assessed, such as linguistic proficiency, use of English in academic contexts, and demonstrated use of target cognitive skills.

CURRICULUM-BASED ASSESSMENTS

Curriculum-based assessments, also known as **curriculum-based measurements (CBM)**, are short, frequent assessments designed to measure student progress toward meeting curriculum **benchmarks**.

Teachers implement CBM by designing **probes**, or short assessments that target specific skills. For example, a teacher might design a spelling probe, administered weekly, that requires students to spell 10 unfamiliar but level-appropriate words. Teachers then track the data over time to measure student progress toward defined grade-level goals.

CBM has several clear advantages. If structured well, the probes have high reliability and validity. Furthermore, they provide clear and objective evidence of student progress—a welcome outcome for students and parents who often grapple with less-clear and subjective evidence. Used correctly, CBMs also motivate students and provide them with evidence of their own progress. However, while CBMs are helpful in identifying *areas* of student weaknesses, they do not identify the *causes* of those weaknesses or provide teachers with strategies for improving instruction.

TEXTBOOK ASSESSMENTS

Textbook assessments are the assessments provided at the end of a chapter or unit in an approved textbook. **Textbook assessments** present several advantages for a teacher: they are already made; they are likely to be accurate representations of the chapter or unit materials; and, if the textbook has been prescribed or recommended by the state, it is likely to correspond closely to Common Core or other tested standards.

Textbook assessments can be limiting for students who lag in the comprehension of academic English, or whose preferred learning style is not verbal. While textbooks may come with DVDs or recommended audio links, ESOL teachers will likely need to supplement these assessment materials with some of their own findings. Finally, textbook assessments are unlikely to represent the range of assessment types used in the modern classroom, such as a portfolio or performance-based assessments.

PEER ASSESSMENT

A peer assessment is when students grade one another's work based on a teacher-provided framework. **Peer assessments** are promoted as a means of saving teacher time and building student metacognitive skills. They are typically used as **formative** rather than summative assessments, given concerns about the reliability of student scoring and the tensions that can result if student scores contribute to overall grades. Peer assessments are used most often to grade essay-type written work or presentations. Proponents point out that peer assessments require students to apply metacognition, builds cooperative work and interpersonal skills, and broadens the sense that the student is accountable to peers and not just the teacher. Even advocates of the practice agree that students need detailed rubrics in order to succeed. Critics often argue that low-performing students have little to offer high-performing students in terms of valuable feedback—and this disparity may be more pronounced in ESOL classrooms or special education environments than in mainstream ones. One way to overcome this weakness is for the teacher to lead the evaluation exercise, guiding the students through a point-by-point framework of evaluation.

Spelling Development

STAGES OF SPELLING DEVELOPMENT

Students typically progress through a series of stages of spelling development. Researchers name the stages differently, but they contain common characteristics.

In the **pre-phonetic stage**, students spell using random letter and number strings. There are no letter-sound relationships evident in words. In the **semi-phonetic stage**, some letter-sound relationships are used to spell words. Students typically learn to correctly spell the beginning and ending sounds in words first, followed later by the medial sounds. In the **phonetic stage**, some simple words begin to be spelled correctly, such as CVC words. In addition to initial, medial, and final sounds, some more complex sounds are accurately represented. This includes some consonant blends and digraphs. In the transitional, or **word extension stage**, students learn to use syllable patterns to spell more complex words. Most words are spelled correctly in this stage. In the **derivational constancy stage**, students use knowledge of roots and affixes to spell related words. Most or all words in students' writing pieces are spelled correctly in this stage.

ORTHOGRAPHY

Orthography refers to the conventional spelling of words in a language. Because many words are spelled using the same patterns, studying orthography helps students increase the number of words they can spell correctly. Learning to apply orthographic patterns is an important part of any literacy program.

Word studies, or word work, should be regularly included in the school day. Word work should be sequential and built upon the knowledge of orthographic patterns that students already possess.

There are three layers of orthography that students can explore during word work. The **alphabet layer** refers to letter-sound relationships. Activities in which students combine letters or letter groups to form words will help them explore the alphabet layer. When students explore the **pattern layer**, they look for larger patterns that guide the spellings of words. Activities in which students build words within word families, such as CVCe words, help them explore the pattern layer. The **meaning layer** explores the relationships between word meanings and spellings. Sorting and writing words that contain the same Latin roots will help students explore the meaning layer of orthography.

PHONETIC SPELLING

Phonetic spelling is common in the early stages of writing development. When writing words, students consider what sounds they hear. They use knowledge of phonics rules to select letters or groups of letters to represent those sounds. For example, a student who is familiar with CVC words might write *love* as *luv*.

Parents are sometimes concerned with the amount of misspelled words in their children's writing. However, phonetic spelling plays a role in reading and writing development and is a stepping stone to conventional spelling.

At this stage, students know how to automatically spell a limited number of words. Using known phonics rules helps them efficiently encode words they do not know how to spell. If students are worried about spelling every word conventionally, they must continuously ask others for help. This slows the writing process and puts more emphasis on spelling than on recording ideas. Therefore, teachers typically tell students in this stage to write the sounds they hear and move on. This process also allows students to apply the phonics skills they use while reading.

Over time, students learn more complex spelling patterns and automatically remember how to spell more words. At this point, spelling becomes more conventional.

ROLE OF MEMORIZATION IN SPELLING DEVELOPMENT AND INSTRUCTION

There are some words that students cannot learn to spell by learning spelling patterns. These include many high-frequency words with irregular spelling patterns, such as the word *the*. Students should have frequent and repeated exposure to these words to memorize their spellings. Practice activities are helpful, such as building these words with letter tiles.

Some academic vocabulary words are also difficult for students to spell using knowledge of spelling patterns. For example, second graders may learn about camouflage as part of a science unit on animal adaptations. However, it would be difficult for students of this age to spell the word *camouflage* using knowledge of spelling patterns. Frequent exposure to these academic words in print will help students learn to spell them over time. Adding these words to word walls or classroom charts can serve as tools to assist with spelling initially. Being given numerous opportunities to write these words with scaffolding will assist with memorization.

Although memorization plays a role in spelling some words, its use as an instructional strategy should be balanced with explicit instruction in spelling patterns. When choosing weekly spelling lists, teachers should focus on patterns that can be applied to multiple words.

DIFFERENT APPROACHES TO TEACHING STUDENTS TO SPELL

There are many methods and commercial programs available to teach spelling. Although they vary in approach, the methods that are most effective share some common characteristics.

Effective spelling instruction should be explicit. Although students naturally learn to spell many words through frequent reading experiences, some explicit spelling instruction is still helpful to teach common spelling patterns and relationships among words. The instruction should be both incremental and sequential.

Teachers can introduce weekly spelling patterns, and students can complete activities to familiarize themselves with the patterns. Depending on the ages of the students, this may include word sorts, word hunts, and tracing. Multisensory activities are also helpful, such as building words with letter tiles and writing words in sand. Teachers may assess students' applications of the spelling patterns at the end of each week. Some teachers give students lists of words to study ahead of time. Other teachers assess students by asking them to spell new words that follow the patterns they have been studying.

Cultural Influences on Language Development and Use

ROLE OF SOCIAL CONTEXT IN LANGUAGE DEVELOPMENT AND USAGE

Members of a group have a shared social identity that is formed by reading, writing, listening, and speaking with one another. Group members develop common expressions, mannerisms, and favorite stories that are understood by other members. For example, members of a professional

33

group may use academic language specific to their field at conferences and work events. However, they will not likely use these terms while talking with people outside the field.

Additionally, **social context** plays a role in how people select the appropriate language to use. When asking a stranger for directions, a person would likely consider social norms and begin with an expression like "Excuse me." When talking with a good friend on the phone, a person might use an informal, joking tone. It is important for people to consider each situation and determine which approach to use.

Teachers can provide frequent opportunities for students to communicate with others for a variety of authentic purposes. This can include communicating with classmates, other students and adults within the school, family members, and community members.

ROLE OF CULTURAL CONTEXT IN LANGUAGE DEVELOPMENT AND USE

Language involves not only the words people say but also the ways in which these words are interpreted by recipients. Differing backgrounds and cultures can affect how messages are received, so it is important for people to consider that others may view communications differently. For example, in some cultures, students are encouraged to ask questions and initiate discussions in class. In others, students are expected to defer to their instructors and not speak unless they are directly questioned. A student who tells an instructor that something doesn't make sense may be praised for using metacognitive strategies in one class while perceived as being rude in another.

Cultural context also affects how nonverbal communications are interpreted. For example, different cultures have their own norms about making eye contact while speaking or the use of gestures during greetings.

Teachers should be sensitive to these cultural differences and consider the roles they may play in student participation and communication. Additionally, teachers should help students view situations from multiple perspectives and consider how their attempts at communication may be perceived by others in various situations.

INTERDEPENDENT RELATIONSHIP BETWEEN CULTURE AND LANGUAGE

The ways that people use language and interpret language directed toward them is related to their cultures. Additionally, as cultures change over time, so do languages. Existing words can take on new meanings, and new words may be added to languages. These changes sometimes occur as a result of popular culture, including television, video games, and music. As people with different cultural backgrounds interact, they must negotiate these differences to make meaning.

Because culture and language are so intertwined, understanding the cultural contexts in which language is used is an important part of learning any new language. English language learners should be taught English skills in context, helping them understand how the language is used in realistic social interactions. Additionally, it is important for teachers to understand the cultural backgrounds of ELLs and the roles their cultures may play in their language interactions and expectations. Teachers should incorporate a variety of teaching strategies and methods into their classrooms to meet the needs of all students.

Types of Literacies

DIGITAL LITERACY

Digital literacy refers to the ability to communicate effectively using digital sources. It involves many component skills, such as locating, processing, analyzing, evaluating, and creating information in digital form. Information can be communicated digitally through websites, social media, apps, digital textbooks, multimedia presentations, emails, texts, and more.

The continually evolving nature of digital communication presents challenges for teachers. Tools, software, and equipment should be selected carefully based upon the ability to help students achieve learning objectives.

Teachers also need to help students locate and synthesize information from multiple sources and evaluate the sources for reliability. Students must also learn to share information responsibly and adhere to acceptable use policies. Additionally, students need to be taught to consider their audiences and purposes for communicating in digital environments, just as they do when communicating through speaking and writing. For example, different language and sentence structure will likely be used in business websites than in text messages. With global business and distance education now common, students also need to be taught how to use modern tools to collaborate with others.

MEDIA LITERACY

Media literacy refers to the ability to comprehend, evaluate, and create media. Media includes methods of communication, such as newspapers, magazines, videos, television, radio, and books.

Students need to critically evaluate the authors' messages and points of view to determine what biases may exist. They also need to determine whether the information presented is supported by reliable sources. Advertisements and testimonials may contain unsubstantiated information, for example.

Because there are many different types of media, students also need the ability to flexibly apply different comprehension strategies. For example, they may skim through newspaper articles to locate and highlight key information, whereas they may take notes during videos. Teachers should incorporate forms of media into classroom instruction and teach strategies for comprehending and evaluating each type.

Teachers can also allow students opportunities to present their learning using different forms of media, such as creating podcasts, writing newspaper articles, filming videos, and more. Students should be taught to consider which types of media will best convey their messages and reach their intended audiences. In addition to helping students develop media literacy, these project options will also accommodate students who prefer different learning modalities.

> **Review Video: Different Types of Media**
> Visit mometrix.com/academy and enter code: 785859

VISUAL LITERACY

Visual literacy refers to the ability to comprehend, evaluate, and create visuals. It includes all types of visuals, such as cartoons, photographs, illustrations, graphs, infographics, and maps.

Visual literacy is important from an early age. Before students can read words, they "read the pictures" to tell stories and make predictions. They are later presented with other visuals, such as graphs to explain data in nonfiction texts and infographics on websites.

As with all forms of media, students need to evaluate author bias and verify the sources used to create visuals. For example, they can be taught to consider where the data used to create graphs comes from. Students also need to extract key information from visuals by looking for clues, such as bolded print or use of color. Additionally, students need to be taught about the legal issues involved in creating visuals, including copyright issues. They also need to consider design and aesthetics issues.

Teachers can assist students with visual literacy by presenting information using a combination of print and visual forms and allowing students choices when completing assignments. For example, students can create posters to convince other classmates to read favorite books.

Data Literacy

Data literacy refers to the ability to comprehend, evaluate, gather, and organize data. With the increasing reliance on data analytics to drive business and education-related decisions, data literacy must be addressed in the classroom.

Students need to learn how to read and interpret **different representations of data**, such as charts, graphs, and tables. They also need to draw informed conclusions from the data and recognize potential author bias and data misuse.

Additionally, students must decide which types of data will be **useful** to answer specific questions and convey certain information. They need to determine the most effective ways to gather data and present it to others.

Teachers should incorporate data gathering and analysis into classroom activities across all subject areas. Students can gather data when completing science experiments and create tables and graphs to represent their findings. Teachers can conduct surveys with students and record their responses using poll-generating tools on the web. Mini-lessons can be focused on interpreting and evaluating data found in nonfiction texts.

Financial Literacy

Financial literacy refers to making informed decisions about financial resources to prepare for a secure future. It includes skills such as saving and spending money, creating budgets, and paying bills. It also includes business-related terms like profit, expense, and revenue.

Although financial literacy is commonly linked to math skills like balancing checkbooks, it relates to traditional literacy as well. People must be able to read banking and billing statements and understand their terms and conditions. They must also critically evaluate financial offers, such as credit card deals, and consider authors' biases and underlying intentions. These skills are needed to make informed financial decisions.

While teaching about financial literacy, teachers should include a variety of realistic materials for students to read, analyze, and evaluate. They should be given opportunities to make and justify realistic financial decisions based on research and analysis.

INFORMATION LITERACY

Information literacy refers to the ability to locate, analyze, and evaluate information. It also refers to the ability to responsibly share information with others. Information can be obtained from a variety of sources, including websites, interviews, newspapers, books, and more.

Students first need to recognize when more information is needed. Teachers can encourage students to self-monitor their thinking and recognize when they need to learn more about topics before drawing conclusions. When planning a school garden, for example, students may recognize that they need to learn more about which plants grow well in their area. They may then consult gardening guides to select plants that are well suited for their climate and soil type.

Once information is located, it needs to be critically analyzed so students can comprehend it. They also need to consider author bias and reliability of sources. When sharing information, students need to ensure that they are using reliable sources and not misleading their audiences.

TECHNOLOGY LITERACY

Technology literacy involves the ability to use technological tools, equipment, and software to communicate effectively. It includes using technology to access, analyze, evaluate, and share information.

Technological tools are now commonly used in education, and teachers must dedicate instructional time to teaching students how to use them effectively and responsibly. Teachers can assist students with learning to use technology to locate information, such as teaching them to enter specific key words in search engines and skim the results for relevant matches. They can also teach students how to carefully select which technological tools they will use to accomplish specific tasks. For example, if students want to create visual representations of information for a class project, they may consider and evaluate the effectiveness of different infographic building tools.

Technology literacy also involves recognizing the possibilities and limitations of technology in accomplishing specific learning objectives. Additionally, it involves troubleshooting common technological problems and using technology in ethical and responsible ways.

Instructional Activities that Support Reading and Writing Skills

ACTIVITIES THAT SUPPORT READING, WRITING, LISTENING, AND SPEAKING DEVELOPMENT

Reading, writing, listening, and speaking are the four main components of English language development. All of these components are important and interdependent. They all play roles in making and conveying meaning, which are goals of literacy instruction.

These skills are sometimes practiced in isolation, such as when students listen to audio texts without any follow-up activities. However, when solving real-world problems, these skills are often used together. For example, doctors must listen to their patients' symptoms, make notes on the patients' charts, and then explain their treatment plans. Therefore, it is important for teachers to plan activities that integrate these four skills.

Project-based learning activities and performance assessments are useful for integrating these four skills. As an example, students could read about the benefits of recycling. They could then speak to the school principal to recommend implementing a school-wide recycling plan, listening and responding to the principal's concerns. They could then create posters to advertise the new program to other students.

CLOZE READING PROCEDURE

Cloze reading is an instructional strategy in which students read brief passages containing omitted words. They rely on background knowledge, semantic clues, and/or syntactic clues to determine the unknown words.

When designing cloze reading passages, teachers should consider a few key factors. The passages should be at the appropriate reading levels for the students. Students should be able to guess the omitted words by using reading strategies. If students need additional scaffolding to determine the missing words, word banks can be provided.

Cloze reading activities can be done independently or with partners. They can also be done as whole-class activities, with teachers reading the main passages and students supplying the missing words.

Cloze reading has several benefits. It requires students to use a variety of reading strategies, including using context clues, to determine the missing words. Students also cross-check their use of cueing systems to determine unknown words in cloze passages. If students read the passages multiple times to determine the missing words, it builds fluency as well.

LANGUAGE EXPERIENCE APPROACH TO READING INSTRUCTION

The **language experience approach** focuses on using students' own experiences as the topics of literacy experiences. Students think about experiences they would like to share. They dictate the experiences to teachers, who write the students' words down in front of them. The teachers then read the texts aloud while pointing to each word, modeling appropriate fluency. Students are then invited to join the teachers in rereading the texts.

The language experience approach can also be done as a whole-class activity, with classes writing about shared experiences together. For example, they could write about projects recently completed at school. Teachers help students generate ideas for what to include and list relevant vocabulary words that may be used. Students then dictate sentences to their teachers, who record them on chart paper. The classes then reread the texts multiple times.

A benefit of the language experience approach is that it involves reading, writing, listening, and speaking. It also builds upon students' prior knowledge and interests. If students are given multiple opportunities to reread the texts they have created, it also assists with fluency.

GUIDED READING INSTRUCTION

Guided reading is an important part of any balanced literacy program. During **guided reading**, teachers arrange students in flexible groups and meet with each group separately. While meeting with each group, teachers provide students with their own copies of leveled texts that are within their instructional reading levels. Before reading, teachers conduct picture walks, pre-teach vocabulary, and review strategies that will be helpful when reading the given texts. Students then read the texts independently in whisper voices while the teachers observe and make notes about students' reading. After students have read the texts independently, the teachers conduct mini-lessons on skills that are targeted in the texts, such as specific spelling patterns that are repeatedly used. Students then take the texts to reread later, helping build fluency.

The flexible nature of guided reading groups ensures that students are always reading books within their instructional reading levels. Because the groups are small, teachers also have frequent opportunities to observe students' use of reading strategies, make notes about their progress, and determine which skills need additional practice. Guided reading also allows teachers to deliver targeted mini-lessons to groups of students with similar needs.

SHARED READING EXPERIENCES

During **shared reading experiences**, teachers read aloud to students using materials like large print books, texts written on chart paper, and projected texts. Students follow along as teachers read and point to each word. Shared reading is an interactive experience, and teachers stop frequently to ask questions and model use of strategies. Depending on the ages and reading levels of the students, teachers focus on different teaching points. For example, kindergarten teachers may model and discuss concepts of print, whereas teachers of students in older grades may model and discuss comprehension strategies. Students may join the teachers in reading the texts as well.

Shared reading can be used across all subject areas and has several benefits. It allows students to see teachers modeling the use of reading strategies and practice using these strategies with scaffolding. It also allows students to participate in reading and discussing quality texts that they may not yet be able to read independently. Students learn about text features like punctuation marks and spelling patterns that they can incorporate into their own writing. They also have opportunities to hear examples of fluent reading.

READ-ALOUDS

During **read-alouds**, teachers read texts aloud to students. Depending on their purposes for reading, they may or may not pause to model the use of strategies or ask questions. Some read-alouds may be done strictly for entertainment purposes, whereas others may be done to provide background knowledge in content areas or allow for the modeling of reading strategies.

The key difference between read-alouds and shared reading experiences is that students do not have access to the texts during read-alouds. They listen as teachers read aloud, and they are sometimes shown the pictures. The focus is on listening to the texts and the teachers' use of strategies; students do not join in reading.

BENEFITS OF INDEPENDENT DAILY READING TIME

Independent daily reading has several benefits. Reading self-selected books can boost engagement with reading and help students develop a love of reading. When given opportunities to reread favorite texts, fluency may also increase. Independent reading also gives students opportunities to apply reading strategies to new texts autonomously.

Books for independent reading are usually self-selected. Students in the early stages of reading development who cannot read texts independently can be encouraged to "read the pictures." Teachers can model how to use prior knowledge and picture clues to tell the stories in their own words. Students who are able to read the words can be encouraged to select appropriate texts for independent reading time. Depending on the ages of the students, teachers may need to help readers build reading stamina. They can schedule a few minutes of daily independent reading time early in the school year and gradually add additional minutes. Teachers may schedule whole-class independent reading time or establish it as one station for students to complete during literacy stations.

Students can also be encouraged to have book boxes that contain several texts at the appropriate reading levels for use during independent reading time.

ROLE OF FLEXIBLE GROUPINGS IN EFFECTIVE READING INSTRUCTION

Flexible groupings are one way that teachers can differentiate instruction. When using **flexible grouping**, teachers strategically group students together to accomplish specific instructional goals. The groups may be large or small, and they vary depending on the activity. For example, a teacher may work with a small group of students who are all having difficulties with cause-and-effect relationships. The teacher is able to target instruction in this skill area to only the students who need extra practice. Guided reading groups are also flexible because students typically progress through instructional reading levels at different rates. Teachers can use both formal and informal assessment data to group students.

Flexible groupings have several benefits. They allow students to receive targeted instruction, often in small-group settings that allow for more teacher interaction. Students who have mastered these skills are able to work on other things, preventing them from becoming bored or frustrated. Additionally, students may feel more comfortable participating in small groups of their peers. Flexible groupings also mean that students will have opportunities to work with many other students throughout the year.

CONSIDERATIONS WHEN GROUPING STUDENTS FOR INSTRUCTIONAL PURPOSES

When determining when and how to group students for instructional purposes, teachers should take many factors into consideration. They should consider what instructional goals they want to accomplish. These goals are often based upon specific learning objectives.

Once teachers know what goals they want to accomplish, they can consider what types of groupings to use. Possibilities include partner learning as well as small or large group instruction. Teachers also need to consider the characteristics of the students in each group. For example, teachers may group students who need to practice specific skills together to target instruction. Other times, they may group students who have differing perspectives on topics to facilitate active discussion and sharing of viewpoints. These decisions should support the learning objectives. Teachers also need to consider what types of learning activities to use within the groups. Additionally, they need to consider what roles students will be assigned within their groups, if any. It is common for classrooms to use a variety of grouping arrangements throughout the year to accomplish different instructional goals.

CLASSROOM MANAGEMENT STRATEGIES FOR EFFECTIVE GUIDED READING GROUPS

Guided reading groups are important components of balanced literacy programs because they allow students to receive differentiated, small-group instruction on a routine basis. However, they may be ineffective if frequent interruptions or classroom management issues occur. Clearly established and practiced routines can prevent these issues from occurring.

Students who are not working with their teachers in guided reading groups should be engaged in activities they are able to successfully complete either independently or with the help of their peers. If center rotations are being used, students should know in what order to proceed through the centers and what the expectations are for each rotation.

Additionally, routines should be in place for how to solve problems without interrupting the guided reading groups. There should be clear criteria in place for when the teachers can be interrupted, such as in the case of emergencies. Students should be taught how to independently access any materials they may need to complete their activities. Hand signals or sign-out sheets may be utilized to minimize interruptions when students need permission to leave the classroom. Students can also be taught to ask a set number of classmates for assistance with problems before asking their teachers.

CHARACTERISTICS OF SHARED WRITING EXPERIENCES

During **shared writing experiences**, teachers and students collaboratively plan the content of shared writing pieces. Teachers assist their students with choosing topics, deciding which details to include, selecting words, and organizing text structure. Students are asked to share their ideas, and teachers help students organize their thoughts and put them into writing. Teachers control the writing instruments and put the words down on paper. Along the way, they may ask students for assistance with spelling words, determining how to punctuate, and other issues. Teachers model their thinking and use of writing strategies throughout the process. Once the drafting is finished, students may assist with revising, editing, and reading the texts aloud.

Shared writing experiences give students opportunities to be active participants in scaffolded versions of the writing process and work collaboratively to develop quality writing pieces. Additionally, they benefit from observing their teachers as they model the use of writing strategies.

CHARACTERISTICS OF INTERACTIVE WRITING EXPERIENCES

During **interactive writing experiences**, teachers and students work together to create shared writing pieces. With teacher guidance, students help plan writing topics, determine which details to include, and organize text structure. Students share the writing utensils with teachers and contribute to recording the words on paper. Teachers provide guidance along the way. For example, they may remind students of recently learned spelling patterns while students are spelling the words on paper. Classes may also work together to revise, edit, and read the writing pieces.

Giving students control over the writing utensils is what differentiates interactive writing from shared writing. In shared writing, teachers record the words on paper.

Interactive writing allows students to be active participants in the writing process while receiving scaffolding from teachers. It also allows students to collaboratively create quality writing pieces they are unable to produce independently at their current stages of writing development. Additionally, teachers can build targeted mini-lessons into the interactive writing process.

Selecting Appropriately-Leveled Texts

SELECTING APPROPRIATE TEXTS TO SUPPORT THE BACKGROUNDS AND INTERESTS OF DIVERSE LEARNERS

When selecting appropriate texts to support diverse learners, teachers should take several factors into consideration. First, they should consider students' reading levels and stages of reading development to determine how much text support is needed. For emergent and early readers, teachers should consider how much picture support is present, how many words are printed on each page, and the predictability of the text. They should also consider how easily students will be able to decode the words based on spelling patterns, text clues, and use of high-frequency words.

For transitional and fluent readers, teachers should consider text complexity. This includes the vocabulary, language use, and sentence structure used in the texts. They should also consider how the texts relate to students' prior knowledge and interests and whether the content supports learning objectives. If topics are unfamiliar to students, some scaffolding or pre-teaching may be needed.

DETERMINING IF TEXTS ARE AT STUDENTS' INDEPENDENT READING LEVELS

When determining reading levels, teachers typically consider both accuracy rate and comprehension. Different reading programs vary slightly in their cutoff levels, but texts are generally considered to be at the independent level if they are read with 95% to 100% accuracy. Additionally, responding correctly to 90% to 100% of comprehension questions may indicate that texts are at students' independent levels. Texts at the independent reading level can be read by students with no assistance.

Texts that students can read independently are good candidates for free choice reading time. They also can be used when practicing comprehension strategies, such as inferring and drawing conclusions. Because students do not struggle to decode words in these texts, they have the mental energy available to do more complex analysis. Additionally, students can repeatedly read favorite books at their independent reading levels for fluency practice. They can also read these books to partners or family members.

DETERMINING IF TEXTS ARE AT STUDENTS' INSTRUCTIONAL READING LEVELS

Different reading programs vary slightly in their cutoff levels, but texts are generally considered to be at the instructional level if they are read with 90% to 94% accuracy. Additionally, responding correctly to 70% to 89% of comprehension questions may indicate that texts are at students' instructional levels. These books present some challenges for readers, but they can still be read without frustration.

Texts at the instructional level are appropriate for use in guided reading groups. Students are able to decode most words, yet a few miscues may occur that can be used as teaching points. Teachers may analyze student errors and use this information to plan mini-lessons. Additionally, students are able to apply comprehension strategies to analyze and discuss these texts. Texts at the instructional level allow students to have successful and positive experiences with reading while learning from their challenges.

DETERMINING IF TEXTS ARE AT STUDENTS' FRUSTRATION LEVELS

Different reading programs vary slightly in their cutoff levels, but texts are generally considered to be at the frustration level if they are read with less than 90% accuracy. Additionally, responding correctly to less than 70% of comprehension questions may indicate that texts are at students' frustration levels. These books are considered difficult for students to read.

Texts at the frustration level are not good candidates for students to read independently during guided reading groups, when teachers need to observe students' reading and help them apply strategies. Students may become frustrated with too many unknown words or lose the meanings of the texts.

However, these texts can be used in other beneficial ways. Students may enjoy exploring difficult texts on topics of interest, which may help them develop a love of reading. Because these texts can provide valuable information that students cannot access independently, teachers can also read these texts aloud or provide digital versions with audio. Teachers can model using reading strategies with these difficult texts during shared reading experiences. Additionally, students can be encouraged to read these texts with family members.

SYSTEMS USED TO LEVEL BOOKS

There are several different systems that are used to level books. **Lexile** measures consider both text complexity and word frequency to level books. Specialized assessments are used to determine students' Lexile levels, which can then be used to select appropriate books.

Irene Fountas and Gay Su Pinnell developed another system for leveling books based on their recommendations for guided reading groups. Their system, sometimes known as **guided reading levels**, considers several factors to assign book levels. These factors include word frequency, sentence complexity, vocabulary, and text features. Running records can help identify guided reading levels.

The **Developmental Reading Assessment (DRA)**, also provides a system for leveling books. Students can take the DRA to determine their instructional reading levels. Results can then be used to select books using the DRA system.

Because there are many different leveling systems, conversion charts are available online to help teachers and parents identify book levels using their preferred systems.

Assessment Methodology for Language Skills

PURPOSES OF LITERACY ASSESSMENT

Literacy assessments can serve many purposes. Assessments can be used to monitor the progress of students toward achieving district and state benchmarks as well as individualized goals. They can identify specific skills that students have mastered as well as those that need additional practice. They can also identify if students are making adequate yearly progress.

Additionally, assessments can be used to guide teacher instruction. By analyzing assessment results, teachers can determine which topics they should focus on for whole-class, small-group, and individualized instruction. This helps ensure that too much instructional time is not spent on topics students have already mastered while ignoring topics that need additional practice.

Assessments can also be used to evaluate the effectiveness of reading programs. By analyzing students' assessment data over time, districts can look for trends in student achievement and progress toward closing achievement gaps.

ADVANTAGES AND DISADVANTAGES OF GROUP AND INDIVIDUAL LITERACY ASSESSMENTS

Group literacy assessments are administered to groups of students at one time. Teachers explain the directions and then instruct all students to begin working, while they observe and answer questions. Assessments are scored after students finish and submit them. Examples of group literacy assessments include state-mandated standardized reading and writing tests. Using the group approach to literacy assessments is more efficient than individualized assessment, freeing up more time for classroom instruction. It also assists teachers with classroom management because all students are being assessed at once.

Individualized assessments are given to one student at a time. Teachers may listen to students read, observe strategy usage, or ask students to retell stories they have read. Dynamic Indicators of Basic Early Literacy Skills (DIBELS) and Developmental Reading Assessment (DRA) are examples of individual assessments. This approach allows teachers to closely observe the strategies each student uses. However, it is more time intensive, and the remaining students in the class must be engaged in other activities.

43

USING PROGRESS MONITORING TO ASSESS STUDENTS AND GUIDE INSTRUCTION

Progress monitoring is used to track students' progress toward achieving certain performance goals over time. Teachers first identify students who may benefit from progress monitoring. This usually occurs as a result of assessment data. Students who score below expectations on certain components of criterion-referenced tests may be progressively monitored in those areas.

Teachers then set performance goals that can be measured and tracked over time. For example, if students are currently decoding five CVC words correctly in one minute, the goal may be for them to decode 15 words per minute. Interventions are put in place to help students with these skills. Teachers then repeat testing in these targeted areas on a regular basis, such as weekly or biweekly. Results are recorded, and teachers look for progress over time. Once students have mastered the initial goals, new goals are set, or progress monitoring is discontinued, depending on students' needs.

Progress monitoring can help teachers identify whether or not current interventions are successful or whether changes are needed. It can also help teachers identify when students have mastered certain skills.

TYPES OF FORMAL ASSESSMENTS USED TO ASSESS ORAL LANGUAGE AND READING SKILLS

There are several types of formal assessments designed to assess readers. Some assessments assess knowledge of concepts of print. These are typically performance assessments. Students are asked to locate titles and authors' names, identify letters and words, track the direction of print, and more. Teachers observe students and mark their responses on recording sheets containing scoring criteria. Other formal assessments ask students to identify letter names, apply phonological and phonemic awareness skills, and decode words. Portions of the DIBELS assessment are examples of this type. Data gained from these assessments can be used to group students, plan differentiated instruction, and develop interventions.

Other formal assessments evaluate students' decoding abilities and reading fluency. Students may be asked to read short texts while being timed. They may also be asked to retell stories or answer comprehension questions. Both DIBELS and DRA are two examples of this type of assessment. State standardized tests often require students to read passages and answer comprehension questions. In addition to helping teachers group students and differentiate instruction, these assessments can also help teachers select appropriately leveled texts. There are also formal assessments that specifically assess students' vocabulary knowledge.

FORMALLY ASSESSING WRITTEN LANGUAGE

Students' writing is often formally assessed using teacher-created, district-mandated, and state-mandated assessments. These assessments typically provide students with specific writing prompts indicating the topics and text structures they are expected to use. Sometimes prompts are based on reading passages that are also contained in the assessments. For example, students may be asked to read two related texts and write responses that explain the common theme they share.

Students' written responses on formal assessments are usually scored using either analytic or holistic rubrics. These rubrics should contain clear criteria that reflect the performance expectations for students. Common criteria include development, organization, language use, conventions, and following the writing process. By analyzing students' performances on different rubric criteria, teachers can plan individualized instruction and develop interventions for struggling students. For example, if students are struggling with language use, teachers can help students analyze mentor texts that contain strong examples.

INFORMALLY ASSESSING LITERACY DEVELOPMENT

One type of informal assessment is **miscue analysis**, which occurs when teachers listen to students as they read and analyze their miscues. By looking for patterns in the miscues, teachers can determine which strategies students are using and which are lacking. This information can be used to guide instruction.

- **Informal reading inventories** require students to read leveled texts while teachers note errors and fluency. Students then respond to comprehension questions about the texts. Information gained from informal reading inventories can be used to select leveled texts, group students, and plan appropriate instruction.
- **Portfolios** are another type of informal assessment. Portfolios consist of collections of student work, which can be used to show progress over time.
- **Performance assessments** can also be used to assess students' literacy development while allowing students to complete authentic tasks. For example, students may research nutritional guidelines and read food labels to create healthy weekly meal plans.
- **Informal assessment** can also occur when teachers observe students engaged in literacy activities, ask them to explain their thinking, and note performance on assignments and homework. These methods can provide valuable information about students' knowledge and skills, which can be used to guide instruction.

RUBRICS

Rubrics are evaluation tools used to assign scores to students' work. They explain the criteria used to assign scores for different levels of mastery. Rubrics can be given to students when projects are assigned to ensure they understand expectations. They can make evaluation more consistent because all students are evaluated using the same criteria. Rubrics can also be easily adapted to reflect different types of activities and assignments.

There are many ways rubrics can be used to evaluate literacy development. They can be used to assess students' reading fluency, with categories relating to speed, accuracy, and prosody. They can also be used to evaluate projects relating to analysis and comprehension.

Additionally, rubrics can be used to assess students' writing. Categories relating to development, use of language, conventions, and other topics can be included. The rubrics can be adapted to reflect the genres or text structures used.

ANALYTIC VS. HOLISTIC RUBRICS

Analytic rubrics assign separate scores for each criterion being evaluated. For example, if a writing rubric has criteria for development, use of language, and conventions, each of these areas receives its own score. These scores are then added together to determine the overall score for the assignment. Analytic rubrics provide targeted feedback and help students understand their strengths and weaknesses. However, they can be time-consuming to create and adapt.

Holistic rubrics provide one overall score for the assignment rather than evaluating each criterion separately. They list varying levels of performance, and each level describes the characteristics of assignments earning that score. For example, a writing assignment might be assigned a score ranging from 1 to 4. Assignments earning a score of 4 would be well developed, have effective use of language, and have few or no errors with conventions. Holistic rubrics can be faster for teachers to create and adapt for different assignments. However, the feedback is less targeted than it is when using analytic rubrics, which evaluate each criterion separately.

RUNNING RECORDS

Running records are tools used to record students' behaviors and use of strategies during reading. To administer running records, teachers provide students with books in their developmental reading levels and ask them to read the books aloud. While students are reading, teachers record the words read correctly with check marks. They also note errors by recording the actual words in the texts and the words students substituted for them. Word repetitions, omissions, and self-corrections are also noted using special symbols.

By analyzing errors, teachers can determine which cueing systems students are consistently using. They can plan mini-lessons to encourage students to use the cueing systems they are not currently using. Teachers can also note fluency and how students track the texts. Analyzing self-corrections can indicate whether or not students are self-monitoring their reading. Additionally, accuracy rates can be calculated. To calculate accuracy rates, teachers first divide the number of words read correctly by the total number of words in the texts and then multiply the answers by 100. Accuracy rates can be used to determine if the texts are in students' frustration, instructional, or independent reading levels. This assists teachers with selecting appropriate texts and differentiating instruction to meet students' needs.

ROLE OF PERFORMANCE-BASED ASSESSMENTS IN LITERACY ASSESSMENT

Performance-based assessments require students to solve real-world problems and accomplish authentic tasks by applying literacy skills and strategies. An example of a performance-based assessment is writing a letter to a government official in support of a new law, citing evidence-based reasons for the position. Depending on the types of tasks involved, performance-based assessments may require students to synthesize information from multiple sources, defend positions with text evidence, write texts following the writing process, and create materials to convey information to others.

Performance-based assessments are open ended and do not contain right or wrong answers. Typically, there are multiple ways that students can approach the tasks. The assessments are evaluated using rubrics, with clear criteria determined and shared with students in advance.

An advantage of performance-based assessments is that they allow students opportunities to solve real-world problems, thereby increasing learner engagement. They also require higher-level thinking skills, such as analysis, application, synthesis, and creation. Additionally, they often allow students some choices in how they present their learning. A disadvantage is that performance-based assessments may be time-consuming to create and implement. Grading can also be subjective.

ROLE OF PORTFOLIOS IN LITERACY ASSESSMENT

Portfolios are collections of students' projects and work gathered over time. They can serve many purposes in assessing literacy development. They can be used to track students' progress over time and check for mastery of certain skills, which is useful for planning differentiated instruction. Portfolios can also be passed along to students' future teachers, helping them determine students' instructional levels. Additionally, portfolios can be used to help students self-evaluate their own progress and set future goals.

If using portfolios, teachers must make several decisions. They must determine how the portfolios will be used, which will influence the criteria used to select portfolio entries. They also need to determine how entries will be selected. Will teachers or students select the entries, or will both play roles in the process? Teachers also need to decide if the portfolios will be graded. Checklists and rubrics are possible tools that can be used to grade portfolios.

Some advantages of portfolios include the ability to see concrete evidence of student progress over time and the possibility of having students actively involved in assessing their own progress. However, evaluating portfolios is subjective, and teachers may be unsure of how to use them to guide instruction.

DETERMINING WHEN TO RESPOND TO STUDENT MISCUES IN READING

Even proficient readers make errors at times. Fluent readers often read texts rapidly and may occasionally omit or substitute words without changing the meanings of the texts. For example, they may substitute "her house" for "the house" in a text. These types of errors do not impact meaning and, if occasional, can be ignored. Stopping to correct these types of minor errors can interrupt fluency and comprehension.

Readers in the emergent and early stages of development may make frequent errors and become frustrated if corrected each time. Overcorrection may interfere with confidence and reading enjoyment. Teachers should strategically choose which types of errors to respond to during each reading session. One approach is to focus on a single type of error each time, such as errors where syntax cues are ignored. Another approach is to intervene only when errors affect the meaning of the text. Minor errors can be ignored to build fluency and confidence.

Supporting Advanced Readers

CHARACTERISTICS OF ADVANCED READERS

Advanced readers can display many different characteristics. They are sometimes identified by above-average scores on standardized reading assessments. Other times, observed reading behaviors and performances on classroom assignments can provide clues.

Advanced readers typically read fluently and have strong word recognition and decoding abilities. They are also able to flexibly apply a variety of reading strategies to figure out unknown words and meanings.

Advanced readers may also have well-developed vocabularies and incorporate varied words into their speech and writing. They may show a strong interest in reading and get deeply immersed in the texts they have selected. Advanced readers often love to talk with others about the books they have read, and they may make connections between the texts and themselves, other texts, and real-world events. Additionally, they are often able to analyze texts using high-level comprehension skills, such as evaluating and drawing conclusions.

CHALLENGING/ENGAGING HIGH-ACHIEVING READERS
COLLABORATIVE LEARNING OPPORTUNITIES

High-achieving readers can often benefit from participating in collaborative, project-based learning opportunities that allow them to apply higher-level reading and writing skills with others. Collaborative projects draw upon the strengths and unique problem-solving abilities of all group members and allow high-achieving readers to work with others to solve realistic problems. The projects allow students to share ideas and receive feedback from others of all skill levels, including other high-achieving students who may enjoy analyzing and discussing the same types of complex texts that they do.

High-achieving readers can benefit from forming collaborative relationships with teachers. They can be taught to use metacognitive strategies to self-monitor their own reading and set realistic but challenging goals for their own reading and writing development. They can collaborate with teachers to select literacy projects that pertain to their interests. This involvement in the learning process can help high-achieving readers stay interested and engaged in literacy instruction.

OPEN-ENDED ASSIGNMENTS AND PROJECTS

High-achieving readers often benefit from having some choices about what and how they learn. This can include choices about the types and topics of texts they explore. For example, if classes are learning about persuasive writing, students may choose the texts they will analyze from a range of genres and topics.

Students can also have some choices about the complexity of the projects they complete, with options to delve deeper into topics if desired. For example, if students in a class are identifying characteristics of fairy tales, some students may choose to compare and contrast multiple versions of the same tale and note identifying features.

High-achieving readers may also benefit from having choices about the formats of their projects. Possible project ideas include creating multimedia presentations, writing alternative endings to texts, creating three-dimensional artistic representations of story events, and more. These options also accommodate different learning modalities. Teachers may create a menu of options for students to choose from or encourage them to come up with their own ideas.

Although students may be directing some of their own learning, teachers should still conference with high-achieving readers frequently to assess progress and collaborate on ideas.

ISSUES AND FRUSTRATIONS OF HIGH-ACHIEVING READERS

High-achieving readers are sometimes required to read the same texts as the other students in their classes during reading instruction and in other content areas. Because these texts are often designed for on-level readers, they may be easy for high-achieving readers to decode and comprehend. Without any challenges in the texts, high-achieving readers may **finish quick**ly and possibly become bored.

High-achieving readers are also sometimes given extra work to complete when they finish their on-level work early. They may view this extra work as a punishment, and the new work may not be challenging for these students either. **Boredom** and **frustration** may then occur.

Additionally, high-achieving readers may become bored during whole-class lessons on concepts they have already mastered. For example, readers who are successfully decoding complex multisyllabic words will likely become bored during lessons on CVCe spelling patterns.

These high-achieving readers may sometimes appear disengaged, resist coming to school, or have behavior issues within the classroom. To prevent these issues from occurring, teachers can **differentiate instruction** and provide high-achieving readers with opportunities to read texts within their **instructional levels**. These students can also be encouraged to complete alternate assignments that are more challenging.

Motivating Students to Read

CREATING SCHOOL ENVIRONMENTS THAT PROMOTE A LOVE OF READING

Helping students develop a lifelong love of reading is an important goal of literacy instruction. Teachers can model their own love of reading by talking about their favorite books and authors and modeling their own use of reading strategies. They can share stories of how reading has positively affected their own lives and opened up new opportunities.

- Teachers can also help develop **communities of readers** within their classrooms, making reading a social experience. Fun and interactive read-alouds and shared reading experiences can help create communities of readers, along with organizing literature circles and reader's theater activities. Favorite books can be reread multiple times, with students participating in the reading.
- Teachers can give students frequent opportunities to read **books of choice**. They can create classroom libraries containing multiple types of texts that students can access easily. Comfortable reading spaces, such as reading chairs and pillows, are also beneficial. Students should also have opportunities to visit their school libraries regularly.
- Additionally, teachers can guide students in completing **author studies**. Students may form connections to favorite authors and seek additional books they have written.

> **Review Video: Characteristics of Literacy-Rich, Content-Area Classrooms**
> Visit mometrix.com/academy and enter code: 571455

PROMOTING SUCCESSFUL INDEPENDENT READING EXPERIENCES AT SCHOOL

Independent reading is beneficial for students' reading development and is sometimes necessary when teachers are working with other students. Therefore, some strategies can be used to make independent reading experiences successful.

It is important to teach students to select appropriate texts that will not lead to boredom or frustration. Some teachers instruct students to apply the five-finger rule. In this approach, students randomly select a single page of text to read. If they struggle to decode five or more words, the book is too difficult. Other teachers inform students of their reading levels and keep labeled boxes of leveled texts available. Students can also be encouraged to maintain personal book boxes that contain several appropriate books so that they are ready for independent reading time.

To remind students of decoding and comprehension strategies they can use during independent reading time, teachers can display posters in their classrooms. Students can also be given small, personalized copies of these strategies to use.

Additionally, students can be encouraged to analyze and discuss what they have read to build interest and engagement. They can maintain reader-response logs or join literature circles with others who have read the same texts.

MOTIVATING STUDENTS TO READ

One technique to motivate students to read is to make reading an enjoyable part of the daily routine. This includes designating daily time for reading, providing a comfortable, relaxed atmosphere, helping students select texts of interest, and showing genuine interest in discussing the texts together. This technique is easy to implement, and students who look forward to this reading time as children may continue reading for enjoyment in adulthood. A disadvantage is that some students may not respond to this approach.

Another technique is to use rewards and incentives for reading. Some programs reward students after they have read a certain number of books or for a certain number of minutes. Sometimes students are tested on the books they have read to assess comprehension. Read-athons are one example of this approach. Peer participation, competition, and opportunities to earn rewards may increase short-term motivation to read. Disadvantages include the costs of the incentives and the possibility that motivation will decrease once the rewards are removed.

Teachers frequently use a combination of these techniques by providing daily reading time while also incorporating some incentives for reading.

Print-Rich Learning Environments

CHARACTERISTICS OF LITERACY-RICH, CONTENT-AREA CLASSROOMS

Literacy-rich, content-area classrooms include frequent teacher modeling of academic behaviors. This includes teacher modeling of thinking aloud, use of reading and writing strategies, and incorporation of academic vocabulary into regular activities.

These classrooms also include daily reading, writing, listening, and speaking activities. Students are engaged in reading, writing, and discussing a range of different texts and media in both print in digital form. Depending on the content area, this may include lab reports, journal articles, maps, historical fiction, diaries, graphic organizers, narratives, and more.

Students in literacy-rich classrooms are encouraged to make connections between different sources and content areas. For example, readers may make connections between a historical fiction text about the Dust Bowl and what they have learned in science about weather patterns.

Additionally, teachers in literacy-rich classrooms encourage the respectful sharing of information and ideas among classmates.

CREATING LEARNING ENVIRONMENTS SUPPORTIVE OF CULTURAL AND LINGUISTIC DIFFERENCES

Classrooms should incorporate **culturally** and **linguistically diverse materials**, including those that represent the cultures of students. Reading materials, artwork, classroom labels, and posters are all examples of diverse materials that can be included. Students should also have opportunities to share items that are meaningful to them with other classmates.

Additionally, ELLs should not be punished for reluctance to participate in discussions. Instead, they should be offered **support** and **scaffolding** when needed. When ELLs are in the early stages of English language acquisition, teachers can also use simple sentence structures and provide visual clues to support students' comprehension.

Teachers should also work to create nonthreatening and supportive classroom environments by modeling accepting attitudes. They can model and explicitly teach how to compare and contrast different cultures respectfully. When studying historical and current events, teachers can help students explore the events from different perspectives and discuss how culture can affect people's experiences.

> **Review Video: Importance of Promoting Literacy in the Home**
> Visit mometrix.com/academy and enter code: 862347

USING WORD WALLS TO SUPPORT READING AND WRITING DEVELOPMENT

Word walls are collections of words that are prominently displayed in classrooms. Words selected for display on word walls should be meaningful for students. They might include high-frequency words that students need to read and write often or academic vocabulary words related to units of study. Word walls are flexible, and words may be added or removed throughout the year based on students' needs.

Teachers should model how to use word walls to locate and spell high-frequency words. Words may be attached using Velcro, magnets, or other methods that allow them to be removed. This allows students to take the words down while using them and return them to the wall when finished.

There are many ways to organize word walls. Words can be listed alphabetically under letter headings, helping young writers quickly locate them for spelling assistance. If focused on academic vocabulary, the words can be grouped by topic. Visuals can be included with vocabulary words to assist students with remembering meanings.

LEVELED BOOK ROOMS

Leveled book rooms are consolidated collections of leveled readers that can be checked out by all teachers within a school. Reading specialists often help organize and maintain leveled book rooms as part of their responsibilities. Because teachers frequently have students who read both well above and well below grade level, these types of book rooms ensure that all students have access to books within their instructional reading levels.

To implement successful leveled book rooms, books should be clearly organized and labeled according to level. The same leveling system used by classroom teachers should be used in the leveled book rooms for consistency. Books may also be organized in additional ways, such as by genre, topic, or author. Teachers should be taught the procedures for checking out and returning books. Records should be maintained in order to keep track of where all books are located.

INSTRUCTIONAL TECHNOLOGIES SUPPORTING LITERACY DEVELOPMENT

There are many ways that instructional technologies can be used to create classroom environments that support literacy development. Computer programs and apps can be used to practice and assess literacy skills, and there are many options that differentiate instruction based on students' existing skills. Many of these programs and apps also save and track students' progress, helping both students and teachers track progress toward goals.

- Projectors, document cameras, and interactive whiteboards can also be used to **magnify texts** so students can follow along during instruction. Interactive whiteboards also allow students to actively participate in literacy activities with classmates.
- **Digital texts** can be used to support listening development and assist students with reading texts that are too difficult for them to read independently. Interactive storybooks that display and track text for emergent and beginning readers can also be used.

- There are many **digital tools** and **software options** that can be used to create forms of media such as slideshow presentations, infographics, digital storybooks, and newsletters. Modern tools can also be used to help students collaborate on projects, even if they are working remotely.

Print-Rich Environments for Early Childhood

PRINT-RICH CLASSROOMS

In early childhood classrooms, print-rich environments contain books and texts of different genres and topics, including both audio and digital texts. Walls and shelves have signs and labels to help with classroom procedures and organization. Posters display information related to content students have been studying. Reading, writing, and listening centers are available for students to explore during center time. Puppet theaters and flannel boards are present to encourage oral language and storytelling. There are also many literacy-related materials, such as letter tiles and sight word cards. Word walls are posted.

In **print-rich environments**, students are encouraged to share and display texts they have created. They may add their own stories to the classroom libraries or hang up signs they have made. Materials created during shared and interactive reading and writing experiences may also be displayed.

In classrooms for older students, signs and posters are displayed containing academic vocabulary, content students have been studying, and classroom procedures. Written and digital texts from a range of genres are present. There are also ample resources available for students to use to locate and share information, such as computers, tablets, dictionaries, and thesauri.

PROMOTING LITERACY DEVELOPMENT WITH DRAMATIC PLAY CENTERS

Dramatic play centers are common in early childhood classrooms. These centers allow children to act out realistic situations through play. Examples include pretend restaurants, homes, veterinary clinics, and grocery stores. While engaging in dramatic play, children read, write, listen, and speak for authentic purposes.

As children role-play and interact with other children in dramatic play centers, they develop oral language skills. They engage in conversations and practice using language to accomplish tasks, such as ordering in restaurants. They also listen to peers and follow directions, such as when they are pretending to be restaurant servers.

Children also engage in reading activities in dramatic play centers. Labels and realistic print materials can be included. For example, pretend restaurants may include labeled cabinets and menus. Children can practice writing through dramatic play. For example, children who are pretending to be servers may write down orders on notepads.

BUILDING LITERACY ACTIVITIES INTO DAILY ROUTINES AND ACTIVITIES

Teachers can plan reading, writing, listening, and speaking activities across all subject areas. This can include a mixture of independent literacy activities and shared and interactive reading and writing experiences. Texts focusing on topics that are being studied in all content areas can be accessible in the classroom. Students can also write in all subject areas. For example, they can write the processes used to solve problems in math and create travel brochures in social studies.

Teachers of early childhood and elementary students can plan morning meetings in which daily written messages are read and discussed. Students can share current events and topics of interest with their classmates during these meetings, while other students listen and ask questions.

Early childhood and elementary teachers can also incorporate oral language and listening into daily routines. For example, they may recite specific chants or songs during transitions.

Print-Rich Home and Community Environments

PRINT-RICH HOMES

An important component of print-rich homes is easy access to developmentally appropriate texts in a range of genres. Although favorite texts can be kept and reread repeatedly, children should also have access to new and changing texts over time as their interests and skills develop. Both digital and print-based texts are commonly found in print-rich homes. This may include books, magazines, newspapers, online literacy games, and digital stories.

In addition to books, print-rich homes also contain a lot of environmental print that children can read. This may include cereal boxes, board game directions, recipes, mail, and more. Exploring this environmental print helps children understand different purposes for reading and writing.

Children in print-rich homes have easy access to a variety of writing materials, such as paper, pencils, and crayons. Computers can also be available to type texts. Children should be encouraged to write for a variety of purposes and audiences.

FAMILY MEMBERS' PROMOTING READING

Family members can help children make reading a part of everyday activities both at home and while out in the community. Helping children explore environmental print and its purposes is one important step family members can take. They can point out business and road signs while driving, for example. At home, they can help children explore environmental print like food labels, posters, and mail.

Family members can also help children understand how reading is used to accomplish daily tasks. They can ask children to help create and read lists at the grocery store and select meal choices from restaurant menus. While driving, they can ask children to help read road signs to determine which routes they will take. At home, they can read directions together to assemble new toys and follow recipes to prepare shared meals.

There are many benefits to reading with children for authentic purposes; it helps children understand that reading is part of daily life and learn that it can be used for many practical purposes. This approach also blends learning with daily life and real-world tasks, helping engage children in the learning process.

FAMILY MEMBERS' ENCOURAGING ORAL LANGUAGE DEVELOPMENT

Parents and family members should talk to children frequently from the moment they are born. Children learn how to use language by listening to those around them. Family members can respond to their children's initial sounds and beginning attempts at speech by making eye contact and replying. When children begin speaking words and sentences, family members can respond by repeating what they have said and adding additional information. They can encourage children to imitate their words and actions, using games like peekaboo. Family members can talk about what they are doing and ask their children open-ended questions. They can use varied vocabulary and sentence structure in their speech.

Family members can also engage in wordplay with children. They can read rhyming and repetitive texts, songs, and poems together, encouraging their children to participate. Additionally, they can retell favorite stories orally and make up stories of their own.

FAMILY MEMBERS' PROMOTING A LOVE OF READING AT HOME

Family members can incorporate reading time into their children's daily routines to promote a love of reading at home. This can include a variety of types of reading experiences. Sometimes family members can read aloud to their children, sometimes children can read aloud to their family members, and sometimes they can take turns reading. Each of these experiences has its own benefits. Children benefit from hearing their family members reading fluently and using reading strategies, and they also benefit from practicing their own reading skills in safe environments.

While reading together at home, families can read a mixture of new and favorite texts. The experiences should be fun and relaxing, with opportunities to talk about the stories and characters. They can also listen to audio texts together at various times, such as when they are in the car.

Children can benefit from seeing family members reading frequently and for a variety of purposes. Family members can talk about their favorite books and authors. They can also take children to the library regularly to find new books to read together.

PROMOTING COMMUNITY INVOLVEMENT IN LITERACY ACTIVITIES

Teachers can share information with parents about free public story time events to promote parent involvement in community literacy activities. These events are commonly held at public libraries and bookstores. Teachers can also forge partnerships with their local public libraries. They can inquire about programs that issue library cards to students. Local librarians can be invited to visit classrooms to read aloud to students and share information about upcoming events.

Teachers can set up **community volunteer programs**. Community members can be invited to visit classrooms to read with students. Students can also potentially visit senior centers or other locations to read to adults. Local authors and business people who use reading and writing in their jobs can also be invited to visit classrooms to discuss the role that literacy plays in their lives.

Additionally, teachers can encourage students to communicate with community members for **authentic purposes**. For example, students can send thank-you letters to businesses that hosted field trips or sponsored school events. With parents' permission, student work can also be displayed during community events.

USING INSTRUCTIONAL TECHNOLOGIES TO PROMOTE LITERACY DEVELOPMENT AT HOME

There are many free and inexpensive online games and apps that students of all ages can use to practice literacy skills. These include letter recognition activities, phonics skills practice, digital texts with comprehension questions, and more. School districts that subscribe to certain online programs may provide parents with links and passwords so students can practice at home.

Students can also listen to digital storybooks. Online versions are available that track the text for students and show pictures. Audio versions can be downloaded or checked out from public libraries. Family members can listen to and discuss these stories with their children to practice comprehension strategies.

With guidance and supervision, students can communicate with others using digital tools. They can create presentations and written texts using word processing and presentation tools. They can communicate with family members using emails, texts, and videoconferencing tools. They can also use free online tools to create and publish their own digital stories.

> **Review Video: Collaborating with Families**
> Visit mometrix.com/academy and enter code: 679996

INCREASING FAMILY INVOLVEMENT IN READING DEVELOPMENT

Teachers should communicate with caregivers frequently to increase family involvement in reading development. They should convey to caregivers that they are viewed as partners and assure them that they welcome questions and concerns. Teachers should frequently communicate positive information to caregivers in addition to sharing reading concerns. Teachers should also recognize that different families have different resources available, so they should try communicating through multiple channels. This may include phone calls, texts, classroom websites, paper newsletters, emails, and more. Teachers should also be aware of scheduling, cultural, and linguistic differences. Information can be sent home in multiple languages, if possible.

Teachers can share links to reading activities and strategies using classroom websites and newsletters. They can also send home reproducible books and texts from classroom libraries, that students can read with their families. Consumable supplies can also be sent home, such as cardstock letter tiles that can be used to practice spelling and building words.

Parent and family nights can also be scheduled to share strategies and display student work. These events can be recorded and shared with parents who are unable to attend.

Screening for Reading and Language Delays

SCREENING VS. DIAGNOSTIC ASSESSMENTS

Screening assessments are used to identify students who may be at risk for future academic difficulties. Information gained from these assessments can be used to determine which students would likely benefit from specialized interventions to help prevent academic difficulties in the future.

Adequate literacy screening is important in young children. Studies have shown that literacy difficulties are harder to remedy through intervention after third grade. By identifying these students early and providing appropriate interventions, these difficulties can be prevented or lessened. For example, phonemic awareness screenings are frequently given to early childhood students because phonemic awareness is a key indicator of future reading success.

Diagnostic assessments are used to identify students' existing knowledge and skills before beginning instruction. For example, students may complete diagnostic assessments focused on using comprehension strategies to understand nonfiction texts. Data from diagnostic assessments can be used to help teachers plan differentiated instruction to meet students' individual needs.

IDENTIFYING STUDENTS WHO HAVE NOT MET STANDARDS

It is important to identify concerns with literacy development early to prevent future academic difficulties. Reading, writing, listening, and speaking affect performance across all content areas. Therefore, students who struggle with literacy may struggle in all academic areas.

- **Early screening** is one way to identify students who are not meeting standards and may have literacy difficulties. Depending on the ages of the students, screening can be given on a range of topics, including alphabetic principle, phonological and phonemic awareness, decoding strategies, fluency, and comprehension.
- The results of **criterion** and **norm-referenced formal assessments** can also be used to identify students who have not met standards. Teachers can look for specific skills and standard areas that students struggled with on these formal assessments. They can also look for indications that students are not meeting their adequate yearly progress goals.
- Additionally, **informal assessments** can be used to identify students who are not meeting standards. Classroom observations, running records, responses during literature circles, and other informal assessments are helpful tools for teachers to use.

All of these data points can be considered when determining which students may benefit from targeted interventions.

DETERMINING WHETHER STUDENTS SHOULD BE EVALUATED FOR READING OR LANGUAGE DELAYS

Generally, teachers should collect multiple data points over time before requesting that students be evaluated for potential delays or disabilities. Students may perform below expectations on assessments for a variety of reasons, including illness and fatigue. Therefore, no one assessment score should be used as the basis for an evaluation. However, if students perform similarly on multiple assessments over time, further investigation may be warranted. Assessment data can also be combined with classroom observations for supplementary information. Additionally, interventions can be attempted first to determine if achievement gaps can be closed through targeted instruction.

Parents sometimes request that their children be evaluated. Parents are often the first to notice potential issues because they observe their children's progress from year to year and witness the challenges firsthand. Parents can submit their requests for evaluations in writing to classroom teachers, reading specialists, administrators, or other school officials for consideration.

SIGNS OF DYSLEXIA

Dyslexia is a common disorder that affects reading. Students with **dyslexia** often have difficulties with phonological awareness, accurate word recognition, decoding, and reading fluency. As a result, they may also have difficulties comprehending what they have read. Spelling may also be affected. Teachers may notice that students struggle to decode words and read fluently, and students may become anxious or frustrated when asked to read. Dyslexia does not affect intelligence and is marked by a gap between students' abilities and achievements.

Although there is no cure for dyslexia, targeted interventions are often successful. A multisensory approach to reading instruction is often helpful, along with systematic and explicit instruction in reading skills and sight word recognition. The Orton-Gillingham method is one commonly used approach. Teachers should also maintain supportive classroom environments and not rush students or force them to read aloud. Students with dyslexia may also benefit from some accommodations, such as extra time on tests, increased wait time when responding to questions, and access to audio versions of texts.

> **Review Video: Understanding Learning Disability Needs of Students**
> Visit mometrix.com/academy and enter code: 662775

SIGNS OF DYSGRAPHIA

Dysgraphia is a disorder that affects written expression. Students with dysgraphia may have difficulties holding pencils correctly, forming letters, writing on lines, putting thoughts into written words, and organizing writing in meaningful ways. Handwriting and spelling are also commonly difficult for students. Students with dysgraphia may become frustrated or anxious if asked to write, and they may try to avoid writing when possible.

There are many ways teachers can assist students with dysgraphia. To assist with spelling, explicit instruction on sound-symbol relationships and spelling patterns may be helpful. Graphic organizers can be provided to assist students with written organization. Additionally, students may qualify for occupational therapy to assist with developing coordination and motor skills. Students with dysgraphia may also benefit from some accommodations, such as being allowed to type responses or answer questions orally. They may benefit from receiving extra time to complete assignments and tests.

SIGNS OF DYSPRAXIA

Dyspraxia is a disorder that makes it difficult for the body to coordinate movement. Students with dyspraxia may have difficulties with balance and coordination, and they may have trouble performing tasks that require motor skills. Students with dyspraxia may also be sensitive to noise or touch in addition to spatial or perceptual difficulties, all of which might affect reading and writing. Some types of dyspraxia may also affect language, especially enunciation.

In the classroom, teachers can break large, multistep tasks into smaller chunks. If activities require movement, teachers can begin with simple movements first, and gradually increase the difficulty. Teachers can also provide extra processing time when giving directions and extra wait time when asking questions. Some students with dyspraxia may qualify for occupational therapy services. Students with dyspraxia may benefit from certain accommodations, such as seating that is free from noise and distractions.

CHARACTERISTICS OF READING COMPREHENSION DEFICIENCIES

Students with **reading comprehension deficiencies** have difficulty understanding and responding to what they have read. They may have difficulty summarizing texts, making inferences, differentiating between main ideas and supporting details, and more. They often have issues with reading fluency as well, especially with phrasing and prosody. Students with comprehension deficiencies can often decode words efficiently, yet they struggle with comprehending the texts' meanings. However, some students may struggle with both decoding and comprehension.

To assist students with comprehension deficiencies, teachers can provide advance organizers that offer overviews of the text structures and story events. They can also preview texts or conduct picture walks to familiarize students with the topics. Before reading, they can instruct students to pay attention to specific key information within the texts. Additionally, teachers can model their use of comprehension strategies during think-alouds and shared reading experiences.

CHARACTERISTICS OF READING RETENTION DEFICIENCIES

Students with **reading retention deficiencies** have difficulties remembering what they have read. This may include difficulties summarizing texts, ordering story events, and making text connections after reading. Retention deficiencies may occur due to difficulties transferring information to short- or long-term memory or with difficulties retrieving information that has been previously stored in long-term memory.

To assist students with retention difficulties, teachers can provide students with graphic organizers that they can complete while reading. Story maps and sequencing charts are examples of graphic organizers that may be helpful. Teachers can also provide notes and text summaries to assist students with remembering important concepts and details. Additionally, students can be taught to use specific strategies to activate memory, such as visualizing as they read. They can also be taught to annotate texts by highlighting key phrases and taking notes, making it easier to locate important information in the future.

Effective Literacy Interventions

COMPONENTS OF EFFECTIVE LITERACY INTERVENTIONS

Literacy interventions should be targeted to students' individual needs and based upon assessment data. Interventions can be delivered either individually or in small groups, if multiple students can benefit from the same interventions.

If commercial intervention programs are used, they should be carefully evaluated to ensure they are research-based. Interventions should be based upon clear objectives. They should also incorporate ways to measure students' progress to evaluate if the interventions are successful. Pre-tests are commonly given when interventions are implemented, and the results are used to set goals. Student progress is then monitored regularly to determine if progress is being made toward the performance goals.

Research has shown that frequent interventions are more effective than infrequent interventions, even if they occur for shorter blocks of time. For example, teachers may conduct small-group interventions daily, for 15 minutes each time. Students need frequent opportunities to practice and apply new skills. Interventions should include a mixture of systematic and explicit instruction and guided practice with feedback.

Although students benefit from interventions with classroom teachers and literacy specialists, some carefully selected computer-based interventions may also be used.

EVALUATING THE EFFECTIVENESS OF LITERACY INTERVENTIONS

Literacy interventions are planned for students based upon assessment data. This initial data is used to set performance goals, and progress toward goals is measured using progress monitoring and intervention post-tests. If students make regular progress and achieve their performance goals within the expected time frames, the interventions are usually considered effective. If students make minimal or no progress toward their goals despite receiving interventions, the interventions may be considered ineffective, unless additional factors are impeding success.

However, interventions must be implemented with fidelity to determine their effectiveness. Teachers must use the agreed-upon strategies and instructional methods and meet with students consistently according to their intervention schedules. They must also ensure that the interventions are not interrupted. If issues occur in these areas, lack of student progress may not be the result of ineffective intervention planning. The interventions may have the potential to be successful, but the implementation and delivery methods may need improvement.

READING STRATEGIES VS. READING INTERVENTIONS

Reading strategies and reading interventions are often used interchangeably, but there are some key differences between the two. Reading strategies are methods teachers use to help students learn reading skills. To teach students to comprehend texts, teachers may encourage them to make predictions and inferences. Strategies are taught during regular classroom instruction and may be reinforced individually or in small groups. Meeting informally with a student to review and practice how to make predictions during one class session is not a formal intervention as no set improvement plan, regular meeting schedule, or progress monitoring assessment is involved.

Interventions are specific plans to help students make progress in targeted areas. They are based on assessment data, and they are scheduled for regular, set periods of time. Students' progress is monitored through frequent assessments to look for improvement. Reading strategies may be taught and practiced as part of formal intervention plans.

Role of the Reading Specialist

PROMOTING THE GOALS OF SCHOOLS' READING PROGRAMS TO PARENTS AND FAMILY MEMBERS

Although it is common for classroom teachers to communicate with family members about reading development, reading specialists also play important roles in promoting literacy at home. Reading specialists may conduct family surveys to learn more about home literacy behaviors and to assess parents' literacy-related needs and concerns. They may help organize school- or district-wide family literacy events. These events offer hands-on literacy activities appropriate for different grade levels that family members can complete with their children and take home for additional practice. They also feature interactive read-alouds that model ways parents can encourage reading behaviors with their children at home.

Additionally, reading specialists might be involved in organizing book fairs or lending libraries that supplement their schools' traditional libraries. They may provide families with information about reading goals and interventions or summer reading programs.

PROMOTING COLLABORATION AMONG TEACHERS AND OTHER COLLEAGUES

One role of a reading specialist is to promote collaboration among colleagues. A collaborative approach allows colleagues to develop and work toward shared goals. It can increase motivation to implement reading programs with fidelity and help colleagues share strategies to address common problems and concerns.

In addition to attending staff meetings, reading specialists can attend grade-level team meetings. Reading specialists can help grade-level teams analyze assessment data to identify areas in need of improvement. Together, the teams can create performance goals that will be used to drive reading instruction. They can collaboratively develop instructional plans and activities to help reach the shared goals. This type of collaborative approach can encourage motivation and accountability.

Reading specialists may also look for each colleague's strengths and note strong examples of research-based reading instruction. They can encourage these colleagues to share their strategies and allow others to observe their teaching. Teachers may also be encouraged to share problems they are having with reading instruction, and colleagues can work together to develop solutions to these problems.

ROLE IN IMPROVING SCHOOLS' READING CURRICULA

Reading specialists typically have access to assessment data from multiple grade levels and time periods. They can lead data analysis teams that look for trends that may indicate gaps in their schools' reading curricula. Once these gaps are identified, reading specialists can work with teachers to revise curricula and instructional methods to better address these needs and improve

59

student performance. Reading specialists often also serve on committees to evaluate and select potential reading programs to supplement or replace existing ones. Reading specialists can share their knowledge of research-based approaches to literacy instruction and use this knowledge to evaluate the potential reading programs.

Reading specialists also identify external professional development opportunities that may be beneficial for teachers based on their schools' instructional gaps. They advocate for opportunities for teachers to attend these sessions and share what they have learned with colleagues.

Additionally, reading specialists can recruit teachers who are willing to apply and model specific research-based instructional strategies while receiving coaching and support. For example, reading specialists can recruit teachers willing to try interactive word walls or literature circles.

BUILDING CONSENSUS AMONG COLLEAGUES WHEN MAKING INSTRUCTIONAL DECISIONS

Reading specialists often deal with conflict in their roles. **Conflict** may occur when introducing new reading programs or helping teachers decide upon new instructional strategies and goals. One role of a reading specialist is to help establish a **consensus among the different stakeholders** involved, including teachers, administrators, board members, and other school staff.

To do so, reading specialists need to be seen as leaders who are respected in their area of expertise but also **flexible** and willing to listen to new ideas. By listening to suggestions and concerns while also explaining literacy-related research and best practices, reading specialists can help their teams develop shared visions for school reading instruction. They can help other stakeholders understand their roles in achieving these visions by outlining specific but attainable goals and defining the responsibilities of everyone involved. Other stakeholders will be more likely to cooperate with the plans if they understand the role they will play in accomplishing the shared goals.

RESOLVING CONFLICT AMONG COLLEAGUES REGARDING READING INSTRUCTION

Instructional decisions have lasting effects on teachers and students. This is especially true when major decisions are made, such as selecting new reading programs. Conflict about instructional strategies and ways to implement change can lead to interpersonal conflict. Therefore, reading specialists who are facilitating these changes must often assist with conflict resolution.

- Reading specialists can first acknowledge the issues rather than ignore them, recognizing that conflict can be healthy when it leads to open discussions and sharing of ideas. They can then look for the root causes of the conflict. Although the conflicts may be based on personality differences, they may also be based on other issues, such as concerns about adequate time or resources and differing prior experiences. Helping highlight the true issues may lead to discussions about how the concerns can be alleviated.
- Reading specialists can also bring the discussions back to shared performance goals. Colleagues can be asked to restate the shared goals and the reasons behind them, reminding everyone involved that student success is the focus. Colleagues can then collaborate to find solutions that incorporate the ideas while still addressing the concerns of all parties involved.

ADVOCATING FOR PUBLIC SUPPORT OF READING EDUCATION

It is important for reading specialists to be aware of policies that affect literacy education at the local, state, and national levels. This includes awareness of school board, state government, and US Department of Education policies. Attending local school board meetings and joining professional organizations that track impending legislation are two ways to assist with this goal. Reading specialists can share their knowledge with colleagues and community members and advocate for legislation and policies that support effective reading instruction. Additionally, they can interpret existing legislation for their colleagues and ensure that they understand the implications it has on their classroom instruction.

Reading specialists can assist their school districts with writing grants and educational proposals that can positively impact literacy instruction. This may include proposals for funding that can be used to purchase new materials or hire additional reading specialists.

Reading Specialist's Role in Professional Development

READING SPECIALISTS SUPPORT OF CLASSROOM TEACHERS

Reading specialists often play a variety of roles within their schools. Some reading specialists serve as intervention teachers. These specialists directly provide targeted intervention services to students who are struggling with reading, often in areas including phonemic awareness, decoding, sight word recognition, and comprehension. They may go into students' classrooms to provide intervention services, or they may pull students out for a set number of minutes each week.

Reading specialists can also provide professional development opportunities for classroom teachers. In small or large-group sessions, they often model how to use instructional strategies that are supported by research. They compile literature and resources related to literacy instruction and make these resources available to teachers. They may also work with individual teachers to develop instructional plans or overcome difficulties with literacy instruction.

Reading specialists may also oversee standardized literacy assessments for their schools and train teachers in testing procedures. They work with teachers to analyze assessment data, track students' progress over time, and use the results to plan or change appropriate interventions.

PROFESSIONAL DEVELOPMENT OPPORTUNITIES

Reading specialists provide professional development opportunities for teachers on a wide range of topics. For early childhood teachers, reading specialists may offer training about modeling concepts of print, planning phonological and phonemic awareness activities, creating print-rich environments, and designing effective literacy centers. Other topics may include types of reading and writing experiences and using multisensory approaches to reading and writing instruction.

- Professional development for elementary teachers may include topics such as incorporating reading and writing across content areas, using interactive word walls, using assessment data to guide instruction, modeling comprehension strategies, and designing effective literature circles.
- For middle and high school teachers, professional development topics may include teaching academic vocabulary, incorporating reading and writing across content areas, teaching text structures, and using higher-level comprehension strategies.

Reading specialists may also provide professional development opportunities on specialized topics, such as meeting the needs of students with disabilities and teaching reading strategies to ELLs.

Chapter Quiz

Ready to see how well you retained what you just read? Scan the QR code to go directly to the chapter quiz interface for this study guide. If you're using a computer, simply visit the bonus page at **mometrix.com/bonus948/texesscitread** and click the Chapter Quizzes link.

Reading Development: Foundational Skills

Phonetics, Phonics, and Print Concepts

BUILDING RAPID WORD IDENTIFICATION AND AUTOMATICITY

Rapid word identification and **automaticity** refer to the quick, effortless, and accurate recognition of individual words when reading. Speed and accuracy are strong predictors of comprehension, so the ability to identify words automatically plays an important role in reading development.

When readers come to unfamiliar words in texts, they pause to use reading strategies. This includes applying phonics skills and using semantic and syntactic clues. Using these strategies takes time, which may cause the reader to slow down. Applying strategies to decode words also requires significant processing in working memory, which is limited. This diverts attention away from comprehending the text, and comprehension may be negatively affected. When readers develop the ability to accurately and automatically identify words, they free up space in working memory to use for comprehension. This shift often occurs around second and third grade.

It is also important to remember that rapid word identification and automaticity are necessary for fluency but not sufficient on their own. Fluency also involves reading with appropriate phrasing and intonation.

USING INSTRUCTIONAL STRATEGIES TO BUILD AUTOMATIC RECOGNITION OF HIGH-FREQUENCY SIGHT WORDS

Readers need several opportunities to see words before they can automatically recognize them. Therefore, providing opportunities for repeated exposure to high-frequency sight words is an important goal of reading instruction and should be included along with explicit phonics instruction.

Sight words are commonly introduced to students a few at a time. The most frequently used words, such as *a*, *you*, and *the*, are typically introduced first. Some reading programs coordinate sight word lists with weekly texts, ensuring that students will have frequent exposure to each set of words as they are introduced.

There are several types of activities that can be done to build sight word recognition. Having students go on "word hunts" to locate and circle sight words in texts is one activity. Sight words can be built using magnetic letters or spelled in the air with fingers or wands. Activities that require students to read, build, and write each word are also commonly used. Additionally, flash card drills can be incorporated into the school day.

TYPICAL PROGRESSION OF PHONOLOGICAL AWARENESS SKILLS

One of the earliest phonological awareness skills children develop is the ability to recognize rhyming words. After recognizing rhyming words heard in stories, songs, and poems, children begin to produce their own sets of rhyming words. Alliteration, or identifying and producing words with the same initial sounds, is another early phonological awareness skill.

Later, children develop awareness of syllables. This involves both the ability to blend syllables to form whole words and the ability to break whole words into syllables. They also develop the ability to blend and segment onsets and rimes. **Onsets** are composed of the initial consonants or

63

consonant blends in syllables, whereas **rimes** consist of the vowels and remaining consonants that follow. For example, in the word *star*, /st/ is the onset, and /ar/ is the rime. Phonemic awareness is the most advanced phonological awareness skill, and it is usually developed after the others.

RELATIONSHIP BETWEEN PHONOLOGICAL AWARENESS AND PHONEMIC AWARENESS

Although they are often used interchangeably, phonological awareness and phonemic awareness are distinct terms. **Phonological awareness** is a broader term that refers to the ability to identify and manipulate sounds in spoken language. This can refer to identifying and manipulating sounds at the word, syllable, or phoneme level. Example activities include rhyming, alliteration, breaking words into syllables, dividing syllables into onsets and rimes, and blending and segmenting phonemes.

Phonemic awareness is one specific component of phonological awareness. It focuses on the ability to identify and manipulate sounds at the phoneme level only. Phonemes are the smallest units of speech, and phonemic awareness is therefore the most advanced component of phonological awareness. It usually develops after other phonological awareness skills.

> **Review Video: Phonological and Phonemic Awareness, and Phonics**
> Visit mometrix.com/academy and enter code: 197017

PHONEMIC AWARENESS SKILLS

One early phonemic awareness skill is **phoneme isolation**, which is the ability to identify specific phonemes in spoken words. This includes identifying beginning (initial), middle (medial), and ending (final) sounds. Another skill is **phoneme identification**, which involves identifying the common sound in a list of words that have either the same beginning, middle, or ending sound. In **phoneme characterization**, students are given a set of words in which all but one have the same beginning, middle, or ending phoneme, and they must identify the word that doesn't belong.

In **blending**, a more complex skill, students are given the phonemes that make up a word in isolation. They must then identify the whole word formed by putting the phonemes together. In **segmentation**, students are given a whole word and must identify the individual phonemes that make up that word. **Phoneme deletion** involves removing one phoneme from a word and identifying what new word was formed. **Phoneme substitution** involves changing one phoneme in a word and identifying what new word was formed.

ACTIVITIES USED TO TEACH PHONEME BLENDING AND SEGMENTATION

Children often benefit from a multisensory approach to phonemic blending and segmentation. **Elkonin boxes** are one tool that can be used. Elkonin boxes consist of a series of connected boxes on paper. Students listen to a word and slide a penny or other token into a box each time they hear a new sound. For example, while listening to the word *cat*, students would slide three pennies into the boxes.

Students can also be given strings of beads, and they can move one bead for every sound, or phoneme, they hear. They can slide the beads back together as they blend the sounds to form the whole words again. Rubber bands can be used in a similar manner. Students can say whole words with the rubber bands un-stretched and then slowly stretch the bands as they segment the sounds. They can then push the rubber bands back together again as they blend the sounds to form the whole words.

PHONICS

Phonics refers to the relationship between letters and the sounds they make. After children learn to identify letter names, they learn that each letter makes a predictable sound. They later learn that groups of letters, such as consonant blends and digraphs, make predictable sounds as well. This understanding of letter-sound relationships is known as phonics.

Understanding the predictable relationship between letters and the sounds they make is important for the development of both decoding and encoding skills. When early readers come across unfamiliar words, they use knowledge of letter-sound relationships to decode the words as one common reading strategy. For early readers, this is especially helpful for unknown words that follow predictable spelling patterns, such as CVC words. When children are engaging in early writing activities, they use knowledge of letter-sound relationships to write words, which is known as **encoding**.

PHONEMIC AWARENESS VS. PHONICS

Phonemic awareness and phonics are commonly confused terms, but they are not the same. **Phonemic awareness** refers to identifying and manipulating phonemes in spoken language. **Phonics** refers to the relationship between letters and the sounds they make. A key question to ask when deciding if an activity is related to phonemic awareness or phonics is whether or not any letters are involved. If letters and their sounds are involved, the activity is related to phonics rather than phonemic awareness.

For example, asking students what sounds they hear in the word *cat* is a phonemic awareness activity because they are identifying sounds in a spoken word. However, asking students to decode the word *cat* when it is written in a text is a phonics activity because students must use their understanding of letter-sound relationships to successfully decode the word. Students are also using phonics skills if they write the word *cat* by identifying the sounds that they hear and writing the letters that make those sounds.

FLUENCY

Fluency is defined as reading accurately with the appropriate speed and intonation. Beginning readers typically have to stop and decode unknown words frequently, which affects both speed and intonation. Over time, as readers develop rapid word recognition, their reading speed increases. Appropriate intonation is also developed through frequent shared and guided reading experiences.

RELATIONSHIP BETWEEN FLUENCY AND COMPREHENSION

Research has shown that reading fluency is one major predictor of reading comprehension. Non-fluent readers burden their working memories with decoding. Sentences are read in a fragmented way, making it difficult for the brain to organize and make sense of what was read. After expending the energy to decode difficult words, they may forget what they have previously read. Fluent readers are free to use working memory for comprehending the text. They read using smooth, continuous phrasing, making it easier for the brain to make sense of what has been read.

USING SYNTACTIC CUES TO FIGURE OUT UNKNOWN WORDS AND MAKING MEANING FROM TEXTS

Readers use multiple cueing systems to figure out unknown words and make meaning from texts. When readers use **syntactic cues**, they use knowledge about correct oral language structures and the ways sentences are put together to decode and make meaning. For example, readers may use knowledge about subject-verb agreement and word order to decode new words and make meaning from sentences.

To encourage readers to use syntactic cues, teachers can model types of complex sentences. Sentences from familiar stories can be deconstructed, and students can be asked to put them back together again. Teachers can also provide sample sentences that each have one word covered and ask students to guess the missing word. Teachers can then ask students to explain how they figured out the missing word. Readers should also be encouraged to ask themselves if what they have read sounds right to encourage miscue recognition and self-correction.

DECODING VS. ENCODING

Decoding refers to the process of translating print to speech, which is done by translating graphemes into phonemes. **Graphemes** are letters or groups of letters that represent a single sound, and phonemes are the smallest units of sound in language. When a reader uses strategies to read the printed word *chair*, he or she is decoding the word.

Encoding refers to the process of translating sounds to print using knowledge of letter-sound relationships. This is done by translating phonemes to graphemes. When a writer uses knowledge of the sounds letters make to write the word *hop*, he or she is encoding the word.

> **Review Video: Phonics (Encoding and Decoding)**
> Visit mometrix.com/academy and enter code: 821361

Observing how a developing writer spells can be used to assess phonics knowledge. It can provide information about the writer's understanding of when to apply certain spelling patterns. By observing the writer's work over time, a teacher can determine which phonics strategies the writer has mastered and which are still developing. This information can be used to plan individualized phonics instruction. For example, if a writer frequently spells CVCe words without the e at the end, the teacher may focus on this spelling pattern during guided reading lessons with the student.

> **Review Video: Print Awareness and Alphabet Knowledge**
> Visit mometrix.com/academy and enter code: 541069

INSTRUCTIONAL STRATEGIES USED TO TEACH DECODING OF COMMON SPELLING PATTERNS

Blending is a common strategy to teach decoding of CVC words. Students say the sound represented by each letter in the word and then state the whole word they made. To increase fluency, students can be encouraged to increase the speed of blending over time. Once CVC words have been mastered and students have been introduced to consonant blends and digraphs, they can use the same blending process with CVCC words.

For CVVC and CVCe words that cannot be decoded using blending, students can be introduced to the sounds made by each spelling pattern. They can then build and explore word families that contain the same spelling pattern, changing the initial sounds to build new, related words. For example, after identifying the sound that /ake/ makes, students can build *rake*, *cake*, and *lake* using letter tiles or magnetic letters.

INSTRUCTIONAL STRATEGIES USED TO TEACH DECODING OF MULTISYLLABIC WORDS

Although decoding instruction typically tapers off around second grade, it is at this point that students begin reading texts with more complex, multisyllabic words. Therefore, it is important to teach specific strategies that readers can use to decode these types of words.

One strategy is to teach students to identify the different syllables present in a word. This can be done by clapping each syllable or saying the word while looking in a mirror and observing how many times the mouth opens. Students can then be taught to recognize common syllable spelling patterns and the sounds that they make. These common syllable spelling patterns include the following:

- closed syllables, which end in a consonant and usually have a short vowel sound (e.g., rabbit)
- open syllables, which end in a vowel and usually have a long vowel sound (e.g., bagel)
- r-controlled vowels (e.g., carpet)
- vowel digraph pairs (e.g., detain)
- vowel-consonant-silent-e syllables, which usually have a long vowel sound (e.g., athlete)
- consonant-le words, which are usually found at the end of a word (e.g., maple)

Readers can also be taught to look for known parts of words, such as known prefixes and suffixes.

CONSONANT BLENDS AND CONSONANT DIGRAPHS

A **consonant blend** is a group of two or three consonants that blend together to make a sound, but each individual letter sound is still heard. Examples include *bl*, *fr*, and *sw*. Blends are typically introduced after readers have learned to decode basic CVC words, and they are introduced in groups according to the second consonant they contain. Blends containing two consonants are usually introduced before blends containing three consonants. When introducing each blend, the teacher shows students how the sounds of each consonant are blended together to form the new sound. Common words containing the blend can be listed, and students can go on word hunts to find additional examples of words containing the blend. Students can also sort cards containing pictures of objects whose names are spelled with consonant blends.

A **consonant digraph** is a group of two consonants that form a new consonant sound when combined. Examples include *th*, *sh*, and *ch*. Digraphs are also typically introduced a few at a time, with beginning digraphs introduced before ending digraphs. Creating lists of example words, going on word hunts, and completing matching and sorting activities can also be used to teach digraphs.

R-CONTROLLED VOWELS

R-controlled vowels are vowels that appear before the letter r in a word. Words containing this spelling pattern are sometimes referred to as bossy-r words, because the letter r changes the sound of the vowel. The r-controlled vowel pairs are *ar*, *er*, *ir*, *or*, and *er*.

To teach decoding of words containing r-controlled vowels, teachers can model blending of simple words containing these spelling patterns by sliding their fingers along the words as they blend them. For each word, they can point out that the vowel and r together make one sound, and they can generate a list of other words containing the same letter pair and sound. Students can also be given word or picture cards to sort according to which r-controlled vowel sound they contain. Another strategy is to provide a picture of an object that contains an r-controlled vowel in its name. The word can be written below the picture, with the r-controlled vowel omitted. Students can be asked to provide the missing letters to complete the word.

BENEFITS OF EXPLICIT PHONICS INSTRUCTION

Research has shown that early readers benefit from an explicit and systematic approach to phonics instruction. Developing readers who receive explicit and systematic phonics instruction at an early age often show increased ability to decode and spell, along with increased reading comprehension skills when older.

Explicit instruction means that phonics lessons are purposely planned to address specific skills rather than waiting until problems arise with decoding words while reading. For example, a teacher may plan to focus on a set of consonant blends during one week of reading instruction. Systematic instruction means that the lessons follow a carefully planned scope and sequence, with phonics lessons progressing from basic to advanced. Early phonics lessons for kindergarteners may focus on letter-sound relationships, whereas first grade students may focus on decoding different spelling patterns.

Explicit phonics instruction is only one component of a balanced literacy program and time should be allocated to focus on other components as well.

ROLE OF PHONOLOGICAL AWARENESS AND PHONICS SKILLS IN READING DEVELOPMENT
ENGLISH LANGUAGE LEARNERS

For English language learners (ELLs), research has shown that **phonological awareness** in a reader's first language is a **strong predictor** of his or her ability to learn to read in a second language. This is especially true when the native language is closely related to English. Despite the fact that phonological awareness in the native language can be beneficial when learning English, it may lead to **overgeneralization** of rules of the native language. Continued language experiences in the native language along with language scaffolding can be beneficial to ELLs as they learn English.

Some ELLs may also speak native languages in which there is not a **one-to-one correspondence** between letters and phonemes. They may also speak languages that use the same alphabet as English but where the letters represent different sounds. It is important for teachers to understand their ELLs' prior knowledge and consider this when planning appropriate phonics instruction.

Additionally, some English phonemes may not be used in other languages. Introducing English vocabulary words that contain these phonemes helps give these sounds a meaningful context. Using poems and songs with repetition and rhyme can also be helpful.

> **Review Video: ESL/ESOL/Second Language Learning**
> Visit mometrix.com/academy and enter code: 795047

STRUGGLING AND PROFICIENT STUDENTS

Research has shown that phonological awareness and phonics skills are important predictors of reading success. For struggling readers, daily phonological awareness and phonics practice are important. Explicit and systematic instruction should be tailored to the individual needs of each student and based upon observation and assessment data. Once a teacher has determined which skills the student needs to improve, instruction should be regularly included to target these skills until mastered. Ongoing reading assessments and flexible groupings can help make sure that struggling readers' individual needs are consistently met.

Phonological awareness and phonics assessments are important for proficient readers as well. Some proficient readers have developed strong rapid word identification skills without mastering the underlying phonological awareness and phonics skills. When they get into older grade levels and more frequently encounter unfamiliar vocabulary, they will have difficulty decoding the text. Assessment data can be used to identify specific skills to practice in small-group instruction with these proficient readers.

ROLE OF NATURAL EXPOSURE TO PHONICS IN EARLY READING DEVELOPMENT

Like explicit phonics instruction, natural exposure to phonics also plays a role in early reading development. This exposure occurs when children are involved in natural reading experiences, and they come across words they are unable to decode. Phonics instruction is provided in the moment to address the unknown words.

This type of phonics instruction is known as **implicit** instruction. It differs from explicit instruction, which progresses from part (letter sounds) to whole (whole words). Implicit instruction progresses from whole (unknown words encountered in text) to part (breaking down the words in order to decode them).

Implicit phonics instruction has some benefits. Because it occurs during natural reading experiences, the phonics skills are taught **in context** rather than in isolation. Readers are motivated to learn the skills needed to decode the unknown words and continue reading. Teachers can allow time to address unknown words while reading aloud or listening to students reading independently. However, research has shown that it is still important to schedule time for explicit and systematic phonics instruction as well.

STRATEGIES TO TEACH LETTER IDENTIFICATION

Most reading programs introduce letters gradually. Some suggest introducing letters that have high value to learners first, such as the first letters of their names. Others focus on letters that play prominent roles in the books they are reading for the week, whereas others sequence letters by physical characteristics. In general, it is best to avoid teaching commonly confused letter pairs simultaneously, such as b and d.

To develop **letter recognition**, students can be given texts and instructed to circle certain letters. They can play alphabet bingo and cover specific letters when they are called. They can sing the alphabet song while pointing to each letter. Additionally, they can go on letter hunts, where they search the classroom or building to find examples of specific letters in environmental print. To practice recognizing capital and lowercase forms of letters, students can play memory and find matches consisting of both letter forms.

STRATEGIES TO TEACH LETTER FORMATION

To teach letter formation, students can be given letter stencils to trace with pencils. They can also be provided cutout letters made from different materials, such as felt and sandpaper, to trace with their fingers. Later, they can attempt to write letters independently on writing paper following the school's selected handwriting program guidelines.

To practice letter formation using a **multisensory approach**, students can write letters with shaving cream or fingerpaint. They can also write letters in containers filled with salt or sand. Wax craft sticks, modeling dough, and pipe cleaners can be used to construct letter models. Large-sized letters can also be drawn using sidewalk chalk, and students can hop along the letter shapes to trace them. They can also trace letter shapes in the air with their fingers or toy wands. Additionally, students can be given outlines of letters, which they can fill in with buttons, dried beans, or other common objects.

STRATEGIES TO TEACH LETTER-SOUND RELATIONSHIPS

Once students understand that letters are combined to form words that convey meaning in print, they begin learning that each letter makes a predictable sound. This is known as the **alphabetic principle**. Although different reading programs introduce the letters and sounds in different orders, most introduce the letter-sound relationships gradually.

In some reading programs, each letter has a song, poem, or chant that incorporates repetition of the letter name and sound. In others, a letter character or visual is produced, which includes a hint about the sound it makes. The visual often includes a picture of a common object that starts with the letter. Students can also be encouraged to find objects beginning with the letter sound they are learning. Tactile activities, such as building letters out of wax craft sticks or writing them in shaving cream while repeating the names and sounds, are also commonly used. Bingo and other similar games that require matching letters to their sounds can also be used.

CONCEPTS OF PRINT THAT COLLECTIVELY FORM A FOUNDATION FOR EARLY READING INSTRUCTION

Concepts of print are the conventions used to convey meaning in printed text. Children begin developing an understanding of these concepts from an early age through shared reading experiences with others and interactions with printed materials.

Understanding concepts of print includes recognizing the front cover, back cover, and title of a book. It also includes recognizing that the print, rather than the pictures, carries the message. Additionally, it includes directionality concepts, such as knowing that you read from left to right and from the top of the page to the bottom, with a return sweep at the end of each line of text. One-to-one correspondence between written and spoken words is another concept of print. Letter concepts are also important, such as knowing that words are made up of individual letters, identifying letter names, and identifying both capital and lowercase letters. Identifying the names and purposes of common punctuation marks used to end sentences is also a key concept of print.

STRATEGIES TO TEACH PRINT AWARENESS

Starting at an early age, caregivers and teachers can begin introducing children to concepts of print. While reading storybooks and big books aloud, they can model how to hold the books, where the front and back covers and titles are located, and where to begin reading. They can also model directionality by following the text with their fingers as they read, showing the left-to-right movement and return sweep. They can point out different text features, such as capital letters and punctuation marks, and discuss their purposes.

When students are interacting with texts independently, teachers can ask them questions regarding concepts of print. For example, they can instruct students to follow the text with their fingers and pause after encountering punctuation marks at the ends of sentences. Teachers can also point out text features in environmental print, such as hallway signs.

Reading Development

TYPICAL PROGRESSION OF READING DEVELOPMENT

Readers typically progress through four stages of reading development. The first stage of reading development is known as **emergent reading**. It is the stage in which readers develop pre-reading behaviors and begin understanding concepts of print. The second stage is called **early reading**. Early readers begin to use a combination of reading strategies and cueing systems to decode and comprehend simple texts. The third stage is called **transitional reading**. Transitional readers use a wide range of reading strategies to support comprehension of more complex texts. Rapid word recognition combined with effective use of strategies allows readers to read at an increased pace.

Fluent reading is the last stage of reading development. Fluent readers confidently read and comprehend a wide range of complex texts independently.

Students' individual differences and prior experiences can affect at what ages and rates they progress through the stages.

> **Review Video: Stages of Reading Development**
> Visit mometrix.com/academy and enter code: 121184

CHARACTERISTICS OF THE EMERGENT STAGE OF READING

Emergent reading skills are strong predictors of future reading success. In the emergent stage, readers display **pre-reading behaviors**. They begin interacting with texts without actually reading the words. They learn the concepts of print, such as learning how to correctly hold books and understanding that print holds meaning. They begin to identify capital and lowercase letters, and they understand the predictable relationships between letters and sounds. They begin to understand that letters are combined to form words and words are combined to form sentences.

Readers in the **emergent stage** also develop oral language skills. This includes phonological awareness skills, such as rhyming and alliteration. They develop phonemic awareness skills, including the ability to blend, segment, and manipulate phonemes within words.

Emergent readers enjoy having others read to them. They respond to texts that are read aloud by making predictions, retelling events, and other activities. They react to illustrations and use them to make sense of the texts.

INSTRUCTIONAL STRATEGIES USED IN THE EMERGENT STAGE

Teachers should read aloud to students in the emergent stage often, choosing from a range of genres. When reading, teachers should model concepts of print and how to make predictions, retell story events, and other reading strategies. Concepts of print should be explored in environmental print within the classrooms and the schools. Teachers should create print-rich environments containing several different types of texts for students to explore. Students should be given multiple opportunities to interact with different types of texts daily, both with others and independently.

Teachers should also plan **explicit instruction** on letter identification and letter-sound correspondence and give readers opportunities to practice recognizing and forming both capital and lowercase letters.

Additionally, teachers should plan classroom activities to build emergent readers' phonological awareness and phonemic awareness skills. This includes opportunities to practice rhyming, alliteration, onset and rime manipulation, and phoneme manipulation.

CHARACTERISTICS OF TEXTS DESIGNED FOR EMERGENT READERS

Texts designed for emergent readers should have **pictures** or **illustrations** that strongly support the print. They should have a limited amount of text on each page and use **repetitive words** and phrases. They should include several high-frequency and easily decodable words, and the text should be placed in predictable places on each page. Simple sentence structure should be used.

Additionally, books for emergent readers should be focused on familiar objects and topics that will activate readers' prior knowledge. This assists readers with comprehension and making connections and allows them to focus on print concepts. The vocabulary should also be familiar. Print should be large and contain wide spaces between letters and lines of text.

Some emergent texts follow a pattern in which only the last word in each sentence changes. For example, each page of a text might say, "I like to ___." The missing word could be easily guessed based upon picture support.

CHARACTERISTICS OF THE EARLY READING STAGE OF READING DEVELOPMENT

In the early reading stage of development, readers increasingly use strategies to figure out unknown words and make meaning from texts. They use a combination of **graphophonic, syntactic, and semantic cues**. After guessing unknown words using one type of cueing system, they cross-check their guesses using other cueing systems. They begin to self-monitor their reading and self-correct if they realize that errors have been made. They expand their vocabularies and their automatic recognition of high-frequency words. They use picture clues, knowledge of letter-sound relationships, and repetition to decode unknown words in longer and more complex texts.

Early readers also continue developing comprehension strategies, such as predicting and summarizing. They use a combination of these comprehension strategies to make meaning from what they have read. They begin to read silently and no longer need to point to each word while reading.

CHARACTERISTICS OF TEXTS FOR READERS IN THE EARLY READING STAGE

Texts for **early readers** contain more print than those for emergent readers. They include longer sentences, more sentences per page, and more page**s** per book. The texts also contain more complex and **varied sentence structure**. There is less reliance on picture clues than in books for emergent readers, with the print carrying most of the meaning. More complex and content-specific vocabulary words are included. Multiple spelling patterns are used, requiring readers to use a combination of decoding strategies. There is less repetition, or longer and more complex phrases are repeated than those in emergent texts.

Texts for early readers also frequently focus on more complex story lines. Descriptive language is often included. The content of these books is still typically familiar to readers.

Readers in the early stage understand a variety of genres and purposes for reading. Therefore, texts for this stage are varied in genre and purpose.

INSTRUCTIONAL STRATEGIES USED WITH READERS IN THE EARLY READING STAGE

Students in the early reading stage are beginning to increase their reading rates and build fluency. Teachers can provide students with opportunities to frequently read and reread favorite books, which will help them build fluency. In addition to using picture clues, teachers can also model using a range of reading strategies that incorporate all cueing systems. They can prompt students to use these strategies in their own reading, asking them to check whether their guesses look right, sound right, and make sense.

Early readers still benefit from continued explicit and individualized phonics instruction. Activities that focus on advanced phonemic awareness skills, such as phoneme substitution, are also beneficial. Additionally, students benefit from instruction on complex vocabulary words and spelling patterns. Teachers can also provide students with frequent opportunities to read varied text types and genres that incorporate more sophisticated vocabulary words and sentence structures than emergent texts.

CHARACTERISTICS OF READERS IN THE TRANSITIONAL STAGE OF READING DEVELOPMENT

Readers in the transitional stage of reading development are able to engage in sustained, quiet reading for extended periods of time. They are able to read and comprehend longer, more advanced texts and can automatically identify a large number of high-frequency words. They have knowledge of complex spelling patterns, which they use to independently decode most unknown words, including multisyllabic words. They are also continuing to increase their fluency and reading rates.

Transitional readers utilize more strategies to assist with comprehension than early readers. They have an awareness of text structures and can gather and synthesize information from multiple text features, including print, graphs, charts, and sidebars. They rely more on the print than the pictures for meaning and can identify story elements, such as characters, setting, problem, and solution. Additionally, they develop higher-level comprehension skills, such as making inferences and drawing conclusions.

CHARACTERISTICS OF TEXTS FOR READERS IN THE TRANSITIONAL READING STAGE

Students in the transitional reading phase are able to read more difficult texts than early readers. This includes both fiction and nonfiction texts covering a wide range of genres. It also includes both beginning chapter books and challenging picture books. Nonfiction texts may utilize multiple text structures and include features like graphs, charts, photographs, sidebars, and more. The topics may be either familiar or unfamiliar to readers. Some challenging and unknown vocabulary words may be included along with many high-frequency words. Story elements may be described in detail, using descriptive words and phrases. There are numerous chapter book series designed for transitional readers.

Books written for transitional readers have several lines of text per page. Some pages may be composed entirely of text, as in chapter books. The books have many pages with clearly defined spaces between lines of text.

INSTRUCTIONAL STRATEGIES USED WITH READERS IN THE TRANSITIONAL STAGE

Because **transitional readers** are beginning to read more complicated texts of different genres, it is helpful to teach about text structures. Understanding text structures and where to look for main ideas can assist transitional readers with comprehension. Teachers can also teach strategies to determine the meanings of **unknown vocabulary** words by analyzing word morphology. This includes recognizing and analyzing both affixes and roots.

Teachers can plan several opportunities for students to build reading fluency by rereading texts for meaningful purposes. They can also model advanced analysis and comprehension strategies during shared reading experiences, such as making inferences and drawing conclusions. They can provide students with tools like graphic organizers to assist with comprehension during independent reading. Additionally, they can encourage readers to support responses with text evidence.

Teachers can also assist transitional readers with selecting appropriately challenging texts for independent reading.

CHARACTERISTICS OF READERS IN THE FLUENT STAGE OF READING DEVELOPMENT

Readers in the **fluent stage** of reading development read complex texts both **quickly** and **accurately**. They read with appropriate expression. They automatically recognize high-frequency words and efficiently use multiple strategies to determine unknown words they encounter. These strategies include using cueing systems, context clues, and substitutions.

Fluent readers are able to comprehend a wide range of complex fiction and nonfiction texts. They understand content-specific and technical vocabulary words or use strategies and tools to determine their meanings. They have a strong understanding of different types of text structures and know how to efficiently use text features to locate key information. They understand multiple purposes for reading and writing and are able to understand texts from multiple points of view. Additionally, fluent readers use **high-level thinking skills** to comprehend what they have read. They are able to evaluate texts and argue points using text evidence for support.

CHARACTERISTICS OF TEXTS FOR READERS IN THE FLUENT READING STAGE

Texts for readers in the fluent reading stage are complex, varied, and sometimes abstract. Complex text structures are often used. For example, they may use flashbacks or weave back and forth while comparing and contrasting two things. Fictional texts for fluent readers contain highly developed plots and character development. They often use descriptive and figurative language. Additionally, these texts may have multiple themes or layers that require deep analysis. Content-specific and technical vocabulary words are commonly used. Topics may be either familiar or unfamiliar to readers.

Texts for fluent readers rely mostly on the print to convey meaning. Photos or illustrations are mainly included to convey important information that may be difficult to explain in print. For example, photographs of animals may be included in biology texts. Illustrations may be included in historical fiction texts where the settings or characters may be unfamiliar to readers.

INSTRUCTIONAL STRATEGIES USED WITH READERS IN THE FLUENT READING STAGE

Readers in the fluent stage often read texts about new and **unfamiliar topics**. Therefore, teachers can instruct them to activate related prior knowledge that may assist them with making sense of the new texts. They can also model how to efficiently use **research tools** to learn more about unfamiliar topics.

Teachers can also model and encourage readers to use close reading techniques to deeply analyze texts. This process includes rereading texts multiple times to analyze different layers each time. It also includes evaluating, comparing and contrasting, making connections, and using other high-level comprehension strategies. Teachers can encourage readers to analyze texts from multiple perspectives, using text evidence to support their responses.

Because readers in this stage will frequently encounter content-specific and technical vocabulary words, teachers can continue to model word analysis skills, such as analyzing affixes and roots.

Writing Development

RELATIONSHIP BETWEEN READING AND WRITING DEVELOPMENT

Reading and writing are **interrelated** and should be taught together. Students who read a lot tend to have stronger writing skills, and students who write a lot tend to have stronger reading comprehension skills.

When students read varied types of texts, they learn how authors convey meaning differently through tone, language use, and sentence structure. They learn about different types of genres. They often use the texts as models and experiment with these elements in their own writing. Students also increase their vocabularies through reading, and they develop automatic recognition of high-frequency words. Students may then integrate the new vocabulary words into their own writing and remember how to spell words they have seen repeatedly in texts.

When students learn to write, they learn about and use different sentence and text structures. Awareness of these structures can help students recognize and make sense of them when encountered in other texts. Additionally, when students write about texts they have read, it facilitates additional analysis and comprehension. For example, writing about whether or not they would recommend books to others requires students to evaluate the texts and provide support for their reasoning.

CHARACTERISTICS OF WRITERS IN THE PRELITERATE STAGE OF WRITING DEVELOPMENT

The earliest stage of children's writing development is **scribbling**. Children begin scribbling at random places on the pages and do not proceed in any consistent direction. They typically hold writing utensils, such as pencils or crayons, with their fists. Scribbling helps children improve their fine motor skills and sets the stage for the understanding that writing carries meaning.

Over time, scribbling begins to follow a left-to-right directionality across the pages. Drawings may be included to help convey meaning.

Eventually, strings of pretend, letter-like symbols are used. They are sometimes mixed with numbers. Students are able to explain the meanings they are trying to convey through their writing. This phase demonstrates a beginning awareness of concepts of print. Spacing between words is not initially included but develops over time. There is no evidence of letter-sound relationships in the writing at this stage.

CHARACTERISTICS OF WRITERS IN THE EMERGENT STAGE OF WRITING DEVELOPMENT

In the **emergent stage,** writers begin to form letters correctly. Initially, they often write using all capital letters. They also begin to use their understandings of letter-sound relationships to write words. Some sounds are correctly represented in words, typically starting with the initial sounds.

In this stage, writers also begin spelling some words correctly. The first written words typically hold high personal meaning to students, such as their names and words like *mom* and *dad*. They may also write words found in environmental print, such as the names of popular restaurants frequently seen on signs. Some high-frequency sight words begin to be spelled correctly.

Students in the emergent stage write with left-to-right directionality and begin using spacing to separate words. They also begin to use common punctuation marks to split their writing into sentences, although this skill is still developing. Because it requires a lot of energy to encode words at this stage, writing pieces are typically short.

CHARACTERISTICS OF WRITERS IN THE TRANSITIONAL STAGE OF WRITING DEVELOPMENT

In the **transitional stage** of writing development, students begin using a mixture of capital and lowercase letters appropriately. They also correctly use several different punctuation marks. Their writing includes a broader vocabulary than when they were in the emergent stage.

Transitional writers know how to automatically spell many high-frequency words, and they use multiple strategies to encode words they do not know how to spell. These strategies include considering letter-sound relationships to record the sounds they hear, considering known spelling patterns, and thinking of related, known words. Writing includes a mixture of conventionally spelled words and phonetically spelled words that are readable.

Because transitional writers are able to encode many words quickly, they have more available energy to focus on writing development. They focus more attention on developing story elements and including descriptive details. They write longer texts than they wrote in the emergent stage, and their writing includes a mixture of text structures and genres. Transitional writers also have the ability to reread and edit their work.

CHARACTERISTICS OF WRITERS IN THE FLUENT STAGE OF WRITING DEVELOPMENT

Fluent writers spell most words correctly and use capitalization and punctuation marks conventionally throughout their writing. They are able to edit and evaluate their own writing and provide constructive feedback to others.

With the ability to spell most words quickly and automatically, fluent writers are able to focus more on writing craft, such as using descriptive language and developing story elements. Author's voice begins to develop. Writing may span several pages. Fluent writers consider their audiences and purposes for writing and consider them during the planning process. They use multiple strategies to plan their writing, such as brainstorming and using graphic organizers. They are able to write texts in a wide range of genres and select appropriate text structures to fit their purposes. Additionally, fluent writers are able to independently use tools like dictionaries and thesauri to improve their writing pieces.

> **Review Video: What is Sensory Language?**
> Visit mometrix.com/academy and enter code: 177314

Oral Language and Nonverbal Language Development

STAGES OF FIRST LANGUAGE ACQUISITION

- Until about four to six months of age, babies are in the **cooing stage**. Babies in this stage commonly make vowel sounds, which represent their first attempts at oral language.
- From about four to six months until one year of age, babies are in the **babbling stage**. At first, they commonly make repeated consonant-vowel sounds, such as *ma-ma*. Over time, their babbling begins to show the expressive patterns they hear in the language around them. They repeat sounds that others respond to and reinforce.
- From about 12 to 24 months of age, children are in the **one-word stage**. In this stage, children begin referring to objects by consistent, one-word names. These words may be real or invented, and children begin to use language to convey meaning to others.
- From ages two to three, most children enter the **telegraphic stage**, when they string together words to convey meaning. The words that convey the most meaning in sentences are often included, whereas articles, conjunctions, and other words are omitted.
- After age three, most children enter the beginning **oral fluency stage**. They now use more complex sentences and begin using sentence structure and syntax appropriately. They use language for a variety of purposes.

STAGES OF SECOND LANGUAGE ACQUISITION

- In the **preproduction stage**, English language learners (ELLs) are listening and taking in the second language. Comprehension is minimal at this point. ELLs may not yet speak to others in the second language, and this stage is therefore sometimes referred to as the silent period. ELLs may communicate with gestures or single words.
- In the **early production stage**, comprehension is still limited. ELLs begin responding using one- or two-word answers. Vocabulary in the second language begins to grow.
- The **speech emergence stage** is marked by increased comprehension. ELLs begin speaking in longer sentences, but grammatical errors may be present. Vocabulary in the second language greatly increases.

- In the **intermediate proficiency stage**, ELLs are able to comprehend much of what they hear. They begin speaking in more complex sentences that contain fewer grammatical errors. They are able to fluently communicate with others in the second language for a variety of purposes.
- In the **advanced fluency stage**, ELLs understand academic vocabulary and need little support to participate actively in the classroom. Students in this stage speak with near-native English fluency.

COMPONENTS OF ORAL LANGUAGE DEVELOPMENT

- **Phonological skills** are one component of oral language development. These skills include the ability to recognize and manipulate sounds in spoken words. Rhyming and identifying syllables are examples of phonological skills.
- **Syntactic skills** are another component. Syntactic skills (syntax) include understanding grammatical rules and how to correctly arrange words in sentences. Children begin by using simple syntax, such as combining two words to express needs and wants. Over time, their sentence structure becomes more complex.
- **Oral language** also includes a semantic component, which refers to the ability to understand the meanings of words, phrases, sentences, and longer texts. The semantic component is vital for comprehension.
- **Morphological skills** are another component of oral language development. Morphological skills include understanding the meanings of word parts.
- Finally, **pragmatics** refers to understanding the social rules of language. Examples of pragmatics include knowing how to adjust the formality of language depending on the audience and knowing how to respond in certain social situations.

> **Review Video: Components of Oral Language Development**
> Visit mometrix.com/academy and enter code: 480589

RELATIONSHIP BETWEEN ORAL LANGUAGE DEVELOPMENT AND LITERACY DEVELOPMENT

Most children learn to speak through immersion in language-rich environments, with no formal speech instruction necessary. Starting at birth, these early language interactions help set the stage for later literacy development. Early language play, such as sharing songs, nursery rhymes, and poems, assists young children with the development of phonological awareness skills. Strong phonological awareness skills are a solid predictor of future reading success. Hearing spoken language also helps children understand syntax and how sounds and words are combined to form meaning.

- As children engage in frequent and varied oral language opportunities, they also increase their **vocabularies**. Opportunities to use both social and academic vocabulary during listening and speaking activities assists students with comprehending vocabulary words encountered in texts.
- **Oral language experiences** also help readers understand that language can be used for a variety of purposes, such as meeting needs, social interaction, and persuading others. This assists with recognizing an author's purpose. An understanding of cultural norms and nuances is also developed through oral language experiences.
- Additionally, comprehension requires the ability to combine literal meanings of words with prior knowledge and world experiences. Oral language activities, such as following directions, can assist with this.

ROLE THAT ORAL LANGUAGE PLAYS IN THE DEVELOPMENT OF CRITICAL THINKING SKILLS

Oral language leads to the development of other communication skills. Babies first listen to their caregivers and later say their first words before they learn to read and write. Through listening, children learn to evaluate the messages of others and make sense of newly learned information. Through speaking, they learn to organize and communicate their thoughts to others. All of these skills assist with the development of critical thinking skills.

Teachers can ask students to explain their thinking to others. They can also teach students to defend their answers using support and evidence. Students can also be explicitly taught to use strategic questioning when interacting with classmates. Strategic questions require higher-level thinking to answer, and questions with yes-or-no answers should be limited. For example, students explaining the results of science experiments might be asked to evaluate their processes and explain what they might do differently in the future. Additionally, students can respond to high-level questions about texts during class discussions and literature circles. For example, they can be asked to evaluate the ways that authors use persuasive techniques.

PROMOTING ORAL LANGUAGE SKILLS

When engaging in listening and speaking activities with students, it is recommended to use vocabulary words in context to promote comprehension later. Research has shown that identifying vocabulary words on flash cards and other similar types activities has **little effect** on later reading comprehension, whereas the ability to recognize and use words **in context** does.

Students should also have many opportunities to listen and speak for a **variety of purposes** to both peers and adults. Friendly conversations, academic discussions, formal presentations, and social interactions are all examples of different types of oral language activities. Varied activities will help students learn to change their language structures to fit the purposes of the interactions. Teachers can change their language structures throughout the school day. For example, they might chat informally with students about their interests during a morning meeting and switch to academic language when discussing a novel.

Additionally, students of all ages can benefit from reading and listening to a large variety of texts containing different types of sentence structure, language, and vocabulary. Young children can also benefit from word play and phonological awareness activities.

DEVELOPING LISTENING AND SPEAKING SKILLS

Like reading and writing, listening and speaking activities should be incorporated throughout all content areas rather than taught in isolation. Students should be given multiple opportunities each day to listen and speak for a variety of purposes.

Students can listen to texts in audio form, listen to teachers read aloud, or participate in paired reading activities in all content areas. Before beginning, they can be given specific purposes for listening to focus their attention. They can participate in role-playing scenarios to model common social situations and conflict resolution. They can be given frequent opportunities to present their learning to others using a variety of formats. Audience members can be instructed to ask specific and relevant questions, and presenters can be instructed to provide well-supported and evidence-based answers. Additionally, collaborative, problem-based learning activities can be planned, requiring all students to have roles within their groups.

For ELLs and students who struggle with speaking, partially completed scripts and/or sentence stems can be provided. These tools can assist students with outlining thoughts and organizing sentence structure before speaking.

TEACHING STUDENTS NONVERBAL COMMUNICATION SKILLS

Nonverbal communication, sometimes known as body language, includes gestures, facial expressions, and posture. Verbal and nonverbal communication work together to convey desired messages. If nonverbal communication is inappropriate for the audiences or purposes used, the meaning of the verbal communication may be lost or misconstrued. For example, a child may thank a grandparent for a gift. However, if the child has a disappointed look on his or her face while speaking, the grandparent may believe the child does not like the gift.

Additionally, certain types of nonverbal communication can be interpreted differently depending on culture. What is socially acceptable in one culture may be considered rude in another. Students should be aware of the messages their nonverbal communication sends to different audiences.

Teachers can engage students in discussions about what messages are sent by different types of nonverbal communication. They can role-play common scenarios and have other students evaluate the messages conveyed through both verbal and nonverbal communication. Students can also watch video clips of realistic situations, such as job interviews, and evaluate the nonverbal language of the participants. When giving presentations, teachers also provide checklists outlining expected nonverbal communication, such as eye contact with others and strong posture.

Components of Reading Comprehension

READING COMPREHENSION

A basic definition of **reading comprehension** is understanding what has been read. However, reading comprehension is quite complex. It involves both taking meaning from the text and creating meaning by integrating the text with prior knowledge. It is an active process that requires the use of multiple skills and strategies, such as decoding, fluency, understanding word meanings, predicting, inferring, and more. It involves different levels of understanding, including comprehending both the literal meanings of the words and the unstated themes and implications of the text. Comprehension is one of the main goals of reading instruction.

Comprehension is essential to developing proficient readers. If readers are able to decode the words but cannot comprehend the messages, they won't make any meaning from the texts and will become easily frustrated. Because comprehension is an **active process**, it is also important for developing engaged readers who enjoy reading for a variety of purposes.

LITERAL COMPREHENSION

Literal comprehension refers to understanding the written meaning of a text. It involves a basic understanding of the text's vocabulary, events, main ideas, and other features. Literal comprehension is important because it is the foundation upon which deeper levels of comprehension are formed.

PROMOTING LITERAL COMPREHENSION

Answering **literal comprehension questions** using text evidence is one strategy to support development of this skill. This can be done through class discussions or written activities. Readers can be asked to identify the setting of the story, main characters, sequence of events, or other topics where the answers can be found directly in the text. Readers should be asked to provide text evidence for their answers, which might involve marking the sentences where the answers are found. Graphic organizers, such as story maps and problem/solution charts, can also help students develop literal comprehension skills.

To **scaffold** the development of literal comprehension, the teacher can begin by asking questions about a portion of the text immediately after it is read, using the same wording as the text. Over time, the wording can be varied and the teacher can wait for longer intervals before asking the questions.

INFERENTIAL COMPREHENSION

Inferential comprehension is a deeper level of understanding than literal comprehension. It requires inferring what the author meant. The answers to inferential comprehension questions are not found directly in the text. Readers must instead make inferences, draw conclusions, determine points of view, and make other informed decisions based upon the evidence provided in the text.

PROMOTING INFERENTIAL COMPREHENSION

To develop **inferential comprehension skills**, readers can be asked to make **predictions** or **inferences** and **draw conclusions**. This can be done using class discussions, written activities, or graphic organizers. For predictions, inferences, and conclusions, readers should be asked to provide text evidence to support their choices. This may involve marking parts of the text or recording relevant sentences. They should then be encouraged to evaluate their predictions, inferences, and conclusions as they continue reading. If new evidence conflicts with their initial predictions, inferences, or conclusions, readers should be encouraged to revise them as needed. Proficient readers self-monitor their comprehension and continually revise their understanding as additional evidence is gathered.

EVALUATIVE COMPREHENSION

Evaluative comprehension is a deeper level of understanding than literal comprehension and goes further than inferential comprehension. It requires readers to make judgments and share opinions about what they have read based upon evidence found in the text and prior knowledge. For example, evaluative comprehension questions might ask readers to consider if they would have handled an event in the text differently or explain whether they agree or disagree with the author's point of view.

PROMOTING EVALUATIVE COMPREHENSION

Because evaluative comprehension requires deeper thinking than literal comprehension, it is helpful for teachers to frequently model their thinking when responding to these types of questions. They can model how to identify relevant information within the text and draw upon prior experiences to form judgments about topics.

It is also helpful to provide readers with evaluative question stems they can reference when reading independently. These question stems can also be displayed on charts in the classroom.

SUMMARIZATION

Summarization refers to providing a concise description of the main idea and key details of a text. Summarization assists with comprehension by helping readers separate important information and vocabulary from unimportant information. It also helps readers remember what they have read.

Summarization is often a difficult skill for students to learn. Their initial summaries may provide too few or too many details from the text. Modeling and explicit instruction can help students learn to provide **effective summaries**. Students can be taught to reread a text and cross off unimportant or repetitive information. They can then be encouraged to locate and mark the main idea and key details that are essential to understanding the meaning of the text. Additionally, they can be encouraged to substitute general words for lists of related words in a category. For example, rather than listing all of the animals belonging to a character's family, students could use the word *pets* instead.

Readers can also complete **graphic organizers** to develop their summaries. One common type of graphic organizer asks students to complete the following sentence stems to form summaries: Someone, Wanted, But, So, Then.

> **Review Video: <u>Summarizing Text</u>**
> Visit mometrix.com/academy and enter code: 172903

ROLE OF PRIOR KNOWLEDGE IN READING COMPREHENSION

Research has shown that students learn best when they can relate new information to existing knowledge already stored in long-term memory. This helps them organize and make sense of the new information and apply it in future situations. When reading, prior knowledge can help students determine the meaning of unfamiliar vocabulary words, form predictions about what might happen next, make inferences, and make sense of story events. All of these skills are important for comprehension.

To activate students' prior knowledge, the teacher can ask what students already know about a topic when it is introduced. Students' contributions can be listed on a chart or graphic organizer. Know, want, and learned (KWL) charts can be completed, listing what students already know, want to know, and learned about the topic. The teacher can also ask students to make comparisons by asking how the new topic is similar to and different from something they have already learned.

DENOTATIVE VS. CONNOTATIVE MEANINGS

Words often have multiple meanings. **Denotative** meanings are the literal meanings of words. **Connotative** meanings are the secondary meanings of words and refer to the positive and negative associations that arise from them. For example, the denotative meaning of the word *heart* is a muscular organ in the circulatory system that pumps blood. A connotative meaning of the word *heart* is love.

There are several reference tools that can be used to locate the meanings of words. Dictionaries can be used to find the denotative and connotative meanings of words, along with other information like word origin and pronunciation. Thesauri can be used to find lists of synonyms for words, and antonyms are sometimes included as well. Glossaries list the definitions of important vocabulary words and are often found at the end of texts. All of these reference tools can be found in both print and digital forms.

HELPING LEARNERS RETELL FICTIONAL STORIES

There are specific steps teachers can take to focus readers' attention on key parts of stories to assist with retelling. Teachers can preview the stories with students and point out the key events they should listen for before they begin reading. During reading, they can pause and ask students to summarize the key events they have heard in the stories so far. After reading, teachers can lead students in shared retellings or ask students to retell the stories independently.

Students can fill out graphic organizers or create flip books that describe what happened in the beginning, middle, and end. They can also draw or act out the main story events. Additionally, students can be given sentence strips containing the main story events in a mixed-up order and asked to sequence them. Story ropes can also be used, where students tell story events in order as they move their hands along sets of beads or knots on ropes.

Retelling is important for story comprehension because it requires readers to identify and sequence the main story events. Readers must also consider other story elements, such as characters, setting, and plot, during retellings.

PURPOSES FOR READING

One purpose of reading is for entertainment, which is known as **aesthetic reading**. Sometimes readers select texts because they look interesting to read, and they read them just for fun. Selecting a fairy tale from the library for silent reading time and choosing a bedtime story are examples of times students read for entertainment.

Additionally, sometimes people read for information. This is known as **efferent reading**. It occurs when readers select nonfiction texts to learn something new. This might include learning new facts about a topic or learning the steps needed to accomplish a task. Selecting a book about whales while studying ocean life is an example of reading for information. Reading a recipe to prepare dinner is also an example of reading for information.

Reading to learn opinions is another purpose for reading. This type of reading occurs when people are trying to make decisions about things and look to others for advice. Reading online reviews before purchasing a product is an example of reading for opinions.

ASSISTING WITH COMPREHENSION BY RECOGNIZING THE AUTHOR'S PURPOSE

Recognizing the author's purpose can assist with comprehension in multiple ways. First, it can offer the readers clues about the text structures and features they are likely to encounter. If readers recognize that the author is writing to inform, they will know to look for features of informational texts, such as headings and content-specific vocabulary words. If readers recognize that the author is writing to entertain, they will know to pay attention to character traits, plot development, and other features of entertaining texts.

Additionally, knowing the **author's purpose** can help the reader evaluate the text more effectively. If readers recognize that the author is trying to persuade them, they will know to think critically about any claims that the author makes rather than accepting them at face value.

Knowing the author's purpose can also assist readers with determining if texts will meet their needs. For example, students may need to gather factual background information for a science experiment they are completing. They may preview a text and recognize that it is written for entertainment. They may then decide that the text is not suited to meet their needs in this circumstance.

> **Review Video: What is the Author's Purpose?**
> Visit mometrix.com/academy and enter code: 511819

TEACHING READERS TO RECOGNIZE AN AUTHOR'S PURPOSE

The author's purpose may be stated either explicitly or implicitly in a text. Readers can be taught to recognize text structures and features that help identify the author's purpose. Texts that are written to entertain often contain interesting characters and engaging plots. They may contain entertaining phrases and humor, and illustrations may be present.

Texts written to persuade usually contain evidence to support the author's points of view. This may include statistics, facts, and/or personal opinions. Readers can be asked if the authors appear to be for or against something to determine if texts are written to persuade.

Texts written to inform often include facts, which may be stated using text, charts, graphs, or other features. These texts may contain captioned photographs to provide additional information about the topics. Content-specific vocabulary words are often present. Readers can be asked if the authors appear to be trying to teach them about something to determine if texts are written for this purpose.

It is also important for readers to recognize that authors may have multiple purposes for writing. Readers may recognize text structures and features characteristic of two or more purposes within one text.

MAKING PREDICTIONS

When making predictions, readers gather evidence from the text and pictures to make inferences. They sequence story events and make connections between the text and prior experiences to predict what might happen next. Continually making and revising predictions also helps keep readers engaged. All of these activities support reading comprehension.

To help learners make predictions before shared reading experiences, teachers can conduct picture walks of texts. While showing the pictures, teachers can provide brief overviews of the stories, asking students to contribute their predictions about what each section might be about. During reading, teachers can pause to ask students to summarize what has happened so far and predict what might happen next. Teachers can model using prior experiences, picture and context clues, and memories of similar texts when making predictions.

Readers should be taught to evaluate their predictions to determine if they were correct. They should also be taught to look for additional information that might cause them to revise their original predictions. Readers can fill out charts listing their predictions, the evidence used to support these predictions, and what actually happened in the texts.

Review Video: <u>Predictive Reading</u>
Visit mometrix.com/academy and enter code: 437248

INFERRING

Authors sometimes provide clues in their writing rather than stating things explicitly. When this occurs, readers must make **inferences** or draw conclusions based on facts, prior knowledge, or text evidence rather than explicit statements. For example, an author might state that a character marched off and slammed the door. Although the author did not state it directly, readers may infer that the character is angry based on his actions.

- Making **inferences** is important for comprehension because much of the meaning in a text can be stated indirectly. If readers comprehend only direct statements, they may miss out on major themes or events in the story.
- Because **prior knowledge** can be used to make inferences, it is helpful for teachers to activate students' prior knowledge before reading through previewing and discussing what is known about the topic. Providing students with frequent opportunities to read varied texts can also build prior knowledge that will assist with inferring.
- Teachers can also show **pictures** to students and ask what inferences they can make based upon picture clues. Additionally, teachers can model **thinking aloud** while reading, discussing what inferences they are making and what prior knowledge, facts, or text clues they are using as evidence.

DRAWING CONCLUSIONS

Drawing conclusions is important for reading comprehension because it helps readers understand important events or concepts in a text that are not directly stated. Drawing conclusions about an author's purpose for writing can also help readers better evaluate the text because they will be aware of potential bias.

To help readers learn to draw conclusions, teachers can provide students with several supporting details about common topics and ask what conclusions they can draw. For example, they could describe a house with balloons, streamers, presents, and a cake in the kitchen, leading to a conclusion that it is somebody's birthday. A graphic organizer can be used to organize this information, with the conclusion in the middle and the supporting details branching off from this conclusion. This process can then be repeated using details found in texts. This will show readers how they can use prior knowledge and text evidence to form conclusions when they read independently.

METACOGNITION

Metacognition is when readers think about their own thinking. Proficient readers continuously self-monitor their own reading. They ensure that they are making meaning from the text. If things do not make sense, they use strategies to self-correct the issues. Metacognitive strategies are important for reading comprehension because they ensure that readers are actively engaged while reading and that they understand what they have read. Modeling these strategies by thinking aloud is an important way to help students learn and apply these strategies in their independent reading.

Metacognitive strategies before reading include previewing the text, making predictions, and setting a purpose for reading. Metacognitive strategies during reading include visualizing, making connections, rereading to clarify confusion, and asking self-monitoring questions. Readers also utilize text features to locate and make sense of key information. Metacognitive strategies after reading include summarizing, drawing conclusions, and determining if any unanswered questions remain that need additional clarification.

COMPARING AND CONTRASTING

Readers can **compare and contrast** many things when reading, such as characters, settings, story events, multiple texts, and more. This supports comprehension because readers must recall details and find text evidence to compare and contrast. Comparing and contrasting also requires higher-level thinking skills, can help readers organize information, and can clarify confusion between two things.

Venn diagrams are a common way to help readers **compare and contrast** information. Text evidence and prior knowledge can be used to identify features that are the same and different between two things, and they can then be listed in the appropriate sections of the diagram.

Students can also be taught to identify key words that signal whether two things in a text are the same or different. Word such as *similarly* and *like* signal that two things are the same, whereas words and phrases such as *although* and *on the other hand* signal that two things are different. A

84

chart that lists these key words and phrases can be displayed in the classroom as a reminder for students to use when reading.

> **Review Video: Compare and Contrast**
> Visit mometrix.com/academy and enter code: 798319

RECOGNIZING MAIN IDEAS AND DETAILS

The ability to recognize the main ideas and supporting details of texts assists with comprehension. Main ideas and supporting details help readers identify what the texts are covering and determine what message an author is trying to send.

Understanding paragraph structure can help readers locate the main idea and supporting details. Readers can be taught that the main idea is typically located in either the first or last sentence of the paragraph.

Readers can be encouraged to locate the main idea and mark it and then locate all supporting details and mark them in a different way. Main ideas and details can also be written on webs or other graphic organizers to help readers comprehend what they have read. Scaffolding can be provided when readers are first learning to complete these graphic organizers and then gradually withdrawn.

Prereading activities, such as discussing the title and previewing the pictures, can also help readers form initial thoughts about the main idea of a text. They can revise their initial thoughts as they read.

DISTINGUISHING BETWEEN FACTS AND OPINIONS

Facts are statements that can be proven to be true. For example, stating that George Washington was the first president of the United States is a fact. **Opinions** are statements that cannot be proven true or false. They represent people's judgements or views of something. Stating that cats are easier to take care of than dogs is an opinion.

It is important for readers to distinguish between facts and opinions. Recognizing when statements are opinions can help readers identify any biases the authors may have and recognize that the authors may be trying to persuade them. Distinguishing between facts and opinions is important when reading any text, but it necessitates special consideration when using digital sources. Anyone can post information online, and readers must be able to evaluate the sources effectively to determine if they are based on fact or opinion.

To teach students to identify facts and opinions, teachers can introduce the terms and provide examples of each. Students can be asked to mark examples of facts and opinions in texts using different colors. They can also be encouraged to look for key words that signal opinions, such as *think*, *believe*, *feel*, *best*, and *favorite*.

> **Review Video: Fact or Opinion**
> Visit mometrix.com/academy and enter code: 870899

ANALYZING AND INTERPRETING AN AUTHOR'S CRAFT AND STRUCTURE

An **author's craft** refers to an author's style of writing. It includes all of the choices an author makes when writing a text, such as word choice, text structure, point of view, use of literary elements, message, tone, and more. When focusing on an author's craft, readers analyze all of these choices and consider the effects they have on readers.

Analyzing and interpreting an author's craft and structure helps readers reach a deeper level of comprehension than surface comprehension. It aids them in understanding how different elements of the text work together to convey a certain meaning and tone. It helps them recognize that authors make several deliberate choices throughout the writing process about how to convey their messages most effectively, which will assist readers with making choices in their own writing. Additionally, it encourages active engagement with the text because readers are continuously analyzing and interpreting while they read. Comparing and contrasting an author's craft using different texts and other authors can also help readers make connections.

CLOSE READING

Close reading refers to reading and analyzing a text in a thoughtful manner to develop a deep understanding of its meaning, theme, use of language, and other elements. When close reading, readers first read through the text to determine the general meaning. They then reread the text to analyze the use of language and theme. They also make connections between the text and themselves, other texts, or real-world events and form evaluations. The goal of close reading is to develop independent readers who are able to gather deep meaning from texts with little or no scaffolding. Therefore, close reading activities do not involve previewing, picture walks, or other prereading activities.

Not all texts are ideal for close reading activities. Teachers should choose texts with deep meaning and multiple elements to discuss and analyze. They should consider the **complexity** of vocabulary, syntax, and meaning when choosing appropriate texts for close reading. Teachers should also consider the complexity of text features and structures.

Teachers can model how to reread texts and analyze different elements each time. They can guide students in this process by asking questions that require increasingly higher-level thinking skills after each reading of the text.

IMPORTANCE OF BEING ABLE TO SYNTHESIZE

Synthesis is the ability to gather information from multiple sources and combine it to make meaning. It is important because it requires readers to think critically about which parts of texts hold key information. Synthesis also requires readers to summarize and put ideas into their own words rather than repeat the texts verbatim. All of these skills assist with comprehension. Synthesis is also important when readers need to gather information about topics from multiple sources. The sources may differ in format and viewpoint, and readers must be able to find and combine the important points from each.

To teach students to **synthesize**, teachers can model tracking their thinking throughout the reading of a text and explain how it changes as new information is gathered. They can use phrases such as, "I used to think ____, but now I think ____. My thinking changed because____." Text evidence can be cited to explain the changes.

Readers can also be given **graphic organizers** to fill out as they read, recording key points in their own words. After compiling the key points, students can explain the main ideas they learned from the texts and how their thinking changed as they read.

Figurative Language

TYPES OF FIGURATIVE LANGUAGE

- **Similes** are one common type of figurative language used to compare two things using the terms *like* or *as*; for example, the child grew as fast as a weed.
- **Metaphors** are another common type of figurative language used to compare two things. Unlike similes, metaphors do not use the terms *like* or *as*. They simply state that one thing is another; for example, the star was a glistening diamond.
- **Personification** is a type of figurative language that gives human characteristics to nonhuman things, such as animals, objects in nature, or ideas; for example, the creek danced across the prairie.
- **Hyperbole** is a type of figurative language that uses exaggeration for effect. The exaggeration is so excessive that it is not intended to be taken literally; for example, if I don't eat now, I will starve to death.
- **Symbolism** is another type of figurative language. In symbolism, a writer uses a physical object as a representation of something other than its literal meaning. The symbol often represents something abstract, such as a feeling or idea; for example, diverging physical paths in a text can represent two people making different life choices.

> **Review Video: Figurative Language**
> Visit mometrix.com/academy and enter code: 584902

HELPING STUDENTS RECOGNIZE AND INTERPRET FIGURATIVE LANGUAGE

Some types of figurative language can be identified by recognizing **key words**. For example, students can be taught to recognize the words *like* and *as* in examples of similes. Students can be taught to recognize sound words, such as *buzz*, in examples of onomatopoeia. Charts displaying these key words can be displayed in the classroom.

Figurative language can also be explicitly taught, with teachers explaining each type and providing examples. Mentor texts can be used to provide examples of each type of figurative language, and students can be encouraged to locate additional examples on their own. When examples are identified, students can analyze the messages the authors are trying to convey through the use of figurative language.

Authors use figurative language to make their writing more descriptive and interesting. Because phrases containing figurative language cannot be literally translated, readers must have adequate background knowledge and/or use context clues to determine their meanings. The ability to recognize and interpret figurative language ensures that readers understand the authors' intended messages and are able to comprehend the depth of the story beyond the literal, surface meanings of the phrases.

ALLUSIONS

When authors use **allusions**, they refer to well-known people or events familiar to readers without describing them explicitly. For example, a character being warned to avoid opening Pandora's box is an example of an allusion. It refers to a commonly known story in Greek mythology, and readers are expected to know the meaning of the statement without any further explanation. Biblical, mythological, historical, and literary allusions are four common types. Allusions are commonly found in similes and metaphors.

To help readers recognize allusions, students can be asked to find examples of allusions in texts and discuss their types and meanings. Additionally, they can explore and evaluate the effects that allusions have on the meanings and tones of stories. Students can also be taught strategies for researching the meaning of unknown allusions they encounter while reading independently.

> **Review Video: Allusions**
> Visit mometrix.com/academy and enter code: 294065

IDIOMS

Idioms are a type of figurative language. They are expressions that have unique meanings that differ from the literal meanings of their component words. They are typically passed down within cultures. For example, "It's raining cats and dogs" is an idiom that means it is raining hard.

Idioms can be introduced to students a few at a time, with students contrasting the literal and figurative meanings. They can practice using context clues to determine the meanings of unknown idioms, and they can look for examples of idioms in texts. They can also explore the ways that idioms make writing interesting. For example, they can write a paragraph using the idiom, "It's raining cats and dogs." They can then rewrite the paragraph, substituting the words, "It's raining hard." They can compare the effects of each option on readers.

Special consideration should be given when using idioms with ELLs in the early stages of English language acquisition. Because vocabulary knowledge cannot be used to assist with comprehension of idioms, students may miss the meanings and become frustrated.

PROVERBS

Proverbs are short, well-known sayings that offer wisdom or advice. They are commonly passed down within cultures using oral language. An example of a proverb is: "Actions speak louder than words." Proverbs often use figurative language, and their literal meanings do not make sense. Therefore, students need to be taught to recognize proverbs and understand their figurative meanings to comprehend the overall messages of the texts containing them.

When introducing proverbs, teachers can help students understand the cultural and historical significance behind them. For example, the proverb "Don't look a gift horse in the mouth" refers to the historical practice of assessing a horse's teeth to determine its age. The proverb refers to being grateful for what you are given rather than assessing the worth of a gift. Teachers can help students research these proverbs to provide historical contexts for their meanings.

Students can write proverbs on graphic organizers and list both their literal and figurative meanings. They can analyze what the proverbs have in common, such as offering wisdom or advice about life. Additionally, when they are encountered in texts, readers can analyze how the meanings of the proverbs contribute to the meanings of the stories.

Role of Grammar in Reading Comprehension

RELATIONSHIP BETWEEN UNDERSTANDING ENGLISH GRAMMAR/USAGE AND COMPREHENSION

There is evidence that having a strong understanding of English grammar and usage assists with reading comprehension. When readers are able to untangle complex sentences in texts and understand how the components work together to form meaning, they are better able to comprehend what was read. When answering comprehension questions, they are better able to locate key information within complex sentences. Readers are also better able to incorporate complex sentence structure in their own writing.

Understanding English grammar and usage includes knowledge of parts of speech, the roles that they play, and how they are arranged in English sentences. It also includes knowledge of how simple sentences can be combined to form complex sentences. Readers with strong syntactic knowledge are able to self-monitor their reading and recognize when something does not sound right due to decoding errors. The ability to self-monitor and make corrections when needed is important for comprehension.

> **Review Video: The Link Between Grammar Skills and Reading Comprehension**
> Visit mometrix.com/academy and enter code: 411287

TEACHING ENGLISH GRAMMAR AND USAGE TO AID COMPREHENSION

One strategy to teach English grammar and usage to aid comprehension is to **break sentences apart** and analyze their components. Depending on the age and prior knowledge of the student, this may include **sentence diagramming**, dividing sentences into subjects and predicates, and splitting compound sentences into simple sentences. Students may also be asked to label sentence types—choosing from simple, compound, and complex sentences.

An alternative strategy is to combine words to form different types of sentences. Young readers may begin by combining only subjects and predicates to form the most basic types of sentences. As new parts of speech are learned, students can add additional words to form more complex sentences. Students can also be given word cards containing scrambled sentences. They can be asked to arrange the cards to form sentences, analyzing each attempt by asking if the sentences they have built sound right and make sense.

When given comprehension questions about texts, students can also highlight the parts of the sentences that contain the relevant information needed to respond.

SPOKEN VS. WRITTEN ENGLISH

Although there are some occasions for formal, scripted speech, most spoken English is informal and conversational in nature. Speech often includes a mixture of fragments and complete sentences and may include interrupting and switching between speakers. Grammar in spoken English tends to be less strict, and there is more flexibility in word order. There may be differences in pronunciation, pacing, and intonation among speakers, and listeners must adjust to these differences to comprehend what was said. Speakers can gauge the understanding of listeners and rephrase or re-explain when necessary. Unlike written text, there is no formal record of what was said to review later unless notes were taken or the speech was recorded. If speaking is part of an instructional lesson, listeners may benefit from being given overviews of the topics and guiding questions in advance to help focus their attention on key information.

On the other hand, written English allows for careful and deliberate organization. It is typically more formal and features more complex structures than spoken English. Word order is more rigid. Writers cannot gauge readers' understanding or re-explain if necessary, so the meaning needs to be clear. Readers are able to review the text later to further clarify information.

ROLE OF FREQUENT AND VARIED READING EXPERIENCES

Frequent and varied reading experiences allow readers to see diverse examples of how authors write. They can compare and contrast different writing styles and analyze how the audience, topic, and purpose of writing may affect formality and structure. For example, expository science texts will likely differ from graphic novels in formality. The science texts may also include more content-specific vocabulary words and use sentence patterns designed to present facts rather than resemble conversations. Additionally, readers can see vocabulary words and different parts of speech in context and observe how they work together to build meaning. They can also see the effects of different writers' word choices on the moods of the texts. Overall, frequent and varied reading experiences help readers become more comfortable with language.

Being exposed to varied texts also provides students with models of sentence structure and writing styles to emulate in their own writing. Students often consider examples of familiar texts that fit certain genres or themes, called mentor texts, when they write their own. Being exposed to a variety of reading experiences gives students more examples to draw upon when they are writing.

INDUCTIVE VS. DEDUCTIVE METHODS OF TEACHING GRAMMAR

- In **inductive** teaching, students read and analyze texts that contain similarities. They look for patterns and identify grammar rules by themselves. For example, a teacher might give students several compound sentences that contain semicolons to join the two component sentences. Students might be asked to determine what the sentences have in common, leading them to identify and discuss the use of semicolons to join two simple sentences. Benefits include active participation by students to determine the grammar rules and use of critical thinking skills.
- **Deductive** teaching is another method. In deductive teaching, students are explicitly told grammatical concepts and rules before being asked to apply them to their own reading and writing. For example, a teacher might present a lesson on using semicolons to create compound sentences and then ask students to look for examples of this rule during independent reading experiences. One benefit of this approach is that it can be quicker than inductive teaching. Some students may also be more accustomed to this teacher-centered type of approach.

Both methods of teaching grammar can be useful, and teachers often use a combination of both in their teaching.

Many teachers also use writing workshops to introduce grammar through mini-lessons and conferences with students. Using students' writing as informal assessment tools, teachers can determine which grammatical concepts and rules individual students need to practice.

ROLE OF GRAMMAR IN HELPING ELLS WITH COMPREHENSION

Understanding grammar can assist English language learners (ELLs) with reading comprehension. It helps them comprehend different types of sentences. Understanding punctuation marks and word order of different types of sentences helps ELLs determine if something is a statement, a command, or a question.

Additionally, discerning the functions of different **parts of speech** helps ELLs identify the parts of sentences that carry the most meaning. This aids in focusing their attention on the most important words in each sentence. Recognizing words and affixes that signal verb tense also helps ELLs determine when the action takes place. For example, an ELL might recognize that the verbs in a text end in -*ed* and realize that the story takes place in past tense.

Using **syntactic clues** is one important strategy readers use to make meaning from texts. To use syntactic clues, readers must have an understanding of what sounds right in English. When ELLs develop an understanding of English grammar and word order, they are better able to self-monitor their reading and determine if something sounds right. They are also better able to use context clues if they have an understanding of correct word order in English sentences.

TEACHING ELLS ENGLISH GRAMMAR AND USAGE

English language learners (ELLs) should be taught grammar and usage skills in realistic contexts rather than in isolation. It is also helpful to design grammar lessons around familiar topics and vocabulary so learners can focus on the grammar and usage concepts rather than trying to decipher the meaning.

Teachers should frequently **model** correct grammar and sentence structure through listening, reading, and speaking activities. One strategy is to read texts that model a specific grammar rule and ask ELLs to listen for examples of its use or apply it in their own writing. They can also be encouraged to look for patterns in grammar and usage, such as *-ed* and *-ing* endings.

Teachers need to carefully consider when and how to address grammatical and usage errors made by ELLs. Frequent and immediate corrections can cause **frustration**. However, if specific errors are not addressed over time, they may become **fossilized** and difficult to correct. One strategy is to note repeated errors and address them later in mini-lessons rather than at the time they are made. Teachers can also pick a small number of errors to focus on at any one time.

ENGLISH LANGUAGE PARTS OF SPEECH

The following are the eight parts of speech in the English language:

1. **Nouns** describe people, places, and things, for example, he ate a chocolate **cupcake**.
2. **Verbs** describe action or being; for example, the dog **chased** the squirrel around the yard.
3. **Pronouns** are words used in place of nouns, for example, **she** works in the office building downtown.
4. **Adjectives** describe nouns or pronouns. They usually describe which one, what kind, or how many of something, for example, the **yellow** house is located on the corner.
5. **Adverbs** describe verbs, adjectives, or other adverbs. They usually describe when, where, why, or how something happens, and they often end in *-ly*; for example, the fish swam **quickly** away from the shark.
6. **Prepositions** are words that relate nouns or pronouns to other words in the sentence; for example, the chef put the dough **in** the oven.
7. **Conjunctions** join words, phrases, or clauses; for example, the teacher **and** the principal attended the meeting.
8. **Interjections** show emotion in sentences; for example, **ouch**—I bumped my elbow.

When readers come across words whose meanings they do not know, knowing the parts of speech can help them determine the function of the words in the sentences. This will make it easier to guess the meanings using context clues.

> **Review Video: Parts of Speech**
> Visit mometrix.com/academy and enter code: 899611
>
> **Review Video: What is a Noun?**
> Visit mometrix.com/academy and enter code: 344028

TEACHING STUDENTS TO RECOGNIZE DIFFERENT PARTS OF SPEECH

Parts of speech are typically introduced one or a few at a time. **Nouns** and **verbs** are often introduced first because they can be used as the building blocks of basic sentences. If an inductive method is used, students may be given a group of sentences with the same parts of speech highlighted and asked to determine what the words have in common. If a deductive method is used, teachers might explicitly teach what each part of speech does and provide examples.

Mini-lessons can also be used. A **mini-lesson** on nouns, for example, might include listing nouns that fit into the categories of people, places, and things. It might also include finding examples of nouns in texts or sorting words according to whether or not they are nouns. Teachers can also use shared reading and writing activities as opportunities to discuss parts of speech in context.

Sentence diagrams are pictorial representations that show how parts of speech work together to form sentences. Although sentence diagramming can help some students visualize sentence structure, it can be frustrating and tedious for others. Therefore, it can be considered as one component of grammar instruction as long as it fits the needs of the learners.

ACADEMIC LITERACY

Academic literacy refers to the knowledge and skills necessary to communicate effectively in academic situations. It includes content-specific knowledge and vocabulary, such as mathematical terms. It also includes general knowledge and vocabulary used across all content areas, such as the terms *synthesize*, *summarize*, and *evaluate*. Additionally, it refers to the ability to communicate effectively in academic situations through reading, writing, listening, and speaking.

Academic literacy helps students flexibly adapt their use of reading strategies according to the types of text used and the purposes for reading. It helps them acquire content-specific vocabulary needed to comprehend academic texts and effectively communicate their learning using a variety of response types. It helps them summarize, evaluate, and make connections among content acquired from multiple sources and across content areas. Academic literacy also encourages students to effectively communicate and collaborate with others to construct meaning.

TYPES OF KNOWLEDGE COMMONLY USED IN EDUCATION

There are many types of knowledge commonly used in education.

- **Social** knowledge is knowledge about social conventions passed down within members of a community. It includes conventions related to expected greetings, manners, and conversational behavior.
- **Procedural** knowledge refers to the knowledge applied to carry out procedural tasks. An example is solving a complex math problem using a multistep algorithm.
- **Physical** knowledge refers to knowledge learned by observing the features of something. When students discuss the physical properties of rock samples, they are using physical knowledge.
- **Domain** knowledge refers to the knowledge and skills used by experts in a particular field. For example, a student explaining how she completed a division problem using the terms *dividend*, *divisor*, and *quotient* is using domain knowledge.
- **Empirical** knowledge refers to knowledge obtained from scientific experimentation and data collection. Determining the boiling points of different liquids as part of a science experiment is an example of empirical knowledge.

ROLE OF LITERACY IN THE DEVELOPMENT AND APPLICATION OF DIFFERENT TYPES OF KNOWLEDGE

Literacy plays a large role in the development and application of different types of knowledge in the classroom. Social knowledge is passed down through oral language and written texts. Students

92

learn about social norms through the actions of characters in stories and through discussing texts with others. For example, children learn about solving conflict with friends by reading about characters who work through conflict. They also learn how to listen attentively and take turns through participation in literature circles.

- When students read nonfiction **procedural texts**, they develop procedural knowledge that can be used to accomplish tasks. Procedural texts also provide models of text structures students can use when explaining procedures to others.
- Reading texts containing **academic language** helps students develop and apply physical, domain, and empirical knowledge. Developing their academic vocabularies can assist students with expressing their observations and conclusions using academic language.

ACADEMIC READING VS. READING FOR ENTERTAINMENT

- **Academic reading** refers to thoughtfully reading and analyzing academic texts as part of content area studies. Readers usually have specific purposes in mind before beginning academic reading. For example, an entomology student may consult a field guide to correctly classify an insect found during a nature hike. Another student may read a social studies textbook to identify some major causes of the Revolutionary War for an essay assignment.
- **Reading for entertainment** refers to reading for fun. A student may select a fictional book from a favorite series to read on a rainy day.

When completing academic reading, readers often pay special attention to text structures and features to efficiently **locate needed information**. They may skim or skip around in the texts. They may stop to look up the meanings of **unfamiliar vocabulary words**. They may also read more slowly or reread passages multiple times to make sense of unfamiliar content.

When reading for entertainment, proficient readers still self-monitor their comprehension, but they have more freedom about which text elements they wish to respond to and analyze. They may also read at a quicker pace and choose to reread favorite parts for fun.

Development of Reading Fluency

COMPONENTS OF FLUENCY
Reading fluency is made up of several elements including rate, accuracy, and prosody.

- **Rate** refers to reading speed. Proficient readers adjust their reading speed flexibly depending on their purposes for reading. For example, they may read scientific textbooks containing technical vocabulary more slowly than graphic novels they are reading for entertainment. Rate is important for comprehension. If readers read too slowly, they may forget what they have already read and lose the overall meanings of the texts. If readers read too quickly, important points may be overlooked.
- **Accuracy** is another component of fluency. It refers to decoding words correctly without errors. Fluent readers automatically recognize many high-frequency words and use multiple strategies to decode unknown words. Accuracy is important because frequent errors may affect comprehension, especially if errors are made on words central to the meaning of the text.

93

- **Prosody** is another component of fluency. It refers to reading expression, including phrasing and intonation. Prosody affects the ways texts are understood. For example, readers should pause appropriately at commas to emphasize certain phrases. Using the correct intonation associated with each punctuation mark affects the tone of the texts.

PROGRESSION OF FLUENCY DEVELOPMENT IN READERS

- **Early readers** devote most of their mental energy to decoding words. In this stage of reading, the focus is on developing reading accuracy, which is one component of fluency. Early readers practice high-frequency words and learn strategies to decode words with simple spelling patterns. Rate and prosody play lesser roles but are still practiced with scaffolding.
- In the **transitional reading stage**, readers automatically recognize many high-frequency words and more efficiently use strategies to decode unknown words. There is still a focus on accuracy as readers encounter more complex vocabulary and spelling patterns. However, transitional readers increase their reading rates and begin to read independently with prosody. As readers gain confidence with familiar texts, their fluency increases.
- By the time they reach the **fluent stage**, readers are able to flexibly adapt their reading rates based upon their purposes for reading. Automatic recognition of most words results in reading accuracy. Fluent readers read with prosody, and they appropriately match their expressions to the texts.

DEVELOPING FLUENCY IN EARLY READERS

When teaching early readers, the main focus is on developing **accuracy**. This is done through activities to develop automatic recognition of high-frequency sight words and explicit phonics instruction that teaches strategies to decode words with common spelling patterns.

To assist early readers with developing **speed and prosody**, teachers can encourage repeated readings of favorite texts. As readers develop more confidence with the texts through these repeated readings, their reading rates will increase. Because readers already know how to decode the words in these familiar texts, they have more energy available to focus on expression.

Teachers should frequently **model fluent reading**. This includes reading with appropriate speed, phrasing, and intonation. Teachers can also model disfluent reading, such as reading texts without expression, and ask students to explain the effects it has on comprehension. Choral reading of shared texts can also assist students with developing fluency.

> **Review Video: Fluency**
> Visit mometrix.com/academy and enter code: 531179

MAINTAINING FLUENCY IN ON-LEVEL READERS

Like struggling readers, on-level readers can benefit from frequent teacher modeling of fluent reading, choral reading, and opportunities to reread familiar texts. Additionally, they can benefit from partner reading. Partner reading allows students to hear fluent reading modeled by classmates and reread texts repeatedly while receiving feedback. Students should first be taught procedures for how to listen attentively to their partners' reading and provide effective and encouraging feedback. Teachers should always be mindful of individual needs when pairing students.

Reader's theater is another strategy to assist on-level readers with fluency. In **reader's theater**, students read scripts from appropriately leveled texts to perform for classmates. Through rehearsing and performing, students have multiple opportunities to reread the scripts. They must also practice reading with appropriate expression for their characters and reading with appropriate speeds so they can be understood by their audiences. Additionally, reader's theater allows students in the audience to hear models of fluent reading. In reader's theater, the focus is on the reading, and few or no props are used.

INTERVENTIONS TO USE ASSISTING READERS WHO ARE STRUGGLING WITH FLUENCY

Readers who are struggling with fluency can benefit from frequent modeling of fluent reading. As teachers reread familiar texts, students can join in and read chorally, matching their phrasing, speed, and expression to the teachers' reading. Students can also listen to audio recordings of texts.

Readers who struggle with fluency can also benefit from repeated readings of texts. After initial readings, teachers can give feedback to students and help them set goals for rereading. For example, they may encourage readers to pause at the periods between sentences. It is important that readers are given passages within their instructional reading levels. Reading texts far below their instructional levels will not challenge the readers. Reading texts that are too difficult will result in readers stopping frequently to decode unknown words, which interrupts fluency and causes frustration. Encouraging repeated readings of texts with rhyming and repetition, including poetry, can assist readers who are struggling with fluency.

Although teachers may monitor students' reading fluency over time, it is also important to create encouraging environments for readers. Continuously timing readers or forcing disfluent readers to read aloud in front of others may have negative effects.

Supporting the Development of Writing Skills

STAGES OF THE WRITING PROCESS

- In the **prewriting stage**, writers brainstorm ideas, decide on topics, and plan the structure of their writing. This may include brainstorming, using webs or other graphic organizers to map out main ideas and details, and creating outlines. Writers consider who their audiences will be and what their purposes are for writing.
- In the **drafting stage**, writers create their rough drafts. The focus of this stage is recording thoughts. Students are encouraged not to worry about spelling, grammar, and punctuation errors, which will be corrected later.
- In the **revising stage**, writers consider if any portions of their writing lack clarity or if any parts should be added or removed. They examine word choice and consider if there are ways to make the writing more descriptive. They also seek feedback from others about ways their writing could be improved.
- In the **editing stage**, writers carefully check their writing for spelling, capitalization, punctuation, and grammatical errors. They also ask others to edit their writing to ensure no errors are overlooked.
- In the **publishing stage**, writers share their writing with others. This may involve creating illustrated books, reading aloud in authors' circles, putting on plays, or presenting in other ways.

> **Review Video: The Recursive Writing Process**
> Visit mometrix.com/academy and enter code: 951611

TEACHING STUDENTS THE WRITING PROCESS

Modeling is an important strategy to help students become familiar with the writing process. Teachers can lead their classes in creating shared pieces of writing, going through each step as a group. Teachers can also share examples of their personal writing as they introduce each step of the process. Multiple examples that represent writing from various genres should be included to show students how the process can be applied to different types of writing.

Teachers can post charts outlining the **steps of the writing process** in their classrooms. Regular time should be set aside to work on writing so that, at the beginning of each session, students can identify which steps of the writing process they will focus on that day. This will help them establish goals for each session and maintain focus.

Teachers should also schedule time for frequent conferring with students to provide feedback and ensure they are staying focused on the process. Additionally, teachers can provide opportunities for students to reflect on the process and the changes they have made to improve their writing.

BENEFITS OF CONFERRING WITH STUDENTS DURING THE WRITING PROCESS

There are several benefits of conferring with students during the writing process. When writers know they will be frequently meeting with teachers, it increases accountability for following the writing process. It also gives teachers opportunities to provide timely feedback to students and personalize instruction based on their individual needs.

It is important for teachers to model the conference process for students before beginning. Students should be aware of the purposes of the conferences and the expectations for their roles. Additionally, students should practice routines for what to do while their teachers are conferring with others. This modeling and practice will increase the likelihood that conferences can be conducted without interruptions.

There are multiple ways that conferences can be conducted, but they typically include students sharing the progress they have made since their last conference and discussing any questions or concerns they have. Teachers usually pick a few points to focus on with each student, showing specific ways that improvements can be made using examples or mentor texts. Teachers should use the academic language of writing in their conferences. Additionally, conferences should be positive and motivating in nature to help students develop positive feelings about writing.

HELPING STUDENTS WRITE EFFECTIVELY FOR DIFFERENT AUDIENCES

As part of the prewriting process, writers should be encouraged to identify their **intended audience**. Once they have identified their audience, they should consider several factors. One factor is how much **prior knowledge** their audience has about the topics. This will affect what level of background information and detail the writers should go into to meet the **audience members' needs**. For example, writers who are explaining how to use computer programs will focus on different program capabilities depending on whether the audience members are beginners or advanced users. Another factor to consider is what type of relationship the writers have to their audience. This will affect the level of **formality** used in the writing. For example, a friendly letter to a classmate will be less formal than a letter written to a government representative.

Teachers should give students frequent opportunities to complete **authentic writing activities** for varied audiences rather than only submitting assignments for teacher evaluation. They can also provide opportunities for students to compare and contrast texts that are written about the same topics but written for different audiences.

HELPING STUDENTS EFFECTIVELY WRITE IN VARIOUS FORMS AND GENRES

Genre studies are one way to help students learn to effectively write in different genres. In **genre studies**, classes study one genre at a time, in detail, over the course of a few weeks. They read many different mentor texts in the genre and discuss common characteristics. Students can then be encouraged to complete their own writing activities within the genre, using the mentor texts as models.

A similar approach can be used to teach students to effectively write in different forms. For example, when learning to write friendly letters, students can explore many different examples. They can discuss common characteristics and use the examples as models when writing their own friendly letters.

Another strategy is to provide a mixture of **strong and weak examples** of a genre or writing form and ask students to evaluate their effectiveness. They can discuss which examples they think are the most effective and what characteristics these examples display that make them more successful. Similarly, they can discuss which features the weak examples contain or lack that make them less successful. They can then be encouraged to consider these findings during their own writing activities.

DEVELOPING WRITING SKILLS

Developing effective writing skills requires a multifaceted approach. Like reading, writing should be interwoven through the school day and all content areas rather than taught in isolation. It requires a combination of explicit skills instruction and opportunities to freely explore and experiment with writing. Skills instruction should include a wide range of topics, including spelling, grammar, language use, text structures, and more.

It is important to help students develop **positive attitudes** about writing. Building a community of writers where students can freely collaborate, share, and solicit feedback can help students feel safe and supported in the writing process. Students need to be explicitly taught how to solicit feedback from classmates and how to provide constructive and respectful feedback to others.

Because reading and writing are interrelated, students also need frequent opportunities to both read and write texts of different genres and purposes. They need to compare and contrast different texts and evaluate both their own writing and the writing of others. They should be explicitly taught how to participate in the five steps of the writing process, and they should receive frequent feedback on their writing. Feedback should provide specific suggestions for improvement in a positive and encouraging manner.

HELPING STUDENTS EFFECTIVELY COMPOSE WRITTEN TEXTS

While teaching the writing process, teachers should help students understand that quality writing takes time. They can model their own writing processes and share stories about the writing processes of favorite authors. Writing stamina can be developed gradually in younger students, with writing workshop time increasing as the year goes on.

- Although students need models of **quality writing**, they also benefit from seeing **weak examples**. Students can evaluate a range of writing samples and contrast their effectiveness. Comparing both strong and weak examples will help writers identify the characteristics of quality texts and consider them in their own writing.

- Students should also be encouraged to engage in **multiple rounds of revision**. Revisions should be based on feedback from both peers and teachers as well as personal reflection. Students should also be explicitly taught how to consider feedback critically and decide which suggestions to implement and which to disregard.
- Additionally, teachers should monitor students' writing through observation and conferences and plan mini-lessons based on the issues they notice. For writing that will be evaluated, **rubrics** should be given in advance. Students should be encouraged to consult the rubrics and **self-evaluate** their own writing at multiple stages throughout the process.

ASSISTING STUDENTS WITH THE REVISION PROCESS

Revising is often a difficult part of the writing process as students may struggle to see how they can improve their own writing pieces. First, it is important that students understand that the **focus of revision** is on improving clarity, detail, word choice, and other features rather than on the spelling and mechanical issues they will address during editing.

Modeling is often an effective way to help students understand the revision process. Teachers can share their own writing pieces and ask students to identify areas that do not make sense or could be explained in better detail. For example, teachers may ask students to close their eyes and visualize while they read one portion of their written pieces aloud. After asking students to share their visualizations, teachers may revise the writing to include more sensory details. Students can repeat the **visualization process** and note the differences. Teachers can also model writing sentences in multiple ways and ask which ways sound best. They may also help students identify descriptive words that can be used to replace commonly used words, such as replacing the word *nice* with *amiable*. These lists can be posted in classrooms for students to refer to when writing.

HELPING STUDENTS PRODUCE QUALITY WRITING IN THE CONTENT AREAS

In preparation for the workforce and independent living, students must be able to successfully write for a variety of purposes and audiences. This is essential because effective writing is required in many professions. For example, scientists publish research studies, sales professionals write sales reports, and marketing specialists create advertisements.

Going through the steps of the writing process helps students organize, synthesize, analyze, and evaluate complex information. They must make judgments about what information is relevant and which text structures should be used to best convey meaning. Putting content into their own words helps students comprehend difficult information and vocabulary. Therefore, writing in the content areas supports comprehension in these areas as well.

Teachers can provide varied types of texts to support learning in the content areas. This may include fiction books, journal articles, diaries, field guides, research studies, maps, interview transcripts, and more. Students should interact with various quality texts and discuss the roles they play in different professions.

HELPING STUDENTS RECOGNIZE AND USE ABBREVIATIONS AND ACRONYMS

Because there are numerous abbreviations and acronyms, teachers need to selectively choose which ones to focus on for instructional purposes. Therefore, teachers often address abbreviations and acronyms as they come up in students' reading and writing. For example, when writing letters, teachers can explain the abbreviations Dr., Mr., and Mrs. Teachers can also observe issues with abbreviations and acronyms as they occur in students' writing and address them through mini-lessons. Examples of abbreviations and acronyms can be pointed out in texts. Charts displaying common abbreviations and their long-form versions can also be displayed in classrooms to provide scaffolding before they are memorized.

In the age of digital communication and social media, it is also important to teach students when it is appropriate to use abbreviations and acronyms. Students need to consider their purpose for communication and their relationship with their audience. For example, informal acronyms may be appropriate for texts between friends but not for use in business letters.

PRINCIPLES OF EFFECTIVE WRITING

- **Clarity** and **brevity** are two related principles of effective writing. They require writers to include sufficient detail to convey their intended meanings while simultaneously omitting any extraneous or repetitive information. Students should be encouraged to consider the value that each word and sentence adds to their writing to determine whether or not it should be included. They should also consider the background knowledge of their intended audiences to ensure they go into the appropriate amount of detail to meet their needs.
- **Author's craft** and **voice** are also important principles of effective writing that draw readers in and compel them to read more. In fictional texts, they help readers identify with characters and make the stories seem realistic. These principles help maintain reader engagement with the texts.
- Additionally, careful **editing** is important for effective writing. If numerous errors are present, the meanings of the texts may be affected.

HELPING STUDENTS EDIT THEIR WRITING TO CORRECT ERRORS WITH MECHANICS

Frequent modeling is helpful when teaching students to edit. Teachers can model using editing checklists or rubrics to check for errors in their own work. The class can edit writing pieces they have composed together during shared writing experiences or edit texts containing errors written by other authors.

Teachers can also instruct students to **follow routines** when editing. This may include completing editing checklists or recalling mnemonic devices to ensure that all areas have been checked. CUPS is one mnemonic device that can be used to remind young writers to check for capitalization, usage, punctuation, and spelling. Because it can be difficult for students to recognize errors in their own writing, teachers can also encourage students to edit their own work first and then ask other students to edit it as well.

Additionally, students benefit from frequent, shared reading experiences using large print books, projected digital texts, or other means that allow them to follow along as teachers read. Teachers can stop to point out how authors use capital letters, punctuation marks, and other conventions. Frequently seeing these conventions in use will help students understand their purposes and notice when they are used incorrectly in other texts.

HELPING STUDENTS USE CORRECT PUNCTUATION IN THEIR WRITING

Teachers can explicitly teach students about each punctuation mark by introducing it, discussing its purpose, and demonstrating how to use it correctly in writing.

Students should also have frequent opportunities to explore how punctuation is used in context. They can be asked to find examples of certain punctuation marks in texts and examine the roles they play in the sentences. They can try reading the sentences with the given punctuation marks. They can then reread them with the punctuation marks omitted or substituted and discuss the differences in meaning and tone. For example, students could read a sentence in a book ending with a period, using appropriate intonation and pausing. They could then substitute the period for an exclamation point, adjusting their intonation. They could discuss how the meaning and tone of the sentence changed. Students can also edit their own writing by reading it aloud, using the intonation and phrasing suggested by the punctuation marks they included. They can ask themselves if any areas sound unclear, such as if sentences seem to blend together. They can also use punctuation checklists and ask other classmates to edit their work to double-check for errors.

> **Review Video: Consistency in Punctuation**
> Visit mometrix.com/academy and enter code: 169489

HELPING STUDENTS USE CORRECT CAPITALIZATION IN THEIR WRITING

One strategy to teach proper capitalization is to give students texts and ask them to circle all capital letters. Students can then be asked to identify what the words with capital letters have in common, leading to a discussion of capitalization rules. These rules can also be explicitly taught with examples provided.

- Posters can be displayed in classrooms as reminders of when to capitalize letters, such as at the beginnings of sentences, when using proper nouns, or when writing the word *I*.
- Additionally, students can be asked to edit texts, including their own writing pieces, to locate capitalization errors. Students should be reminded that errors may include both randomly capitalized letters and lowercase letters that should be capitalized.
- The ability to differentiate between common and proper nouns is needed to apply capitalization rules correctly. To assist with this skill, students can complete word sorts with common and proper nouns. They can also locate and circle examples of each type in texts.

> **Review Video: Capitalization in Grammar**
> Visit mometrix.com/academy and enter code: 369678

TYPES OF LANGUAGE DISORDERS

Language delays and disorders can fall into three categories. **Receptive disorders** make it difficult for people to understand the messages communicated by others. **Expressive disorders** make it difficult for people to communicate their thoughts and ideas to others. **Mixed receptive-expressive language disorders** involve difficulties in both areas. These disorders can either be developmental or acquired. Acquired disorders are caused by injury or illness.

Within each of these categories, there are many different types of disorders. Apraxia, stuttering, and articulation disorders are some examples of expressive disorders. Students with expressive disorders may find it difficult to produce certain sounds, organize their thoughts into sentences, or use language appropriately in social situations. Therefore, classroom activities that require speaking and/or writing may be difficult. Students with receptive disorders may find it difficult to remember details or follow spoken directions. For example, they may not remember multistep directions that are given verbally for assignments.

MEETING THE NEEDS OF STUDENTS WITH LANGUAGE DELAYS AND DISORDERS

Although students with **language delays** and disorders often receive professional speech therapy, there are many strategies teachers can use to support these students within the classroom.

Teachers should model treating students with language disorders respectfully. They should not interrupt students with expressive disorders or attempt to finish their sentences. Instead, adequate response time should be provided. Students can also be given advance notice of the questions they will be asked, allowing them time to formulate responses.

Students with **receptive disorders** who have difficulties processing or remembering speech may benefit from receiving information in multiple forms. When giving project directions, for example, teachers can provide written directions and explain them verbally. Multistep directions can be broken down into simple steps. Visuals can be used to help students comprehend vocabulary used in speech. Additionally, teachers can ensure that they have obtained students' attention before speaking, and they can monitor students for understanding.

For students who struggle with language pragmatics, role-playing activities can be used to practice appropriate responses for a variety of common social situations, such as asking for help or greeting people.

Reading Development: Comprehension

Morphology and Word Analysis Skills

HOMOGRAPHS

Homographs are words that are spelled the same but may be pronounced differently and have different meanings. An example of a homograph pair is *bat* (baseball bat) and *bat* (the flying mammal).

After explaining the meaning of homographs, teachers can assist students with generating lists of homograph pairs. Teachers can provide sentences using homographs, and students can identify them and their meanings. Students can also look for homographs in texts and play matching games to find cards with two different definitions for the same word.

Homographs have different meanings, so it is important for readers to be able to identify which meanings are being used when they encounter homographs in texts. Readers can be encouraged to use context clues to assist with determining the meanings. Readers can also be encouraged to self-monitor their understanding of each homograph's meaning by asking themselves if what they have read makes sense. Because homograph pairs can also be pronounced differently, readers can be encouraged to try reading the sentences with each possible pronunciation and ask themselves which one sounds right.

COMPOUND WORDS

A **compound word** is formed by combining two or more words to form one word with a new, unique meaning. Examples of compound words include *houseboat*, *moonlight*, and *basketball*.

Identifying compound words rapidly can assist readers with decoding multisyllabic words. Identifying the smaller, known words contained in the compound words will help students decode the words quickly and maintain fluency.

To teach students to identify compound words, they can practice breaking them into parts. Compound words can be provided using letter tiles, magnetic letters, or in writing, and students can be asked to split them into the two smaller word parts. Puzzle cards can be created with which two smaller words join together to create a compound word. Readers can also be asked to find and mark compound words in texts. When students struggle to decode compound words while reading independently, teachers can ask what smaller, known words they see in the unknown words.

TYPES OF CONTEXT CLUES

- There are several different types of context clues that are often provided in sentences. One common type is a **definition clue**. In this type of clue, a definition for the unfamiliar word is provided somewhere within the same sentence; for example, *the precocious toddler surprised her parents by learning to read at a much earlier age than her peers*.
- Another type of context clue is an **antonym clue**. In this type of clue, an antonym or contrasting definition of the unfamiliar word is provided somewhere within the same sentence; for example, *unlike his amiable coworker, Mark was quite unfriendly when interacting with customers*.

102

- **Synonym clues** are a third type of context clue. In this type, a synonym for the unfamiliar word is provided somewhere within the same sentence; for example, *the altruistic donor was so selfless that she donated all of her lottery winnings to her favorite charity.*
- **Inference clues** are another type of context clue. With this type of clue, the unknown word's meaning is not explicitly given, and the reader must infer it from the context of the sentence; for example, *Sam was thirsty after hiking the three-mile trail, so he ordered a cold beverage at the café.*

AFFIXES

Affixes are letters or groups of letters that are added to root words. **Prefixes** and **suffixes** are two common types of **affixes**. Root words may have one or multiple affixes attached to them.

Learning to identify affixes and understand their meanings is important for both fluency and comprehension. Because the same affixes are used repeatedly in English, immediately recognizing them and knowing how they are pronounced can assist readers with decoding multisyllabic words. Decoding the words quickly will help the readers maintain fluency. Because affixes also have predictable meanings, understanding these meanings can help readers comprehend new words in texts and build vocabulary. For example, if readers encounter the word *declutter*, they may know that *de* means the opposite of something, and *clutter* means a messy collection of things. Using this knowledge, they can put the parts together and determine the meaning of *declutter*.

Review Video: Affix Definition
Visit mometrix.com/academy and enter code: 782422

PREFIXES

A **prefix** is a letter or group of letters added to the beginning of a root word. The prefix modifies the existing word's meaning, and a new word is formed. For example, the prefix *dis-* can be added to the word *respect* to form the new word *disrespect*.

Students need to understand the difference between a prefix and base word. It should be emphasized that the base is a whole word, whereas the prefix is a letter or group of letters that cannot stand alone. Examples of words containing prefixes can be provided, and students can practice identifying both the prefixes and root words. Non-examples can also be provided, such as the word *decal. De-* is not a prefix in this example because *cal* is not a word on its own.

The meanings of different prefixes can then be introduced. Root words can be presented, and their meanings discussed. Prefixes can then be added, and students can discuss how the meanings of the words change. They can list other words containing the same prefixes, along with their meanings.

Students can also be encouraged to find examples of words containing prefixes in texts independently and use clues to determine their meanings.

SUFFIXES

A **suffix** is a letter or group of letters added to the end of a root word. When added, it sometimes changes the meaning of the root word and forms a new word. It may also change the part of speech of the root word. An example of a suffix is *-ful*. When added to the end of the root word *thank*, it forms the word *thankful*, which means full of thanks.

To introduce the topic, students can be given lists of words containing suffixes and asked to identify what the words have in common. The suffixes can then be identified, and teachers can explain how the suffixes change the root words. Three-column charts can be created, with columns dedicated to suffixes, their meanings, and example words. Students can be given cards containing root words and suffixes, and they can experiment with pairing them. They can explain whether the combinations form real or nonsense words and define any real words they create. Students can be encouraged to find examples of words containing suffixes and identify their meanings based on context clues in the texts.

DERIVATIONAL VS. INFLECTIONAL AFFIXES

- **Derivational affixes** are letters or groups of letters added to root words to change the meanings of the words or the parts of speech. For example, if the affix *un-* is added to the root *kind*, the new word *unkind* is formed. Both the original and newly formed words are adjectives, but the meanings of the two words are different. However, if the affix *-ment* is added to the root word *fulfill*, the new word *fulfillment* is formed. The original word is a verb, and the newly formed word is a noun. Both of these examples demonstrate derivational affixes.
- **Inflectional affixes** do not change the part of speech of a word, but they do serve a grammatical function. Inflectional affixes include the suffixes *-s*, *-ed*, *-ing*, *-en*, *-'s*, *-er*, and *-est*. For example, adding an inflectional affix can change the word *walk* to *walked*. The part of speech does not change as both words are verbs. The affix only changes the tense of the verb. Inflectional affixes can indicate whether a noun is singular or plural, the verb tense, superlatives, or possessives.

RELATIONSHIP BETWEEN KNOWLEDGE OF ROOTS AND AFFIXES

Knowledge of roots and affixes and the use of **context clues** are closely related. Proficient readers use a combination of these strategies to determine the meanings of unknown words, check their initial guesses, and revise their guesses if necessary.

- When encountering an unknown multisyllabic word, a reader may first look for known **parts** of the word. This may lead the reader to break the word down into the root and affixes. Using knowledge of what each of these components means, the reader may then guess the word's meaning.
- However, both roots and affixes can have multiple meanings. The reader's initial guess may not make sense in this particular context. Therefore, it is important for the reader to also consider **context clues** to check the conjectured meaning. If it does not fit the context, the reader may consider other meanings of the root and affixes that better fit the context clues.
- The reader may also begin by guessing the word's meaning using context clues and then use knowledge of the root and affixes to check the initial conjecture. Teachers should encourage readers to use both of these strategies to **check** and **self-correct** their deductions.

Reading Various Types of Texts

GENRES OF FICTION

Realistic fiction stories are about events that could happen in real life. The characters and settings are realistic. **Historical** fiction stories also contain realistic characters, settings, and events, but they take place in the past—often during important times in history. **Mysteries** contain crimes or puzzling events that the characters must solve. **Fantasies** contain story elements that are unrealistic, such as talking animals or magic. **Science-fiction** stories focus on imagining life with advanced science or technological capabilities and other theorized situations, such as the existence of extraterrestrial life.

Folktales are another type of fiction. They are popular stories that are passed down from generation to generation, often by word of mouth. Fairy tales are one type of folktale. They often contain magical events and creatures, take place in enchanted places, have happy endings, and have good characters battling evil characters. There are often multiple versions of fairy tales. Cinderella is one example. Tall tales are folktales that are portrayed as if they were realistic but include characters with superhuman traits and exaggerated events. Paul Bunyan is an example of a tall tale.

Review Video: Reading Fiction
Visit mometrix.com/academy and enter code: 391411

Review Video: Myths, Fables, Legends, and Fairy Tales
Visit mometrix.com/academy and enter code: 347199

IMPORTANCE OF BEING ABLE TO RECOGNIZE DIFFERENT GENRES OF FICTION

Understanding the characteristics of different genres and being able to correctly classify texts by type is beneficial to readers for many reasons. Knowledge of the typical text structures of each genre assists readers with making predictions. For example, knowing that fairy tales typically end with good overcoming evil can help readers predict how stories will end. It also helps readers analyze texts deeply and incorporate characteristics of the genres in their own writing.

There are different approaches that can be used to teach about genres. One approach is to complete genre studies in which genres are explored in detail one at a time. Teachers may begin by providing explicit instruction on the characteristics of each genre and then give students opportunities to analyze examples. Teachers may also begin by sharing multiple texts of the same genre and asking students to identify common characteristics on their own. Another approach is to present multiple genres at once using a compare-and-contrast approach. No matter which approach is used, readers should have opportunities to explore many texts of each type of genre to develop an understanding of their common characteristics and text structures.

FICTIONAL STORY ELEMENTS

Fictional texts contain characters. There are both **primary characters**, who are central to the conflicts and resolutions of the stories, and **secondary characters**, who play smaller roles. The settings of the stories are another feature. The **settings** include both the times in history and the geographical locations where the stories occur. Fictional stories also contain problems or conflicts. The **conflicts** are usually introduced early in the stories to hook readers and encourage them to continue reading. The **plots** contain the main events of the stories, when the characters work to resolve the problems. The **solutions** contain the resolutions to the problems, which typically occur toward the ends of the stories. Fictional texts also typically contain **themes**, which are the underlying messages the authors are trying to convey to readers.

It is important for readers to understand that not all fictional texts contain every element. However, recognizing the common features will assist readers with making predictions and comprehending the texts.

Review Video: Determining Relationships in a Story
Visit mometrix.com/academy and enter code: 929925

Review Video: How to Make a Story Map
Visit mometrix.com/academy and enter code: 261719

TEACHING STUDENTS TO IDENTIFY FICTIONAL STORY ELEMENTS

A common way for teachers to introduce students to fictional story elements is modeling their thinking during shared reading experiences. For example, teachers may pause their reading when evidence is provided about the story's settings. The teachers may explain what they have gathered about the settings and show students which textual clues they used to make these determinations.

Graphic organizers, including story maps, are commonly used tools that help students locate and record story elements. These story maps typically ask students to locate the characters, settings, problems, events, and solutions in stories. Foldables or flip books can also be used to record these elements. These elements can be recorded using a combination of pictures and text depending on the ages and needs of the students. Students can also fill out these graphic organizers as prewriting activities when outlining their own stories.

Teachers should ask guiding questions to focus students' attention on story elements before reading. For example, they can ask students to listen for the problem in the story before they begin reading.

TYPES OF CHARACTERS FOUND IN FICTIONAL STORIES

There are several common types of characters found in fictional stories. However, not all fictional stories contain all types of characters.

- **Protagonists** are the main characters in fictional stories that readers can relate to and want to succeed. Protagonists can be complex characters with both positive and negative traits. Although readers empathize with protagonists, these characters do not always demonstrate admirable behavior.
- **Antagonists** are characters who stand in the way of protagonists accomplishing their goals. Antagonists are not necessarily bad characters and can also have both positive and negative traits.
- **Flat characters** do not change over time. Their actions and personalities are consistent throughout the stories. They are sometimes known as static characters.
- **Dynamic characters** change over time, usually as a result of experiencing the events in the narrative. Readers can identify changes in these characters as the story progresses. Dynamic characters change over time, usually as a result of experiencing the events in the stories. Readers can identify changes in these characters as the stories progress.

> **Review Video: What is the Definition of a Character in a Story?**
> Visit mometrix.com/academy and enter code: 429493

ANALYZING CHARACTER DEVELOPMENT

Authors of fictional texts present a variety of information about their characters. They describe the characters' physical characteristics, personality traits, hobbies, dreams and goals, and approaches to solving problems. After reading the stories, readers get to know the characters and develop the ability to predict how the characters might react to different types of situations. They also identify the roles that the characters play in the stories, such as being the protagonists or antagonists. Additionally, they determine whether or not any characters have changed as the stories progressed, and they identify reasons for these changes. All of these steps are part of analyzing **character development**.

Students can be asked to discuss character traits and complete character maps using text evidence from the stories. They can be asked to predict how characters would likely react in other situations, based upon their actions in the stories. Students can also be asked to describe how characters have changed from the beginnings of the stories to the ends, using text clues for support. They can compare and contrast characters from different texts or the same characters during different periods of time.

ROLE THAT THE SETTING PLAYS IN A STORY

Setting plays an important role in a story. It describes both the geographical location where the story takes place and the time in history when it occurs. A well-described setting also has the power to set the mood for the story. It can help readers visualize the story's events and imagine that they are present. This can assist readers with comprehension and increase engagement with the text.

To recognize setting, readers can be asked to identify both where and when the story takes place as well as to locate key words within the story that signal the answers to these questions. To explore setting more deeply, readers can be asked to identify how the story evokes their five senses. Using a graphic organizer, they can explore what the characters see, hear, taste, smell, and feel in the story. They can discuss how the use of these details helps readers visualize the setting, and they can be encouraged to use similar details in their own writing.

Teachers can also find examples of mentor texts with detailed settings. Students can explore the ways that the authors describe the settings and discuss how these details affect readers.

ELEMENTS OF POETRY

Discussing and analyzing poetry is a common part of literacy instruction. As part of this instruction, teachers can help students learn to recognize common elements in poetry and use the appropriate terminology to describe them.

There are several elements of poetry. A **verse** is a single line of poetry. Verses can be grouped together to form **stanzas**. The **rhythm** in a poem is developed from patterns of stressed and unstressed syllables. **Meter** refers to a poem's rhythmic structure. Some poems incorporate rhyme, which occurs when words end with the same sounds. **Rhymes** are often found at the ends of verses. Poetry can also use other literary elements, such as alliteration, similes, and metaphors.

Students can learn much about elements of poetry by exploring different types of poems. Students can be asked what they like or dislike about each poem, and these observations can be used to introduce the elements that are used. Students can also compare and contrast different types of poems to see how the elements can be used in different ways. While discussing these observations, teachers can also introduce the correct terminology and provide additional examples to explain how the elements are used by different poets.

> **Review Video: Structural Elements of Poetry**
> Visit mometrix.com/academy and enter code: 265216

HELPING STUDENTS DEVELOP AN APPRECIATION OF POETRY

There are many ways teachers can make learning about poetry fun and engaging for students. Early childhood and elementary students can be introduced to poetry during read-alouds and shared reading experiences. They can be encouraged to participate by clapping, making hand motions, and joining in the reading. As students get older, they can participate by highlighting and annotating poems and presenting them aloud to others.

Students can also be encouraged to explore different types of poetry to find styles that appeal to them. Free verse, sonnets, limericks, haikus, villanelles, and sestinas are just some examples of the many types of poetry. Students can also be encouraged to experiment with writing their own examples of different types of poetry.

Additionally, teachers can design poetry challenges for students. For example, students can be given magnetic words or print media that can be cut apart. Students can then explore rearranging the words into verses and stanzas to create different types of poems—seeing how the rhythm, meter, and other elements change. Students can also explore poetic elements in their favorite songs.

Encouraging Students to Locate and Use Evidence from Nonfiction Texts

Students can use T-charts while reading nonfiction texts. On the left side, they can record opinions, predictions, inferences, and similar thoughts made while reading. On the right side of the T-chart, students can record the **text evidence** used to support these thoughts.

Students can also complete scavenger hunts to find text evidence. Teachers can ask students **broad questions** that require higher-level thinking skills and instruct them to search nonfiction texts to find the answers. Information in the texts that are used to answer the questions can be highlighted or recorded on graphic organizers.

Teachers can also **model** this process for students. They can begin shared reading experiences by identifying what questions they want to answer by reading the texts. They can then model stopping when they reach evidence that answers the questions and making annotations as they go. Possible annotations include strong evidence presented by the author and additional questions that have arisen.

Promoting Close Reading of Nonfiction Texts

Close reading activities are designed to help students deeply analyze texts. In all close reading activities, students begin reading without first completing any pre-reading activities. They reread the text multiple times, analyzing different layers each time.

The first time that students read the text, they can be encouraged to determine the overall main idea and supporting details. The second time they read the text, they can be encouraged to analyze the author's craft and the text structure. This might include determining which text structure the author used, identifying the key vocabulary words and their meanings, locating nonfiction text features, and establishing the author's purpose for writing. The third time that students read, they can be encouraged to evaluate the text, draw conclusions, and make connections to other texts, personal experiences, or real-world events.

Teachers can model this process for students during shared reading experiences. They can also provide students with graphic organizers to help them record information during each reading. Additionally, they can encourage students to highlight or make notes in the text to label key information.

Role Reading Fluency Plays in the Comprehension of Nonfiction Texts

Fluency is important in comprehending any type of text. When readers are able to recognize words quickly and accurately, their working memories are available to focus on comprehension. Additionally, their thinking is not interrupted by stopping frequently to decode words.

Nonfiction texts present some special considerations for readers because they can utilize many types of structures. They also may contain several **content-specific vocabulary** words. Readers who are unfamiliar with these text structures and words may have difficulty locating key information and predicting what will come next, impeding comprehension.

Therefore, it is important to expose readers of all ages to a variety of text genres and structures. When practicing fluency passages, a combination of fiction and nonfiction texts should be included. Teachers should also model reading nonfiction texts so students will recognize what fluent reading sounds like.

PROMOTING COMPREHENSION OF NONFICTION TEXTS WITH WRITING ACTIVITIES

Writing can assist students with comprehension of nonfiction texts in many ways. Students often read nonfiction texts to learn new information or figure out how to accomplish tasks. They can create lists of questions they would like to have answered by the texts and record their answers as they read. They can also add additional questions that are generated by reading the texts.

Readers can **take notes** to record the main ideas and supporting details of nonfiction texts. There are many note-taking formats that can be used, such as outlining. Readers can also write text summaries or record the main concepts on semantic maps.

Additionally, there are many written response activities that can be used to encourage the use of **higher-level thinking skills**. Readers can write evaluations, compare and contrast essays, alternate endings, recommendations, and other similar responses.

APPLYING COMPREHENSION STRATEGIES TO DIGITAL TEXTS

Digital literacy includes the ability to make meaning from **digital texts**. Because the use of digital texts is now commonplace, teachers should give students opportunities to interact with both digital and print-based texts frequently.

Readers need to develop the ability to search **efficiently**. This includes generating lists of questions they want to have answered before they begin searching. It also includes selecting relevant search key words. Once search results are displayed, readers need to be able to scan the options and identify the links most likely to be relevant to their needs.

Digital texts are often nonlinear and contain multiple hyperlinks, so readers need the ability to break down the texts and **locate key information**. They can be taught to use note-taking strategies. This may involve using digital tools, like highlighting and annotation tools, or using graphic organizers.

Readers also need to develop the ability to identify author **bias** in digital sources. They should be encouraged to verify the sources and the validity of authors' claims.

Digital communications vary in **formality**. Readers should develop the ability to identify the **main points** in formal texts, like research articles, and informal texts, like blog posts.

PROMOTING COMPREHENSION BY BUILDING STUDENTS' ACADEMIC LANGUAGE

Academic language is language used in textbooks, class discussions, tests, and other school-related situations. It includes both vocabulary and syntax that differs from social language, which is less formal and structured.

Understanding the **vocabulary** of academic language is vital to understanding the authors' messages. If readers do not know the meanings of several key words, they will not understand the meanings of the texts and will be unable to analyze them deeply. Understanding academic syntax is also important because it helps students break down complex sentence structure to locate key information.

Students need **frequent exposure** to academic language and opportunities to use it across all content areas. For example, rather than asking students how texts are arranged, teachers can ask them to describe the *text structures*. Using these terms builds familiarity over time. Additionally, teachers can provide partial scripts that students can use to incorporate academic language when making presentations. To help students see the differences between social and academic language, teachers can also help students translate texts from one type to the other.

TYPES OF INFORMATIONAL TEXTS

- **Literary nonfiction** texts contain true information about topics but are presented using structures similar to fictional texts. They often include clear beginnings and endings and contain literary elements such as figurative language and imagery. Biographies, memoirs, and travel writing are examples of literary nonfiction.
- **Expository** texts are written to explain things using facts. They are structured differently than literary nonfiction texts. They often contain headings, tables of contents, glossaries, charts, graphs, and similar features. These text structures help readers navigate expository texts and locate specific information quickly. A science book explaining the water cycle is an example of an expository text.
- **Persuasive** texts are written to influence readers. They contain evidence to support the authors' claims. An advertisement urging readers to vote for a specific candidate is an example of a persuasive text.
- **Procedural** texts provide step-by-step directions for how to complete tasks. A manual describing how to complete office tasks using specific software is an example of a procedural text.

> **Review Video: What is Informational Text?**
> Visit mometrix.com/academy and enter code: 924964

TEACHING READERS TO IDENTIFY DIFFERENT TYPES OF INFORMATIONAL TEXTS

Readers can look for specific features to identify types of informational texts. These features can be explicitly taught using example texts, and charts outlining each type of informational text and its features can be displayed in the classrooms.

- To identify **literary nonfiction** texts, readers can look for accurate and factual texts that are written using text structures commonly used in fiction. Although true, these texts read more like stories, with clear beginnings and endings. Literary elements such as figurative language and symbolism may also be included.
- To identify **expository texts**, readers can look for common expository text structures, including tables of contents, headings, sidebars, glossaries, charts, and other similar features. Readers should also be encouraged to check that the texts are factual because some fictional texts may contain these text features as well.
- To identify **persuasive texts**, readers can look for key phrases that signal opinions. These phrases include *I believe*, *you should*, and *in my opinion*. Readers can also look for details provided by the authors to support their viewpoints.
- To identify **procedural texts**, readers can look for clues that indicate sequence. This might include numbered steps or key words like *first*, *next*, and *finally*.

PURPOSES OF NONFICTION TEXTS

- One purpose of nonfiction texts is to **persuade**. In this type of text, authors try to convince readers to adopt their points of view using supporting statements. An article written by a doctor urging parents to limit their children's soda consumption is an example of a persuasive text.
- Another purpose is to **compare and contrast** two things. An essay comparing and contrasting the forms of government in two different countries is an example of this type.
- Other nonfiction texts are written to **inform**. These texts describe and explain topics using facts. A nonfiction book about characteristics of reptiles is an example of a text written to inform.
- Some nonfiction texts are written to **instruct**. These texts explain how to do something. A text about how to change a tire is an example of this type.
- Other nonfiction texts are written to **narrate** real-world events. These texts convey real information in entertaining and/or engaging ways. A personal narrative describing a funny event that occurred on a family vacation is an example of a text written for this purpose.

ADJUSTING READING STRATEGIES WHEN READING DIFFERENT TYPES OF TEXTS

It is important for students to self-monitor their reading and adjust their use of strategies depending upon the situation. This will help them focus their attention on key information. It will also ensure that they are comprehending the text and meeting their expected purposes for reading.

When students are reading fiction, they typically read from beginning to end rather than skipping around. This helps them understand the plot and correctly sequence story events. When reading nonfiction texts to answer specific questions, readers may utilize text features like the table of contents to jump to specific sections. This helps readers locate the desired information quickly.

When students are reading for entertainment, they may read the text at a faster rate than when they are reading to analyze specific literary elements or answer comprehension questions. Slowing the reading rate or rereading passages may allow for deeper interaction with the text.

FEATURES OF EXPOSITORY TEXTS

Expository texts often contain some common features. These features help readers locate and organize key information, and they also provide additional information about the content of the text.

The **table of contents** and **index** help readers know what information is presented in the text and on which pages to find certain topics. **Titles** and **headings** are used to separate content into sections of related information. Enlarged and/or **bolded print** is often used to draw attention to these titles and headings. Important vocabulary words are often highlighted or written in bold print to catch readers' attention. A **glossary** or set of sidebars is often included to provide definitions for these vocabulary words. Photographs or **illustrations** are used to convey information visually, and captions are used to explain their content. Charts, graphs, and tables are frequently used to present relevant data. Maps are also included to provide additional information about places discussed in the text.

HELPING READERS LOCATE AND IDENTIFY FEATURES OF EXPOSITORY TEXTS

There are many instructional strategies that can be used to help readers locate and identify features of expository texts. Leading students in feature walks is one common strategy. Using this strategy, teachers share informational and expository texts with students, previewing each section of the texts together. They point out each of the text's features, such as the titles, headings, table of

111

contents, captions, and charts, and discuss the purposes of each. When reading the texts out loud, they model how to use the features to locate and make sense of key information.

To help readers locate and use these text features independently, charts listing the features and their functions can be posted in classrooms. Students can also be given blank charts they can use to record text features found while reading independently. Additionally, students can be given comprehension questions that require the use of text features to answer.

NONFICTION TEXT STRUCTURES

Some nonfiction texts use a **compare-and-contrast** structure. In this type of structure, both similarities and differences between two or more topics are explained. Sometimes the author presents each topic separately and then includes a discussion of similarities and differences. Other times, the author weaves back and forth between the two topics, comparing and contrasting different features along the way.

- **Cause and effect** is another nonfiction text structure. In this structure, the author describes an event and provides reasons why it happened.
- Another nonfiction text structure is **chronological order**. An author who retells the details of an event or period of time in the order that they happened is using this text structure.
- In the **problem/solution** text structure, a problem is introduced by the author. Possible solutions to the problem are then discussed.
- A **description** or **list** structure can also be used. In this type of structure, a topic is introduced. Descriptive details about the topic are then listed.

FAULTY REASONING IN NONFICTION TEXTS

Faulty reasoning occurs when conclusions are not supported by facts and evidence. The ability to recognize faulty reasoning is important because it helps readers evaluate the claims made in texts to determine if they are factual or not. It also helps readers identify potential author bias.

To assist readers with recognizing faulty reasoning, teachers can explicitly teach several different types and provide examples of how they are used in real texts. **Overgeneralizations** occur when authors draw conclusions based upon insufficient data. An example is stating that all fourth graders must like pizza because one fourth grader likes pizza. **Personal bias** occurs when authors base conclusions on personal opinions rather than factors or data. **Illogical conclusions** occur when authors draw conclusions about the relationships between things without data supporting the relationships. An example is stating that because someone was outside in the rain and later got a cold, the rain must have caused the cold.

Students can be encouraged to locate and share examples of faulty reasoning found during their independent reading experiences. They can also be encouraged to verify the sources used by authors to validate their claims and be wary of unsubstantiated online sources.

Reading Comprehension Tools and Strategies

GRAPHIC ORGANIZERS THAT PROMOTE READING COMPREHENSION AND ANALYSIS

Know, want, and learn (KWL) **charts** can be filled out before and after reading to identify what readers know, want to know, and learned about a topic. These charts help activate prior knowledge and give readers a purpose for reading. **Story maps** can be used to help readers identify the main elements of a story, such as characters, setting, problem, events, and solutions. **Character maps** can be used to describe traits of characters in the story.

Other graphic organizers can be used to help readers explain the relationships among events or ideas in a story. **Graphic organizers** can be used to help readers identify the problem and solution in a story, along with the events that led to the solution. Other graphic organizers can be used to record inferences and the text evidence used to make them. Graphic organizers like webs can be used to record the main idea and supporting details of a story. Venn diagrams can also be used to compare and contrast two stories, characters, or other elements.

SQ3R READING STRATEGY

SQ3R is a strategy used to help students comprehend textbooks. The S stands for **survey**. In this step, students preview the text and note features like headings, graphs, and charts. They use this information to predict what the text is about. In the Q or **question** step, students reread the headings and convert them into questions. They then predict the answers to these questions. The first R stands for **reading**. In this step, students read the text and attempt to answer the questions they listed. They may also make annotations to note important points or additional questions. The second R stands for **recall**, and this step involves summarizing each section of the text immediately after it is read. The last R stands for **review**. Students attempt to answer their original questions without using the text. If they are unable to answer any questions from memory, they review the text and their notes for assistance.

The SQ3R strategy has several benefits. By surveying the text, students activate prior knowledge and set purposes for reading. Listing questions helps focus students' attention during reading. Annotating helps students analyze and make meaning from the text. Summarizing and reviewing help students remember key information.

Instructional Strategies to Support Reading Skills

SUPPORTING READING COMPREHENSION IN ELLs AND STRUGGLING READERS

It is helpful to build background knowledge before introducing new texts to English language learners (ELLs) and struggling readers. Readers can then draw upon this background knowledge to make meaning from the new texts. After assessing what students already know about the topics, background knowledge can be developed using other texts, charts, graphs, photographs, videos, discussions, and additional methods.

- ELLs and struggling readers can benefit from **previewing** new texts before reading them independently. This may include picture walks or receiving text outlines that identify the **main ideas** covered in each section.
- **Pre-teaching vocabulary** can also help ELLs and struggling readers comprehend new texts. Teachers can introduce the vocabulary words and use photos or real objects to help explain their meanings. The vocabulary words can be frequently incorporated into class discussions to familiarize students with them.
- Additionally, **graphic organizers** can be used to help ELLs and struggling readers identify and organize key parts of texts that assist with comprehension. To offer scaffolding, partially completed graphic organizers and/or sentence stems can be provided initially, and support can be gradually withdrawn over time.

SUPPORTING READING COMPREHENSION IN PROFICIENT READERS

Proficient readers can be encouraged to comprehend at the inferential and evaluative levels in addition to the literal level. They can analyze texts deeply and make inferences, draw conclusions, and form evaluations. They can also be encouraged to complete activities that require higher-level thinking skills. Rather than listing the main characters, for example, proficient readers can be asked to retell the stories from each character's point of view or evaluate the choices the characters made.

To **challenge proficient readers** and encourage them to be enthusiastic about reading, they can also be given choices about book selection. Teachers can guide students in expanding their text selections to include different topics and genres but allow them to make their own selections. Teachers can also encourage students to choose texts that are appropriately challenging. Proficient readers can benefit from ownership in reading-related activities. Teachers can create menus of challenging questions or projects that readers can choose from based on their interests.

ENGAGING IN COLLABORATIVE DISCUSSIONS ABOUT PRINT AND DIGITAL TEXTS

Engaging in **collaborative discussions** can have several benefits for readers. It allows them to learn from other people's experiences and perspectives, which may differ from their own. Readers may hear additional evidence that strengthens their own initial understandings and conclusions. Conversely, they may hear evidence that challenges their initial thoughts and requires them to make revisions. Readers also have to support their points with text evidence to explain their thoughts to classmates. Locating and analyzing text evidence can assist with comprehension.

Discussing texts with others also has broader social benefits. It gives students opportunities to be **active and social learners**. Sharing ideas and collaborating helps build a community of learners who are able to communicate and respect different points of view. It also allows students to experience different social roles within the group and develop conflict resolution skills.

INFLUENCE OF CULTURE ON READING COMPREHENSION

Culture affects the ways people view and interact with the world around them. As a result, readers of different cultural backgrounds may comprehend the same texts differently. Readers rely on prior knowledge and existing schemata to make sense of what was read. Texts that are culturally familiar and related to readers' existing cultural schemata are more easily comprehended than those that are unfamiliar. When reading culturally familiar topics, readers are better able to make predictions, inferences, and conclusions based on existing schemata.

Therefore, it is important for teachers to activate both students' content knowledge and cultural knowledge prior to reading. For example, students may read a text describing a birthday celebration. The teacher can activate students' knowledge about how birthdays are celebrated in different cultures.

Research has indicated that cultural differences in syntactic complexity are less likely to affect comprehension.

METHODS OF STRUCTURING COLLABORATIVE DISCUSSIONS ABOUT PRINT AND DIGITAL TEXTS

Literature circles are one way to structure collaborative discussions about print. **Literature circles** consist of small groups of students who lead discussions about shared texts, which may or may not have been self-selected. Students collaboratively analyze the texts, discussing topics such as character development and theme. In some classrooms, guiding questions are provided by the teachers, whereas discussion questions are student-generated in others. Sometimes students are assigned roles within the group, such as summarizer and discussion leader.

Other times, there may be whole-class collaborative discussions. These types of discussions may occur when the whole class is completing an author study, for example, and are comparing and contrasting the events of different texts. These discussions are typically teacher-led.

There may also be small-group, teacher-led, collaborative discussions about teacher-selected texts. For example, discussion time may be included during guided reading groups.

RECIPROCAL TEACHING STRATEGY

Reciprocal teaching is a strategy designed to assist students with reading comprehension. In reciprocal teaching, students and teachers **share the responsibilities** of leading small-group discussions about texts. Teachers initially take the lead and model using four main comprehension strategies, including generating questions, summarizing, clarifying, and predicting. They gradually share more responsibility with students, who eventually take over leading the groups in applying these strategies to analyze texts.

Reciprocal teaching has several benefits. It requires students to be actively engaged in the reading process, as they must understand and apply the reading strategies to guide their classmates. It encourages the use of higher-level reading strategies that can then be applied to other texts. It also encourages discussion and collaboration among class members. Additionally, reciprocal teaching can help build students' confidence in their abilities to independently read and analyze challenging texts.

ACTIVITIES PROMOTING READING COMPREHENSION

Before reading, teachers can set the purposes for reading and activate students' prior knowledge by making connections to what they already know. They can **preview** the texts and important vocabulary words and encourage students to make **predictions**.

During reading, teachers can model thinking aloud to demonstrate how they **monitor** their own understanding. They can check and revise predictions, make inferences, and form connections. They can provide students with guiding questions or graphic organizers to use as they read independently to encourage the same reading behaviors.

After reading, teachers can **model** summarizing, drawing conclusions, and evaluating the texts. They can also discuss how their thinking changed as they read and were presented with new evidence. They can encourage students to use the same strategies after reading independently by setting up literature circles, creating written response activities, and designing other reading response projects.

TYPES OF CONNECTIONS READERS CAN MAKE TO TEXTS

- Readers can make **text-to-text connections**. These are connections made between two or more different texts that have been read. Readers might make connections between the texts' events, characters, themes, or any other features. An example is when a reader identifies that characters in two different books both persisted to overcome challenges.
- **Text-to-self connections** refer to connections readers make between texts and their own personal experiences. An example is when a reader understands the sadness a character feels when losing a pet after having personally experienced the same thing.
- **Text-to-world connections** refer to connections readers make between events in texts and events that have happened in the real world. An example is when a reader makes connections between a text about an astronaut and news about a recent space launch.

To encourage readers to make these connections, teachers can model their own thinking during shared reading experiences. They can model thinking deeply about similarities rather than making surface connections. For example, rather than pointing out that two characters are both girls, they can compare their character traits. Teachers can also encourage the use of Venn diagrams to show the similarities and differences between two texts, people, or events.

BENEFITS OF COMPARING DIFFERENT BOOKS BY THE SAME AUTHOR

When students read and compare multiple books by the same author, they use several reading strategies important for comprehension. They compare and contrast story elements between texts, such as characters, settings, problems, and solutions; they make text-to-text connections. They also consider how the author's life experiences may impact his or her writing style and content.

After completing multiple author studies, readers may also begin to identify favorite authors. These authors can serve as **mentors** for students, providing models of how to use language and incorporate story elements in their own writing. The connections readers feel to their favorite authors can boost engagement with reading and encourage them to seek out additional texts. Students can learn about the authors' lives and the paths they have taken as writers. They may be inspired by learning that people similar to themselves have become published authors.

BENEFITS OF LEARNING ABOUT TOPICS USING DIFFERENT TEXTS AND/OR GENRES

Reading different texts on the same topic can give readers a more comprehensive understanding of the topic. Each text reflects the personal writing style and bias of the author. Reading multiple texts allows readers to hear different perspectives and form their own judgments.

Reading texts from **multiple genres** about the same topic is also beneficial. Each genre presents the information differently and serves unique purposes. Reading an **informational text** about the Civil War may provide readers with an understanding of the war's causes, events, and major figures. Reading a **historical fiction** book written from the perspective of a soldier may give readers a more personalized account of this period in time, engaging the readers and helping them form personal connections.

When reading multiple texts, readers also need to identify the important points from each and synthesize the information. They need to consider the authors' purposes for writing. These skills assist with reading comprehension.

Supporting Vocabulary Development

ENCOURAGING VOCABULARY ACQUISITION THROUGH READING AND WRITING ACTIVITIES

If a new text contains unfamiliar vocabulary words that are central to the meaning and/or may be difficult to decode, a teacher may **preview** the words with the group. After introducing the topic of the text, the teacher may flip to the words, show students their spellings, and ask students to share what the words may mean based on prior knowledge and picture clues. Exposure to these words before reading will build readers' confidence and help them recognize and decode the words faster, maintaining fluency. Knowing the meanings in advance will also assist with comprehension.

When reading aloud to students, teachers may pause at new vocabulary words and model how to use context clues, prior knowledge, and picture support to decode and comprehend the new words. Students can be encouraged to use these strategies when reading independently.

Readers need repeated exposure to vocabulary words to develop automatic recognition and comprehension. Teachers may display classroom charts containing vocabulary words and their meanings, possibly using picture clues for young readers.

Students can also be encouraged to incorporate vocabulary words in their own writing. Word walls or charts containing the words can assist students with spelling and remembering the meanings of the words.

HELPING READERS RECOGNIZE AND EXPLORE THE MEANINGS OF UNKNOWN VOCABULARY WORDS

First, it is important for students to identify unknown vocabulary words when reading. Readers who are not monitoring their own comprehension may decode the words and continue reading, even if they do not understand their meanings. Teachers can model how to stop when they reach words they don't understand, even if they can decode them, and encourage students to do the same.

Next, readers need to determine which unknown words are central to the meanings of the text and worth exploring further. This is important because there may be many unknown words and, if readers stop extensively at each one, fluency and comprehension may be interrupted. Therefore, students can be encouraged to consider whether or not they can comprehend the sentences and overall meanings of the texts without devoting more energy to these particular unknown words.

If readers determine that the unknown words are central to the meaning of the text, they can be encouraged to use strategies such as using context clues, looking for known roots or affixes, or consulting dictionaries. Overall, readers should be encouraged to monitor their own reading and comprehension and determine when to apply known strategies.

> **Review Video: Acknowledging the Unknown When Reading**
> Visit mometrix.com/academy and enter code: 712339

SUPPORTING VOCABULARY ACQUISITION AND USE THROUGH LISTENING AND SPEAKING

Young children begin their vocabulary development through listening well before they begin to read and write. Through listening to family members, caregivers, and others, children develop their meaning (oral) vocabularies. These are words that children understand when heard and eventually use in their own speech. These vocabularies can be developed by talking to the children frequently and for a variety of purposes, reading to them, exposing them to songs, rhymes, and poems, and many other language activities.

Children continue to build vocabulary through listening and speaking activities when they begin school. Teachers can read aloud to students often, varying the genres and purposes for listening. Engaging students in discussions about what was read aloud can give students a purpose for listening and opportunities to use text-related vocabulary in their own oral responses. Teachers can also incorporate key vocabulary words in class discussions.

Students should also have frequent opportunities to speak in the classroom. In addition to informal class discussions, students can present projects to classmates and explain their thinking during problem-solving. They should be encouraged to use content-specific vocabulary when appropriate.

TEACHING WORD ANALYSIS SKILLS AND VOCABULARY TO ENGLISH LANGUAGE LEARNERS

Focusing on cognates is one way to help build word analysis skills and vocabulary for English language learners (ELLs). Cognates are words in different languages that share the same roots. For example, the English word *directions* and the Spanish word *direcciones* are cognates. ELLs can be encouraged to look for known parts of unfamiliar words. They can then use knowledge about the meanings in their native languages to determine the meanings of the English words. This strategy builds upon ELLs' prior knowledge. Explicitly teaching common roots and affixes can help ELLs quickly increase their vocabularies as well.

Scaffolding should also be provided when introducing ELLs to new words. This can be done using visuals that help demonstrate the meanings of the words. Real objects, pictures, and gestures can all be used. Graphic organizers can also be used to show how new words are related and how they connect to specific topics.

TEACHING WORD ANALYSIS SKILLS TO STRUGGLING READERS

Struggling readers require consistent and explicit instruction, which often includes a combination of both whole-class instruction and targeted individual or small-group instruction daily. They also need frequent opportunities to manipulate words. Both building and breaking apart related words using letter tiles can help struggling readers develop understandings of patterns in the ways words are made.

Struggling readers can also benefit from explicit instruction on chunking words into component parts. Depending on the ages and prior knowledge of the students, this might include identifying syllable patterns, onsets and rimes, roots and affixes, or smaller sight words that are part of the larger words.

Struggling readers also need frequent opportunities to practice their word analysis skills using real texts. After explicit instruction on recognizing prefixes in words, for example, students can read texts that contain several prefixes. They can identify these words and their meanings. This will help them transfer their word analysis skills to realistic contexts. Scaffolding can be provided through anchor charts, graphic organizers, and teacher support during these independent reading experiences to provide reminders of known strategies.

TEACHING WORD ANALYSIS SKILLS TO HIGHLY PROFICIENT READERS

Proficient readers still have a need for differentiated reading instruction, even if they are meeting or exceeding grade-level expectations. They can benefit from developing the same word analysis skills as other readers, such as looking for known parts in unfamiliar vocabulary words, breaking words into components, and finding relationships between the meanings and spellings of different words. These strategies should be presented using materials and interactions that are both engaging and appropriately challenging for proficient readers. Use of texts that have some unfamiliar words will ensure that readers have opportunities to apply these strategies and continue to increase their vocabularies. Using assessments to determine reading levels or teaching readers to self-select appropriate texts can help ensure that the selected materials offer some challenges and learning opportunities for proficient readers.

Because proficient readers often devote less energy to decoding words than struggling readers, they are able to allocate more energy to reading comprehension, analysis, and reflection. Proficient readers can be asked to evaluate authors' word choices and discuss the effect that certain words have on the meaning or tone of the texts.

ASSISTING READERS WITH COMPREHENSION USING GRAPHOPHONICS, SYNTAX, AND SEMANTICS

Proficient readers understand how to use a variety of reading strategies and are able to apply them to different situations as needed. The types of text a student reads may differ greatly in terms of vocabulary, quality of context clues, picture support, and connections to the reader's prior knowledge. Therefore, the strategies that work to determine an unknown word in any one sentence or text may not work as well in another.

Decoding words using **graphophonic** clues is a strategy where readers consider the letter-sound relationships in the word. Another strategy is to consider **syntax**, or how the word sounds in the sentence and fits into the overall sentence structure. A third strategy is to consider **semantics**, or the meaning of the text, to guess the unknown word. To be correct, a guessed word should fit all three criteria. It should look right (graphophonics), sound right (syntax), and make sense (semantics).

When they come to unknown words, proficient readers try one strategy first and then cross-check their guesses using other strategies. If they realize they have made errors, they self-correct. Using a combination of these strategies helps ensure that readers make sense out of what they are reading.

HELPING BEGINNING READERS USE CONTEXT CLUES TO FIGURE OUT UNKNOWN WORDS

Like older readers, beginning readers also turn to context clues to figure out unknown words. The types of context clues available to beginning readers may differ, however, because the texts they read often contain simple sentence structures and picture support.

One strategy beginning readers can use is to look for picture clues. When a reader is stuck on an unfamiliar word, the teacher can guide the student to look to the picture for hints.

Another strategy is to ask the reader to skip the unknown word and read the rest of the sentence. After finishing the sentence, the teacher can ask the reader to fill in the blank with a word that makes sense. Context clues found in the rest of the sentence can often help the reader guess the missing word. If the reader guesses a word that makes sense but does not match the text, the teacher can guide the student to look for phonetic clues within the word, such as the first sound, and try again.

Texts for beginning readers sometimes contain other context clues, such as rhymes and repetitive vocabulary, that can be used to figure out unknown words.

> **Review Video: Using Context Clues**
> Visit mometrix.com/academy and enter code: 613660

HELPING STUDENTS USE CONTEXT CLUES TO FIGURE OUT THE MEANINGS OF UNKNOWN WORDS

Teachers should explicitly introduce students to different types of context clues, including definition, antonym, synonym, and inference clues. Examples of sentences containing each type can be provided, and students can be asked to mark the clues, label each type, and explain the meanings of the unknown words. They can also be asked to find examples of each of these types of context clues in other texts. An anchor chart listing the different types of context clues and examples of each can also be posted in the classroom.

Students can also be given sets of words that are related in some way, such as pairs of synonyms or antonyms. They can be asked to write sentences that incorporate the word pairs, creating context clues for other readers. The students can then share their sentences with peers, asking them to identify the context clues and meanings of the unknown words.

IMPORTANCE OF KNOWING LATIN AND GREEK ROOTS

Many English words are formed from Latin and Greek **roots**. Therefore, recognizing these roots and knowing their meanings can help readers with both decoding and comprehending.

When readers automatically recognize Latin and Greek roots, they will be able to quickly decode the main parts of words that contain them. If they automatically recognize the affixes as well, they will be able to break words into parts and decode them effortlessly. This will allow the readers to maintain speed and fluency while reading.

The roots also hold most of the meaning in words and form the bases of entire word families. Knowing the meanings of these roots will help readers quickly determine the meanings of many newly encountered words, especially if they also know the meanings of any attached affixes. For example, if readers know that the Latin root *port* means to carry, they will have clues about the meanings of the words *transport*, *transportation*, *import*, and *export* as well.

HELPING READERS IDENTIFY LATIN AND GREEK ROOTS IN UNFAMILIAR WORDS

When teaching readers about Latin and Greek roots in English words, one strategy is to help them see the relationships between words in the same word families. This can be done by creating charts or other visual representations of word families and their meanings. For example, a root and its meaning can be written in the middle of a web, and words containing the root and their meanings can be written in circles branching off from the root.

Another strategy is to create three sets of cards, including prefixes, suffixes, and roots. Students can experiment with combining the sets of cards to try to form real words. When real words are created, students can explain their meanings. Students can also be given words containing prefixes, roots, and suffixes. They can be asked to break the words into their components and identify the meanings of each part.

Additionally, students can be encouraged to locate words containing Latin and Greek roots in the texts they read independently. They can use their knowledge of the roots to define the words.

APPROACHES TO VOCABULARY LEARNING

- A **definitional approach** to vocabulary learning is the most traditional. Students are either provided definitions of words or look them up in a dictionary, and they are drilled until they commit the meanings to memory.
- A **structural approach** to vocabulary learning emphasizes the morphological features of words—the roots, prefixes, and suffixes. Once students learn the recurring morphemes in English, they can deduce the meaning of a word in isolation without relying on its context.
- A **contextual approach** to vocabulary learning provides the students with multiple examples of a word used in realistic contexts, allowing them to infer the meaning without resorting to a dictionary or an explicit definition.
- A **categorical approach** to vocabulary learning groups words into categories based on a semantic similarity. For example, a student might be given a list of words associated with driving a car, such as "steering wheel," "to brake," "to accelerate," and "gear shift."
- A **mnemonic approach** to vocabulary learning builds associations between target words and mental images so that hearing a target word evokes the image, facilitating recall of the word's meaning.

> **Review Video: Types of Vocabulary Learning (Broad and Specific)**
> Visit mometrix.com/academy and enter code: 258753

ROLE OF NON-CONTEXTUAL STRATEGIES IN VOCABULARY DEVELOPMENT

Non-contextual strategies are used when new vocabulary is learned without seeing or hearing the words in context. For example, teachers may give students lists of new vocabulary words they have not yet encountered in texts. The teachers may ask students to define the words, use them in sentences, and memorize them. Quizzes may then be given in which students must match the words to their definitions or provide examples of the terms.

There are times teachers may use non-contextual vocabulary strategies, such as when students are learning content-specific words that are not often found naturally in texts. When studying parts of speech, for example, teachers may have students memorize the definitions of *noun*, *verb*, and *adjective*. These words are important for students' understanding of sentence structure, yet students are not likely to encounter these words written in texts with contextual clues. However, it is recommended that teachers do use contextual strategies whenever possible.

Students can be taught to use tools such as dictionaries to define unknown words when contextual clues are not available. They can be prompted to draw pictures to explain word meanings or use graphic organizers to show the relationships among words.

ROLE OF CONTEXTUAL STRATEGIES IN VOCABULARY DEVELOPMENT

Contextual strategies are used to determine the meanings of unknown vocabulary words when they are encountered in context. The ability to use these strategies to quickly determine word meanings is important for both reading fluency and comprehension. Because words can have multiple meanings, readers also need to use contextual strategies to determine which meaning makes sense in a given sentence.

Teachers can explicitly teach students about the different types of contextual clues often found in sentences. They can encourage students to highlight the words and phrases that provide clues about meanings of the vocabulary words.

Contextual clues often include synonyms or antonyms for the unknown vocabulary words. Therefore, when introducing new words, teachers can assist students with creating lists of synonyms and antonyms. Teachers can also ask students to solve analogies or determine which word does not belong when given a group of related words. These activities will help students recognize synonyms and antonyms and understand relationships among words when they are encountered in context.

CRITERIA FOR SELECTING VOCABULARY WORDS FOR INSTRUCTION

Vocabulary words can be divided into three tiers. Teachers should consider these tiers when determining which words to focus on during instruction.

- **Tier one words** are common words used in everyday speech. They are typically learned by the early grades through normal conversation. Explicit instruction on the meanings of these words is seldom needed.
- **Tier two words** are found in both fiction and nonfiction texts and are common enough that readers will likely encounter them in multiple texts. Tier two words carry a lot of meaning and can negatively affect comprehension if they are not understood by readers. When deciding which tier two words to focus on, teachers should consider how the words affect the overall meanings of the texts and their morphologies. They should consider if students will be able to form connections between these words and other words, helping them understand unfamiliar words encountered in the future.
- **Tier three words** are mostly found in nonfiction texts and are domain-specific. These words are important for understanding the texts and their domains. Because students are unlikely to have encountered these words before, explicit instruction is needed. This often includes pre-teaching the words and analyzing them in context.

TExES Practice Test

Want to take this practice test in an online interactive format?
Check out the bonus page, which includes interactive practice questions and much more: **mometrix.com/bonus948/texesscitread**

1. A syllable must contain:

a. A vowel
b. A consonant
c. Both a vowel and a consonant
d. A meaning

2. A teacher wants to select books for her emergent readers to add to the classroom library. Which set of text features are most appropriate for emergent readers?

a. Predictable text placement, repetition, and picture support
b. Complex and varied sentence types, multiple sentences per page, little picture support
c. Sidebars and charts, several lines of text per page, descriptive words and phrases
d. Complex text structures, figurative language, technical vocabulary words

3. "Code knowledge" facilitates reading fluency because:

a. It brings the entirety of the student's previous experience to bear on decoding a text.
b. It offers a framework for organizing new information by assigning code words to sets of ideas.
c. There is no such thing as "code knowledge." The correct term is "core knowledge."
d. It offers a systematic approach to untangling the wide variety of vowel sounds when an unfamiliar word is encountered.

4. A teacher is working with a group of third graders at the same reading level. Her goal is to improve reading fluency. She asks each child in turn to read a page from a book about mammal young. She asks the children to read with expression. She also reminds them they don't need to stop between each word; they should read as quickly as they comfortably can. She cautions them, however, not to read so quickly that they leave out or misread a word. The teacher knows the components of reading fluency are:

a. Speed, drama, and comprehension
b. Cohesion, rate, and prosody
c. Understanding, rate, and prosody
d. Rate, accuracy, and prosody

5. What is the purpose of targeted instruction?

a. Deliver instructions that are precise, clear, and direct so that students understand exactly what is expected.

b. Accurately rank a group of learners from low achievers to high achievers so that the teacher knows from the beginning of the school year which students have less ability and will therefore need support.

c. Teach students how to take information from a text and reorganize it into bulleted lists.

d. Assess and target areas needing improvement as well as areas of greatest strength for each student to ensure that all members of a class are receiving instruction tailored to their specific needs.

6. Cause and effect, compare and contrast, and time order are all examples of what?

a. Literary devices
b. Literary elements
c. Genres
d. Text structures

7. An understanding of the meanings of prefixes and suffixes such as *dis, mis, un, re, able*, and *ment* are important for:

a. Reading comprehension
b. Word recognition
c. Vocabulary building
d. Reading fluency

8. How can reading comprehension and vocabulary best be assessed?

a. They should be assessed with brief interviews and tests every two months to determine how much learning has taken place. Students learn in spurts, and in-depth assessments of comprehension and vocabulary are a waste of time.

b. They should be assessed by a rough a combination of standardized testing, informal teacher observations, attention to grades, objective-linked assessments, and systematized charting of data over time.

c. They should be assessed by giving students weekly self-assessment rubrics to keep them constantly aware of and invested in their own progress.

d. They should be assessed by having students retell a story or summarize the content of an informational piece of writing. The degree to which the material was comprehended, and the richness or paucity of vocabulary used in such work, provides efficient and thorough assessment.

9. A reading teacher is assessing an eighth grader to determine her reading level. Timed at a minute, the student reads with 93% accuracy. She misreads an average of seven words out of 100. What is her reading level?

a. She is reading at a Frustration level.
b. She is reading at an Excellence level.
c. She is reading at an Instructional level.
d. She is reading at an Independent level.

10. Olivia, a first-grade student, has a reading intervention plan to improve her decoding of CVCe words. In addition to working with the teacher in a small group each day, Olivia's teacher gives her 10 new CVCe words to decode each Friday. The number of words read correctly is recorded on a graph, and the teacher notes any improvement made from the previous weeks. Which type of assessment is the teacher demonstrating?

    a. Progress monitoring
    b. Screening assessment
    c. Summative assessment
    d. Norm-referenced assessment

11. The use of analogies is most appropriate for helping students achieve which instructional objective?

    a. Analyzing common roots and affixes
    b. Defining words
    c. Identifying word origins
    d. Recognizing the relationships between words

12. A teacher takes a running record while Charlie, a second grader, reads a new text. Part of the running record is shown below.

> *home*
> The witch's house was deep in the woods, hidden behind some
> *grumpy*
> trees. A grouchy cat guarded the entrance to the house, hissing
> *omission*
> loudly when any strangers approached. Nobody had dared to go
>
> near it in years.

Which strategy would be most appropriate for the teacher to focus on during the next guided reading session?

    a. Using semantic cues
    b. Using syntactic cues
    c. Omissions
    d. Self-corrections

13. Which statement best describes phonemic awareness?

    a. Phonemic awareness is the ability to identify and manipulate sounds at the sentence level.
    b. Phonemic awareness is the ability to identify and manipulate sounds at the word level.
    c. Phonemic awareness is the ability to identify and manipulate sounds at the syllable level.
    d. Phonemic awareness is the ability to identify and manipulate sounds at the phoneme level.

14. A student is taking a reading test. The teacher has blocked out a number of words. Each blank is assigned a set of three possible words. The student must select the correct word from each set so that the text makes sense. The student is taking:

    a. A cloze test
    b. A maze test
    c. A multiple-choice quiz
    d. A vocabulary test

15. Students in Mr. Henderson's science class are conducting research for their science fair projects. Today, they are typing keywords into a search engine to identify sources that may be relevant for their background information. Which reading strategy should Mr. Henderson teach and practice with his students prior to this activity?

a. Skimming
b. Scanning
c. Close reading
d. Extensive reading

16. It is the beginning of the school year. To determine which second-grade students might need support, the reading teacher wants to identify those who are reading below grade level. She works with students one at a time. She gives each child a book at a second-grade reading level and asks the child to read out loud for two minutes. Children who will need reading support are those who read:

a. Fewer than 100 words in the time given
b. Fewer than 200 words in the time given
c. More than 75 words in the time given
d. The entire book in the time given

17. Which of the following choices will be most important when designing a reading activity or lesson for students?

a. Selecting a text
b. Determining the number of students participating
c. Analyzing the point in the school year at which the lesson is given
d. Determining a purpose for instruction

18. _Train, brain, spring._ The underlined letters are examples of:

a. Consonant digraph
b. Consonant blend
c. Consonant shift
d. Continental shift

19. Which of the following options best describes the use of environmental print in a prekindergarten classroom?

a. Including real food packages and menus in the dramatic play area
b. Setting aside 10 minutes each day for students to read books independently
c. Displaying sight words on a word wall
d. Creating anchor charts of vocabulary words from content areas

20. Before asking students to read a new fiction book independently, the teacher conducts a picture walk with the class. What is the teacher's primary goal for conducting the picture walk?

a. Encouraging the use of syntactic cues
b. Setting a purpose for reading
c. Activating students' prior knowledge
d. Developing students' metacognitive skills

21. Which of the following options is true of children in the pre-alphabetic stage of word learning?

    a. Children do not use any letter/sound relationships to decode words.

    b. Children use letter/sound relationships to correctly decode the initial or final sounds in words.

    c. Children use letter/sound relationships to correctly decode all sounds in simple, age-appropriate words.

    d. Children recognize and use letter groupings, along with letter/sound relationships, to decode words.

22. Which classroom activity best demonstrates constructivism?

    a. Students complete a close reading of a persuasive text using questions outlined by the teacher. They first read and discuss the main idea of the text. Next, they read and discuss the reasons the author provides to support her opinion. Finally, they reread the text and evaluate the author's effectiveness in persuading others to agree with her.

    b. Students collaboratively decide to research costs and benefits of additional flexible seating options to the classroom, while the teacher assists with research strategies. Students then write a persuasive letter to the school board asking for funding for the seating.

    c. Students complete a set of reading stations in a predetermined order. In one station, they complete phonics practice activities on the computer. In another, they match word cards to create compound words. In a third station, they sort words according to vowel sounds and check their work using an answer key.

    d. Students in different grade levels are paired up. The older students read to the younger students and help them draw pictures of their favorite parts of the stories.

23. A teacher is teaching students analogizing. She is teaching them to:

    a. Identify and use metaphors

    b. Identify and use similes

    c. Identify and use groups of letters that occur in a word family

    d. Identify and use figures of speech

24. Which of the following activities would best help to create a classroom environment that promotes a love of reading for kindergarten students?

    a. Going on a word hunt to locate words starting with a specific letter

    b. Tracing sight words using stencils

    c. Practicing phonics skills on the classroom computer

    d. Reading a favorite rhyming text aloud together and discussing favorite parts

25. While reading an expository text aloud to students, a teacher makes the following comments.

> "'The cheetah can accelerate to its top speed in about three seconds.' Hmm, I'm not sure what accelerate means. Let me read that again to see if the sentence has any clues. 'The cheetah can accelerate to its top speed in about three seconds.' It has something to do with the cheetah getting faster, so I think accelerate means to speed up."

What is the teacher demonstrating in this activity?

    a.   Forming mental images
    b.   Making a prediction
    c.   Thinking aloud
    d.   Visualizing

26. A struggling reader has difficulty comprehending vocabulary words when they are encountered in unfamiliar texts. She frequently uses a dictionary to look up the unknown words. While this helps her figure out the meanings of the words, it interrupts her fluency and affects comprehension. Her teacher, Mr. Palmer, would like to teach her other strategies she can use instead that will minimize the disruptions to her fluency and increase her comprehension. Which strategy would likely be most effective?

    a.   Quickly asking a classmate for the meanings of the words
    b.   Creating a list of the unknown words and looking them up later
    c.   Trying to determine the meanings of the words from context clues
    d.   Skipping over the words she does not know as long as the sentences make sense

27. A fourth-grade teacher gives students a character chart to fill out while reading a fictional text. Students are instructed to record traits of the main character as they read. One student, Daniel, turns in a map that lists the following traits: short, has blond hair, has freckles, is a girl. Which strategy would be an appropriate next step for the teacher to focus on?

    a.   Analyzing character development from the beginning of the story to the end
    b.   Identifying the character as a protagonist or antagonist
    c.   Differentiating between internal and external character traits
    d.   Comparing and contrasting the character with a character from another book by the same author

28. A teacher has a child who does not volunteer in class. When the teacher asks the student a question the student can answer, she does so with as few words as possible. The teacher isn't sure how to best help the child. She should:

    a.   Leave the child alone. She is clearly very shy and will be embarrassed by having attention drawn to her. She is learning in her own way.
    b.   Ask two or three highly social children to include this girl in their activities. She is shy, and she probably won't approach them on her own.
    c.   Observe the child over the course of a week or two. Draw her into conversation and determine if her vocabulary is limited, if she displays emotional problems, or if her reticence could have another cause. Note how the child interacts with others in the class. Does she ever initiate conversation? If another child initiates, does she respond?
    d.   Refer her to the school counselor immediately. It is clear the child is suffering from either a low IQ or serious problems at home.

29. Maria, a third-grade student, is reading a new chapter book for the first time. Her teacher observes as Maria struggles to decode the word *scapegoat* in the following sentence: "John frowned when he realized he was being made the scapegoat." Which of the following strategies would most likely assist Maria with decoding this word?

    a. Using syntactic cues
    b. Blending the sounds
    c. Using context clues from the sentence
    d. Chunking

30. A student is reading a fictional book and reaches the following sentence: "Unlike Mark, whose college plans were tentative, Ana already had firm plans to attend the state university." Which type of context clue is present in this sentence to help the student determine the meaning of *tentative*?

    a. Synonym clue
    b. Definition clue
    c. Antonym clue
    d. Inference clue

31. Based on assessment data, a teacher identifies a small group of students who would benefit from targeted instruction on using textual evidence to support their answers. Which strategy would be most helpful for the teacher to model to assist students with this type of test question?

    a. Underlining passages in the text where answers are located
    b. Reading the passage once to identify the main idea, and then rereading to look for details
    c. Reading each answer choice carefully before selecting an answer, crossing out answers as they are eliminated
    d. Completing a story map while reading the story

32. What are homographs?

    a. Words that are spelled differently but pronounced the same way
    b. Words that are spelled the same way but have different meanings
    c. Words that have the same Latin root
    d. Words that are members of the same word family

33. For their monthly project, a group of students can choose to read and respond to one book on a list supplied by their teacher. The books are grouped according to genre. Most students choose books listed under the genre that is described as "modern-day stories that are not true, but seem as though they could really happen." Which genre did most of the students choose from?

    a. Historical fiction
    b. Autobiography
    c. Realistic fiction
    d. Fantasy

34. Early in the school year, all members of a group of kindergarten students are able to chant the alphabet. The teacher is now teaching the students what the alphabet looks like in written form. The teacher points to a letter, and the students vocalize the corresponding sound. Alternatively, the teacher vocalizes a phoneme and a student points to it on the alphabet chart. The teacher is using _____ in her instruction.

    a. letter–sound correspondence
    b. rote memorization
    c. predictive analysis
    d. segmentation

35. The most effective strategy for decoding sight words is:

    a. Segmenting sight words into syllables. Beginning readers are understandably nervous when encountering a long word that isn't familiar. Blocking off all but a single syllable at a time renders a word manageable and allows the reader a sense of control over the act of reading.
    b. Word families. By grouping the sight word with similar words, patterns emerge.
    c. A phonemic approach. When students understand the connection between individual words and their sounds, they will be able to sound out any sight word they encounter.
    d. None; sight words cannot be decoded. Readers must learn to recognize these as whole words on sight.

36. Aidan, a fifth-grade student, writes a letter to the cafeteria manager at his school asking her to implement a schoolwide composting program. He outlines reasons why the composting program would benefit the environment and save the school money on waste disposal costs. He ends his letter by politely asking her to consider the proposal. What is Aidan's primary purpose for writing?

    a. To inform
    b. To persuade
    c. To entertain
    d. To describe

37. Which of the following words contains a phonogram produced by three letters?

    a. Tack
    b. Hit
    c. Bleak
    d. Light

38. Which classroom instructional strategy would most likely assist ELLs with developing phonemic awareness skills?

    a. Practicing phonemic awareness skills on familiar vocabulary words in English
    b. Practicing phonemic awareness skills using only words in their native languages
    c. Introducing phonemes that are not part of their native languages first
    d. Teaching the English alphabet and alphabetic principle before teaching phonemic awareness skills

39. A second-grade class is listening to a read-aloud of a fictional text about Thanksgiving Day in America. One student has recently moved to America and is unfamiliar with the holiday. Which of the following options is the most effective way for the teacher to address this issue with the student?

    a. Ask the student to retell the story after listening to it to assess comprehension.

    b. Provide background information on Thanksgiving before reading, relating it to traditions the student is familiar with.

    c. Provide the student with a written outline of the key elements in the story before reading.

    d. After reading, describe the key features of the story and holiday again with different language than what was used in the book.

40. Which learning theory is based on the idea that students are actively involved in constructing their own meaning, and that teachers should guide students through scaffolding rather than using instructor-led teaching techniques?

    a. Behaviorism

    b. Cognitivism

    c. Constructivism

    d. Social learning theory

41. After students have studied metaphors for several days, a teacher wants to assess their abilities to apply their knowledge of what a metaphor is. Which assignment would be most appropriate for this purpose?

    a. Underlining the metaphors in a sample text

    b. Explaining what a metaphor is to a classmate

    c. Writing a paragraph that includes at least two metaphors

    d. Critiquing the author's use of metaphors in a poem

42. Which of the following represents a main difference between the conventions of spoken and written language?

    a. Syntax is more relaxed in spoken language, with more flexibility in word order.

    b. Body language plays a bigger role in sharing meaning in written language than in spoken language.

    c. Written language tends to be less formal and more conversational in nature than spoken language.

    d. Written language includes a greater mixture of fragments and complete sentences than spoken language.

43. Which of the following sentences would best help model the concept of figurative language?

    a. The sky was dark and gray, warning that a storm was approaching.

    b. The snow was a wet blanket covering the earth.

    c. Taking care of a puppy requires time and patience.

    d. The cold, wet raindrops splashed on my glasses and made it difficult to see.

44. A parent of a first-grade student is concerned about her child's use of phonetic spelling. She is concerned that her daughter is not spelling enough words conventionally and is developing habits that will be difficult to overcome. She presents the following sentence that her daughter recently wrote as an example:

> A leprd haz spots.

What would be the most appropriate response to the parent?

    a. Going forward, a grownup should assist the child during writing tasks and confirm the spelling of each unknown word.
    b. Students in this stage typically write the sounds that they hear, and this stage is a stepping stone to conventional spelling development.
    c. At this age, the student should be using more conventional spelling, and a phonics intervention plan should be created.
    d. The student should be encouraged to use a dictionary to confirm spellings of unknown words.

45. A teacher asks her students to say the word _map_. She then says, "Change the /m/ sound to a /t/ sound. What word do you have now?" Which phonemic awareness skill are students practicing?

    a. Alliteration
    b. Segmenting
    c. Blending onset and rime
    d. Phoneme substitution

46. Which of the following statements is true regarding word walls?

    a. They should mainly focus on content-related words.
    b. They should contain only words that are difficult for students to spell independently.
    c. They should be flexible, allowing words to be added and removed throughout the year.
    d. They are only needed for students in the emergent stage of reading development.

47. Which statement best describes the relationship between reading and writing?

    a. Reading is a prerequisite skill that should be taught before writing.
    b. Writing is a prerequisite skill that should be taught before reading.
    c. Reading and writing are interrelated and should be taught together.
    d. The order of instruction does not matter, but one should be taught first to avoid cognitive overload.

48. The first-grade teacher wants her class to understand that stories have a certain order. She reads them a story, then orally reviews how each event that happened in the story caused the next event to happen. To reinforce the lesson, the teacher should:

    a. Give each child a piece of drawing paper that has been folded in half and then in half again, creating four boxes, along with a piece that has not been folded. The teacher should then ask the students to draw a cartoon about the story. Each of the first four boxes will show the events in order. The second page is to show how the story ends.

    b. Give each child a piece of drawing paper and ask the students to draw the most important scene.

    c. Give each child a piece of drawing paper and ask the students to draw the story's beginning on the front of the page and ending on the back.

    d. Give each child a piece of drawing paper that has been folded in half and then in half again, creating four boxes, along with a piece that has not been folded. The teacher should then ask the students to draw a cartoon about anything they want. She reminds them to put their story cartoons in proper order.

49. Prekindergarten students tell their teacher, Mr. Clark, that they want to write about their field trip to the zoo. Mr. Clark writes down the students' sentences on chart paper, and then reads them back to the class, pointing to each word and modeling appropriate fluency. After reading the story multiple times, Mr. Clark invites the students to read with him. Which type of interaction is Mr. Clark demonstrating?

    a. Language experience approach
    b. Writing workshop
    c. Trait-based writing
    d. Modeled writing

50. Kindergarten students learn one new letter and its corresponding sound each week. They participate in songs and chants that include repetitive use of the letter name and sound. Which concept are students practicing?

    a. Alphabetic principle
    b. Concepts of print
    c. Phonological awareness
    d. Automaticity

51. Which of the following words has the most phonemes?

    a. Sheet
    b. Hand
    c. Right
    d. Sea

52. Silent reading fluency can best be assessed by:

a. Having the student retell or summarize the material to determine how much was understood.

b. Giving a written test that covers plot, theme, character development, sequence of events, rising action, climax, falling action, and outcome. A student must test at a 95% accuracy rate to be considered fluent at silent reading.

c. Giving a three-minute Test of Silent Contextual Reading Fluency four times a year. The student is presented with text in which spaces between words and all punctuation have been removed. The student must divide one word from another with slash marks, as in the example: The/little/sailboat/bobbed/so/far/in/the/distance/it/looked/like/a/toy. The more words a student accurately separates, the higher her silent reading fluency score.

d. Silent reading fluency cannot be assessed. It is a private act between the reader and the text and does not invite critique.

53. Students in a fourth-grade classroom read a novel about Alicia, a character who moves from a farm to a big city and struggles with the resulting changes in her lifestyle. After reading and discussing the text together, the teacher asks students to make a text-to-self connection. Which student response demonstrates a text-to-self connection?

a. Alicia reminds me a lot of Jacob in the book we read last semester. His family moved across the globe, and he had to adapt to the cultural differences in his new home.

b. I saw a story on the news about a girl who moved to a big city, and she helped set up a community garden in her new neighborhood.

c. Last year, I had to attend a new school because my family bought a new house in the city. It was hard at first to make new friends because everyone else already knew each other.

d. This was one of my favorite books we read this year because Alicia learned to make the best out of a difficult situation.

54. Liz, a third grader, is completing a reading assessment with her teacher. During the fluency component of the assessment, she reads a short passage aloud. Her teacher notes that Liz's reading rate is in the average range for her grade level, and she correctly decodes 95% of the words in the passage. However, Liz reads in a monotone voice and often forgets to pause before beginning new sentences. Which component of fluency should Liz's teacher target during small-group instruction?

a. Accuracy

b. Automaticity

c. Word recognition

d. Prosody

55. While speaking to his friend, a fifth-grade student says, "Hey, you should read this book. It's awesome." Later, while presenting an oral book report in front of his class and teacher, he says, "This book is full of suspense. The author leaves you wondering if the main character will be rescued from the mountain before it is too late. I highly recommend you read it to find out if he is rescued in time." This example best demonstrates the role of what in language usage?

a. Social context

b. Cultural context

c. Contextual clues

d. Personal context

56. Which of the following reading prompts requires the highest level of thinking, according to Bloom's taxonomy?

    a. Compare and contrast the protagonist and antagonist in the story.
    b. Evaluate the author's use of figurative language in conveying the theme of the story.
    c. Identify the setting of the story.
    d. Infer what the author means in the final paragraph of the story.

57. Which instructional strategy would be most appropriate to assist a student with retention difficulties in analyzing the plot of a fictional text?

    a. Providing the student with a story map
    b. Having the student read the story twice before responding to questions
    c. Playing an audio version of the story rather than having the student read a printed version
    d. Asking the student to compete a KWL chart before and after reading

58. Mrs. Lopez teaches second grade. After completing a science experiment, she gathers her students on the carpet to write a summary of what they learned. Mrs. Lopez asks students to help her record the responses on chart paper, sharing the marker. She provides guidance and sentence starters as needed. After everyone has recorded their responses, the class reads them aloud together. Which type of writing experience is Mrs. Lopez demonstrating?

    a. Interactive writing
    b. Shared writing
    c. Independent writing
    d. Guided writing

59. Which statement is a key tenet of Marie Clay's literacy processing theory?

    a. Children have differing prior knowledge and previous experiences and take different paths to literacy development.
    b. Literacy development is enhanced when children learn to write after developing basic reading skills.
    c. Emergent readers learn best using large-group instruction, where they have models of proficient readers to emulate.
    d. Children learn to read best with a whole-language approach to instruction, with little emphasis on assessment.

60. "Verbal dyspraxia" refers to:

    a. Trouble with the physical act of writing
    b. Confusing word or sentence order while speaking
    c. Misplacement of letters within words
    d. An inability to process verbal information

61. Ms. Watson has included a variety of pointers in the classroom reading center. She instructs students to use these pointers or their fingers to point to the words when reading independently. Which of the following concepts of print is Ms. Watson addressing?

    a. Spacing
    b. Book orientation
    c. Directionality
    d. Letter concepts

62. Which of the following instructional strategies best demonstrates a way to prevent letter confusion in kindergarten students?

a. Introducing the letters in alphabetical order
b. Teaching visually similar letters, such as *b* and *d*, separately
c. Requiring students to master each letter before introducing the next letter
d. Focusing more on letter sounds than on letter names

63. A student encounters a multisyllabic word. She's not sure if she's seen it before. What should she do first? What should she do next?

a. Locate familiar word parts, then locate the consonants
b. Locate the consonants, then locate the vowels
c. Locate the vowels, then locate familiar word parts
d. Look it up in the dictionary, then write down the meaning

Refer to the following for questions 64 - 65:

> A reading teacher is working with a student who has just moved to Texas from Korea. The child knows very few words in English. The teacher offers her a picture book of Korean folk tales. Using words and gestures, the teacher asks her to "read" one folk tale. The child "reads" the familiar tale in Korean. The teacher then writes key English words on the board and asks the child to find those words in the book. When the child finds the words, they read them together.

64. The strategy used in this situation is:

a. Useful. The child will feel more confident because the story is already familiar. She will also feel that the lesson is a conversation of sorts, and that she is communicating successfully. She will be motivated to learn the English words because they are meaningful and highly charged.
b. Useful. The teacher is learning as much as the child is. The teacher is learning about Korean culture and language, and she can apply this knowledge when teaching future Korean students.
c. Not very useful. The child needs to be exposed to as much American culture as possible. Encouraging her to remember her own culture will make her sad and will limit her curiosity about her new home.
d. Not very useful. The first things the child should learn are the letters of the alphabet and associative sounds. Only then can she begin to decipher an unfamiliar language.

65. By using this strategy, the teacher is taking care to consider what type of load?

a. Language load
b. Cognitive load
c. Bilingual load
d. Cultural load

66. A cloze test evaluates a student's:

a. Reading fluency
b. Understanding of context and vocabulary
c. Phonemic skills
d. Ability to apply the alphabetic principle to previously unknown material

67. Which of the following spelling patterns is usually taught to children first?

   a. CVCe
   b. CVVC
   c. CVC
   d. CCVC

68. A kindergarten teacher is administering a reading assessment to her students. She dictates some CVC words and asks students to write them down on paper. The words she dictates are *cat* and *cot*. One student writes the following responses on her paper.

   bhp
   wpi

Which skill should the teacher focus on first with this student?

   a. Phonological awareness
   b. Alphabetic principle
   c. Phonics generalizations
   d. Blending

69. VC, CVC, CCVC, CVCC, and CCVCC are among the types of:

   a. Homophones
   b. Closed syllables
   c. Monosyllabic words
   d. Polyglotal indicators

70. A fourth-grade teacher wants to help his students analyze word morphology in order to identify the meanings of unknown words. Which word could he use to best exemplify the strategy of analyzing word morphology?

   a. Trees
   b. Manuscript
   c. Butterfly
   d. Ceiling

71. Which statement best describes the relationship between phonological awareness and phonemic awareness?

   a. Phonological awareness and phonemic awareness are interchangeable terms.
   b. Phonological awareness is one specific component of phonemic awareness.
   c. Phonemic awareness is one specific component of phonological awareness.
   d. Phonological awareness typically develops after phonemic awareness.

72. A teacher wants to help his students identify the types of nonfiction texts they are reading based on their text structures. Which keywords would students likely find in compare-and-contrast texts?

   a. For example and for instance
   b. Similarly and on the other hand
   c. Because and as a result
   d. First, next, and finally

73. *Bi, re,* and *un* are:

   a. Suffixes, appearing at the beginning of base words to change their meaning

   b. Suffixes, appearing at the end of base words to enhance their meaning

   c. Prefixes, appearing at the beginning of base words to emphasize their meaning

   d. Prefixes, appearing at the beginning of base words to change their meanings

74. Using graphic organizers, activating prior knowledge, and shared reading are examples of what type of instructional concept?

   a. Modeling

   b. Scaffolding

   c. Assessing

   d. Inspiring

75. Alex is a first-grade student. His teacher notices that he commonly substitutes words that make sense in the sentences but don't match the print. For example, he recently said, "The car drove down a street," while the text actually said, "The car drove down the street." Which cueing system is Alex using?

   a. Graphophonic

   b. Semantic

   c. Syntactic

   d. Pragmatic

76. Which of the following options best demonstrates a kindergarten teacher differentiating phonics instruction for her diverse group of students?

   a. Asking struggling readers to decode two CVC words and asking highly proficient readers to decode 10 CVC words

   b. Asking struggling readers to decode CVC words and asking highly proficient readers to write CVC words in sentences

   c. Asking struggling readers to decode CVC words and asking highly proficient readers to decode words with consonant blends

   d. Having struggling and proficient readers work in pairs to decode CVC words

77. A second-grade teacher wants to help her students enrich their vocabulary. She's noticed that their writing journals are filled with serviceable but unexciting verbs such as "said" and "went," and general rather than specific nouns. The most effective lesson would involve:

   a. Suggesting students use a thesaurus to replace common words with more unusual words

   b. Suggesting students add an adjective to each noun

   c. Brainstorming a list of verbs that mean ways of talking or ways of going, then adding them to the word wall along with some nouns that specify common topics

   d. Suggesting students look up the meanings of boring words and consider another way to express them

78. Which of the following options best describes decodable texts?

   a. They contain a predictable text structure that allows emergent readers to guess what will come next.

   b. They allow students to apply newly learned phonics skills while reading new texts.

   c. They contain a large amount of content-related words to reinforce vocabulary development.

   d. They are books with complex plot development that are ideal for close reading analysis.

79. In addition to word frequency, sentence complexity, and vocabulary, which of the following factors is frequently used to level books?

   a. Author's purpose
   b. Interest level
   c. Text features
   d. Author's craft

80. *Caret, carrot, to, two and too* share something in common. They:

   a. Are nouns
   b. Are monosyllabic
   c. Are homophones
   d. Represent things in nature

81. A preschool teacher is reading aloud to his students using a big book. He wants to help his students understand that the print carries the meaning of the story. What can the teacher do to foster this understanding?

   a. Show students where to start reading on each page
   b. Point to the words while reading
   c. Model the return sweep at the end of each line of text
   d. Ask students what they see in the pictures

82. A first-grade teacher wants to help students compare and contrast short vowel sounds. Which activity would best assist students with this skill?

   a. Segmenting words with short vowel sounds using Elkonin boxes
   b. Tracing words with short vowel sounds using stencils
   c. Sorting words containing short vowel sounds
   d. Including words with short vowel sounds on the weekly spelling list

83. Research indicates that developing oral language proficiency in emergent readers is important because:

   a. Proficiency with oral language enhances students' phonemic awareness and increases vocabulary.
   b. The more verbally expressive emergent readers are, the more confident they become. Such students will embrace both Academic and Independent reading levels.
   c. It encourages curiosity about others. With strong oral language skills, students begin to question the world around them. The more they ask, the richer their background knowledge.
   d. It demonstrates to students that their ideas are important and worth sharing.

84. A fifth-grade teacher introduces the skill of underlining text evidence to answer comprehension questions. He then models how to use this strategy using a sample text and related questions. Next, the class uses the strategy together to answer a new set of questions, with the teacher providing feedback on each attempt. Which activity would be the best choice to come next?

   a. Give students a passage and questions to complete independently using the underlining strategy.
   b. Reteach how to use the underlining strategy using different examples.
   c. Asks students to use this strategy when they take tests in the future.
   d. Test students on their ability to use the underlining strategy to answer comprehension questions.

85. A teacher gives students the following set of words: *compare, organism, predict, cell, habitat,* and *conclude.* Students are instructed to sort the words into two categories. What is the primary purpose of this activity?

   a. Classifying words according to morphology
   b. Recognizing common spelling patterns used to decode words
   c. Differentiating between academic and content vocabulary
   d. Grouping words with similar meanings

86. Which of the following words has exactly two morphemes?

   a. Defrosting
   b. Realigned
   c. Dogs
   d. Tip

87. What is orthographic processing?

   a. The ability to separate spoken words into component sounds
   b. Understanding the predictable sound each letter makes
   c. Recognizing letter patterns that make up words or word parts
   d. Understanding spoken words

88. Which of the following statements is typically true of literature circles?

   a. All students within a classroom read and discuss the same book.
   b. Teachers predetermine the questions and concepts that will be discussed.
   c. Students have choices about the books they read.
   d. Groups remain static throughout the year.

89. A teacher gives students a list of words, including *care, home,* and *use,* and asks them to record the definitions. Next, she asks them to add *less* to the ends of the words and record the new definitions. Students are then instructed to write down their observations in their writing journals. What is the primary purpose of this activity?

   a. Helping students recognize the meaning of a common suffix
   b. Teaching students the *-less* spelling pattern
   c. Practicing word analysis skills that will assist with decoding
   d. Identifying commonly used prefixes

90. Joseph is reading a book with fictional characters who live in modern times but travel back to the American Revolution to fight with the colonial soldiers. This book contains elements of which two genres of fiction?

    a.   Folktales and realistic fiction
    b.   Fantasy and historical fiction
    c.   Fable and fantasy
    d.   Historical fiction and folktale

Answer Key and Explanations

1. A: A syllable is a minimal sound unit arranged around a vowel. For example, *academic* has four syllables: *a/ca/dem/ic.* It is possible for a syllable to be a single vowel, as in the above example. It is not possible for a syllable to be a single consonant.

2. A: Emergent readers are learning concepts of print, and they benefit from having text in familiar places to assist with tracking and directionality. They are still developing phonics skills and may rely on one or more cueing systems, so picture support is important for determining unknown words. Emergent readers also benefit from simple sentence structure and repetition, which assists them with guessing unknown words. The features in choice B are more appropriate for early readers who are beginning to read more complex texts and are able to use phonics skills and multiple cueing systems rather than relying on picture clues. The features in choice C are more appropriate for transitional readers who are able to read a wider range of genres and text structures independently. Choice D is appropriate for fluent readers who are able to read complex, technical, and abstract texts independently.

3. D: It offers a systematic approach to untangling the wide variety of vowel sounds when an unfamiliar word is encountered. Code knowledge, also called orthographic tendencies, is a helpful approach to decoding a word when multiple pronunciation possibilities exist. For example, in the words *toe, go, though,* and *low,* the long O sound is written in a variety of ways. A code knowledge approach teaches a reader to first try a short vowel sound. If that doesn't help, the reader should consider the different ways the vowel or vowel groups can be pronounced, based on what he knows about other words.

4. D: Fluent readers are able to read smoothly and comfortably at a steady pace (rate). The more quickly a child reads, the greater the chance of leaving out a word or substituting one word for another (for example, *sink* instead of *shrink*). Fluent readers are able to maintain accuracy without sacrificing rate. Fluent readers also stress important words in a text, group words into rhythmic phrases, and read with intonation (prosody).

5. D: Targeted instruction is achieved by assessing areas needing improvement as well as areas of greatest strength for each student, and adjusting instruction to target those areas. This helps to ensure that all members of a class are receiving instruction tailored to their specific needs.

6. D: Text structure refers to how a text is organized. Different text structures are used depending on the purpose for writing, and cause/effect, compare/contrast, and time-order text structures are all commonly used in nonfiction texts. Literary devices are techniques authors use in their writing to set a certain mood, emphasize a point, convey a description, or more. Literary elements refer to parts of texts, such as characters, setting, plot, conflict, and resolution. Genres refer to specific categories of texts, such as fantasies.

7. A: Prefixes and suffixes are important for reading comprehension because they change the meanings of the root word to which they are attached. A student who understands that *un* means "not" will be able to decipher the meanings of words such as *unwanted, unhappy,* or *unreasonable.*

8. B: Reading comprehension and vocabulary cannot be sufficiently assessed with occasional, brief studies. Performing continuous observation, using high-stakes and standardized testing, paying attention to grades, and closely tracking the outcomes of objective-linked assessments are interrelated tools that, when systematically organized, offer a thorough understanding of students' strengths and weaknesses.

9. C: In one minute, a student who misreads one or less than one word per twenty words, or with 95%–100% accuracy, is at an Independent reading level. A student who misreads one or less than one word per ten words, or with 90%–95% accuracy, is at an Instructional level. A student misreading more than one word out of ten, or with less than 90% accuracy, is at a Frustration level.

10. A: Progress monitoring is a type of assessment used to track students' progress towards certain goals over time. When students are receiving reading interventions, frequent progress monitoring should be done to assess their progress and determine if the interventions are succeeding. Screening is done initially to determine if students are at risk for academic difficulties, and it is done at greater intervals, such as the start of each school year. Summative assessment occurs at the end of a unit of study or other larger unit of instruction. Norm-referenced tests compare students' performances to the performances of sample groups of similar students, while progress monitoring is done to assess students' progress towards their own personal goals.

11. D: Analogies are used to help students recognize the relationships between words. Students are commonly given a pair of words whose relationship they must first identify. They then apply the same type of relationship to complete another word pair. Analogies can be used to help students recognize many different types of relationships, including recognizing synonyms, antonyms, and more. While students may explore word structure, definitions, and origins while completing analogies, the overall objective of analogies is to recognize and apply relationships between sets of words.

12. D: Charlie did not acknowledge any errors, but instead kept reading after each one. Proficient readers recognize when something does not look right, sound right, or make sense, and they try again until they find the correct words. The teacher can prompt Charlie to stop and question himself when he makes errors until he begins recognizing and self-correcting them on his own. Because Charlie's errors both make sense and sound right in the sentences, he is already using both semantic and syntactic cues. The student only omitted one minor word, which did not change the meaning of the sentence.

13. D: Phonemic awareness refers to the ability to identify and manipulate sounds at the phoneme level. Because phonemes are the smallest units of spoken sound, phonemic awareness is the most advanced phonological awareness skill.

14. B: A maze test is a specific type of cloze test. In a cloze test, words are deleted, and the reader must supply the missing words using contextual clues and vocabulary that is familiar. A maze test is a multiple-choice application of a cloze test.

15. A: When readers skim, they look through a text quickly to determine what it is mostly about. Skimming would help the students quickly identify which sites listed in the search results are closely related to the science fair topics and warrant further, deeper reading. Scanning involves reading quickly to pick out certain pieces of information from a text, such as a specific fact or date. Close reading involves rereading a text multiple times while analyzing different layers each time. Extensive reading refers to students selecting books that are enjoyable and easy to read independently, which helps increase reading rate and fluency.

16. A: At the beginning of the school year, second-grade students should be able to read 50–80 words per minute. By the time they are well into the school year, second-grade level reading is tracked at 85 words per minute.

17. D: It is impossible to include every text desired into the language curriculum—there are simply too many good books, stories, poems, speeches, and media available. Teachers must first think about what skills their students need to acquire, as well as what skills they have already mastered. In designing activities for class, a good teacher will start first with the purpose for instruction. For example, purposes of reading can include: reading for information, reading for enjoyment, understanding a message, identifying main or supporting ideas, or developing an appreciation for artistic expression/perception. Once the purpose or intended learning outcome has been identified, the teacher will have a much better idea of which texts, strategies, and activities will support that purpose.

18. B: Consonant blend refers to a group of consonants in which each letter represents a separate sound.

19. A: Environmental print is the print people see in their everyday lives. For children, this may include restaurant logos, food labels, and street signs. Environmental print helps children understand that print has meaning, and reading familiar words can boost reading confidence. The remaining options provide students with opportunities to read other types of meaningful words, but not environmental print.

20. C: Picture walks are frequently used to activate students' prior knowledge. When readers look at the pictures, they make connections between the content of the new texts and what they already know from other texts or life experiences. These connections can spark interest in the stories and deepen comprehension. Teachers may encourage the use of syntactic cues during guided reading groups, but this is not typically part of a picture walk. Setting a purpose for reading is another beneficial prereading activity, but it is not always a part of a picture walk either. Metacognitive skills, which assist students with self-monitoring during reading, are also beneficial, but they are not typically the focus of a picture walk.

21. A: In the pre-alphabetic stage of word learning, children do not yet have an understanding of letter/sound relationships they can use to decode words. They may remember some words based on visual features, such as words found in environmental print. Choice B describes the partial alphabetic stage, when children begin to use letter/sound relationships to decode some sounds in words, particularly the beginning and ending sounds. Choice C describes the full alphabetic stage, and choice D describes the consolidated alphabetic stage.

22. B: Choice B best represents constructivism because students are using reading, writing, listening, and speaking skills to perform an authentic task that they collaboratively agreed upon. The teacher acts as a guide to facilitate the process. While students are engaged in higher-level thinking activities during the close reading activity in choice A, the activity is planned and led by the teacher. Similarly, the order and content of the stations in choice C have been determined by the teacher, and the activities do not represent authentic, performance-based tasks. Choice D, while providing beneficial modeling and social learning interaction, does not include students performing authentic, problem-based tasks.

23. C: Analogizing is based on recognizing the pattern of letters in words that share sound similarities. If the pattern is found at the end of a family of words, it is called a *rhyme*. Some examples of rhyme are *rent, sent, bent,* and *dent.* If the pattern is found at the beginning of the family of words, it is frequently a consonant blend such as *street, stripe,* or *strong,* in which all the letters are pronounced, or the pattern is a consonant digraph, in which the letters are taken together to represent a single sound such as in *phone, phonics,* or *phantom.*

24. D: All of the listed options can assist students with developing reading skills, and students will have individual opinions regarding preferred activities. However, reading is a social experience that helps children learn about themselves and the world around them. Using language creatively, such as through rhyming, helps them understand all of the ways that language can be used. Reading and discussing stories together is also a social experience that connects readers and makes them part of a community of learners. These benefits will likely contribute to a love of reading more than practicing isolated skills.

25. C: The teacher is demonstrating a think-aloud, or sharing her thinking process as she uses a reading strategy. In this example, she explains her thoughts as she uses context clues to determine the meaning of an unknown word. Mental images and visualizations both refer to the pictures that readers get in their minds when they read. Predictions are logical guesses about what might happen in a text.

26. C: Using context clues can help the reader determine the meanings of many unknown words quickly and also contribute to reading comprehension. Asking a classmate for the meanings of words may work in the short term, but it does not help the reader develop independent reading strategies, and there may not always be another person present while reading. Looking up the unknown words later may result in the student missing words that are critical to the meaning of the text, negatively affecting comprehension. Similarly, while skipping over the unknown words may result in sentences that appear to make sense, the missing words may play important roles in the meaning.

27. C: Daniel has identified only external character traits, or traits related to the character's appearance. He has not identified any internal traits, or traits related to the character's thoughts, feelings, words, or actions. An appropriate next step would be to help Daniel differentiate between the two types of traits and find examples of each in the text. The remaining options would require Daniel to identify internal traits using textual evidence. For example, it would be difficult to describe how the character has changed throughout the story without using any internal traits to describe her at different points in the story. Similarly, it would be difficult to label the role she plays or compare her with other characters without using any internal traits to support the responses.

28. C: Until the teacher monitors the child's verbal abilities and habits, she cannot determine if the lack of interaction suggests a learning disability, an emotional problem, or simply a shy personality. The teacher should informally observe the child over a period of time, noting if and when she initiates or responds to oral language, if she is reading with apparent comprehension, if her vocabulary is limited, and the degree to which the child is interested in understanding.

29. D: Chunking involves looking for known parts in a word. Because *scapegoat* is a compound word, it is likely that Maria will at least recognize the word *goat*. This leaves a smaller portion of the word to decode. There are many words that would sound right in the sentence, so guessing based on syntax alone is unlikely to result in the correct word. Because the word is multisyllabic and contains multiple spelling patterns, blending may be difficult. Additionally, the sentence provides few context clues to help Maria guess the word correctly.

30. C: This sentence contains the word *firm*, which is an antonym for *tentative*. This antonym, along with the word *unlike*, help the reader determine that *tentative* means not firm. There are no synonyms, or words that mean the same, for *tentative* in the sentence. There are also no definitions for the word. Inference clues give hints about the word's meaning without explicitly listing a synonym, antonym, or definition. No such inference clues are present.

31. A: To help students use textual evidence to support their answers, they should be taught to locate the evidence directly in the text rather than relying on memory. One strategy that addresses this skill is underlining the information within the text when it is located. Rereading the text multiple times may help students remember the information contained in the text, but it does not encourage them to locate the specific answers to questions. Reading and eliminating answer choices is a beneficial test-taking strategy in general, but it does not assist students with locating and verifying specific details. A story map helps to identify key information in the story, but there is no guarantee that it will address any specific test questions.

32. B: Homographs are words that are spelled the same way but have different meanings. For example, *minute* (the unit of time) and *minute* (tiny), are homographs. Note that homographs can also be pronounced differently. Words that are spelled differently but pronounced the same way are called homophones. Words with the same Latin root or words within the same word family are related to one another, but they are not homographs.

33. C: There are many genres from which students can choose to read. The most elemental distinction between genres consists of fiction and non-fiction, the latter referring to stories or texts that are true, or factual. Fictional texts can fall into a variety of categories. Realistic fiction seems as though it could be true. These stories involve realistic characters and settings with which readers can often identify. This type of fiction can consist of different subjects, but it still must be relatable in nature.

34. A: Letter–sound correspondence relies on the relationship between a spoken sound or group of sounds and the letters conventionally used in English to write them.

35. D: None; sight words cannot be decoded. Readers must learn to recognize these as whole words on sight. Sight words have irregular spelling. Segmenting them into syllables or using a phonemic approach are ineffective strategies to aid a reader in recognizing a sight word because these approaches depend on rules a sight word doesn't follow. Word families group words that share common patterns of consonants and vowels. The spelling of those words is, therefore, regular because they follow a predictable pattern. Sight words are irregular, do not follow a predictable pattern, and must be instantaneously recognized for writing fluency. No decoding is useful.

36. B: Aidan is writing to convince the cafeteria manager to act on a specific request, and he supports his request with reasons. This is indicative of persuasive writing. When authors write to inform, they share information about their topics to teach readers new things. When authors write to entertain, they write to provide readers with enjoyable experiences. When authors write to describe, they write to share descriptive details about their topics.

37. D: A phonogram is a letter or group of letters that represent a single sound. In the word *light*, the letters *igh* together produce one sound, $/\bar{\imath}/$. The longest phonogram in choice A contains two letters, *ck*. Choice B contains only one-letter phonograms. The longest phonogram in choice C contains two letters, *ea*, which together produce the $/\bar{e}/$ sound.

38. A: It is beneficial for ELLs to practice phonemic awareness skills on words they know in English. Some English phonemes may not be used in students' native languages. Therefore, introducing English vocabulary words that contain these phonemes helps give these sounds a meaningful context. While phonological and phonemic awareness in students' native languages can be beneficial when they are learning English, it may lead to overgeneralization of rules of the native languages. Therefore, in instructional settings, using familiar words in English will help students practice the phonemes and patterns of English. Students will need to gradually learn phonemes that are not part of their native languages, but it is not ideal to introduce them first. Phonological and phonemic awareness assists with learning the alphabetic principle, so it is beneficial for students to develop these skills first.

39. B: Readers rely on prior knowledge and existing schemata to make sense of newly encountered texts. Therefore, texts that are more closely related to students' existing cultural schemata are more easily comprehended. To increase the likelihood of comprehension, the teacher should provide the student with background information on Thanksgiving before reading the book. Relating it to familiar traditions will also assist with activating the student's prior knowledge. Choice A does not provide any scaffolding to the student to assist with comprehension. Choice C offers some scaffolding in the form of a written outline, but it is less likely to be effective than an interactive discussion about the topic and the connection to the student's own cultural traditions. Choice D waits until after the book is read to offer additional information, even though it would be more beneficial to introduce the topic before reading.

40. C: Constructivism is a learning theory based on the idea that people are actively involved in the learning process, rather than being passive receivers of knowledge. Constructivism suggests that children learn best by solving real-world problems, gathering information, testing ideas, and other active processes, with teachers guiding and scaffolding them along the way.

41. C: Writing their own examples of metaphors requires students to apply their knowledge. Identifying and underlining metaphors assesses the comprehension level of Bloom's taxonomy, and defining a metaphor assesses the knowledge level. Critiquing the author's use of metaphors assesses the evaluation level.

42. A: Spoken language is generally less formal and more conversational in tone than written language. As a result, syntax is more relaxed, and there is greater flexibility in word order. Spoken language also tends to contain a mixture of sentences and fragments. For example, a typical conversation among friends may contain several shifts between speakers, along with brief comments and replies rather than fully developed sentences. Body language plays a greater role in spoken language, as it can either affirm or contradict the meaning of the spoken words. For example, if a person says they are looking forward to something, yet they are frowning and avoiding eye contact, the recipient of the message may not believe the speaker is sincere.

43. B: Figurative language involves the use of words and phrases that differ from their literal meanings. The expression in choice B means that the wet snow covered the ground, not that it was literally a wet blanket. It is an example of a metaphor, which is one type of figurative language. The other options contain some descriptive words and phrases, but they have literal meanings.

44. B: Phonetic spelling is common at this age, as children write the sounds that they hear. They typically know how to spell a limited number of words conventionally. This is a typical stage of development, and over time, they will begin to spell more words conventionally as more phonics rules and spelling patterns are learned. Asking an adult or using a dictionary to confirm the spellings of all unknown words can slow down and inhibit the writing process. Additionally, as phonetic spelling is typical at this age and the student has spelled some words correctly, it is unlikely that an intervention is needed based solely on this information.

45. D: Phonemes are the smallest units of sound in words. In this activity, students are replacing one phoneme with another, which is known as phoneme substitution. Alliteration refers to a series of words in which most words begin with the same sound. Segmenting refers to breaking a word down into its individual sounds, or phonemes. Onset and rime blending involve blending the beginning sound of a word with the rest of the word.

46. C: Word walls should be flexible, meaning words can be removed if students have mastered them, and new words can be added as they are introduced. It is also helpful if the words on word walls are removeable, so students can take them to other areas of the room when they are using them for reading and writing activities. Choice A is incorrect because there are many types of words that can be included on word walls, including content-related vocabulary, academic vocabulary, and high-frequency words. Choice B is incorrect because words can be displayed on word walls for different reasons. For example, words containing the same root can be displayed to help students see relationships between words. Because word walls can contain different types of words and be used for different purposes, they can be helpful for readers in all stages of reading development.

47. C: Research has shown that reading and writing are interrelated processes, and literacy development is enhanced when they are taught together. Even very young children can be encouraged to use writing to communicate, though their early attempts at writing may be scribbles. This helps children develop an understanding that print carries meaning, and it also assists with development of directionality and other concepts of print. Similarly, children learn concepts of print and skills that they use in their writing by seeing them modeled in the books they read.

48. A: The teacher should give each child a piece of drawing paper that has been folded in half and then in half again, creating four boxes, along with a piece that has not been folded. The teacher should then ask the students to draw a cartoon about the story. Each of the first four boxes will show the events in order. The second page is to show how the story ends. When a child is able to visually see the way a familiar story has unfolded, that child can find causal or thematic connections in the action that increases her comprehension of the story overall. Asking the class to draw a single picture or to draw the beginning and end doesn't sufficiently demonstrate the importance of order to meaning. While some first-graders may be able to create their own cartoon stories that demonstrate a logical series of events, many first-graders are not yet ready to organize thought into a linear progression.

49. A: In the language experience approach, students decide on a story they want to tell and dictate it to a teacher, who writes the words down on paper. The teacher then reads the story back multiple times, modeling appropriate fluency. Students are then invited to join in reading the story. In writing workshop, students work on independent writing pieces following the stages of the writing process. They may all be involved in different stages at different times. Trait-based writing teaches students to consider the traits of good writing, such as word choice, throughout the writing process. During modeled writing, teachers think aloud as they record their thoughts on paper or on the board.

50. A: Alphabetic principle is the understanding that each letter of the alphabet makes a predictable sound. Students are practicing this by repeating the letter name and sound each week. Concepts of print are conventions used to convey meaning in text. Examples include knowing how to hold a book and track text correctly. Phonological awareness is the ability to identify and manipulate sounds in words. It does not involve letter/sound relationships. Automaticity refers to the ability to recognize whole words quickly and effortlessly.

51. B: Phonemes are the smallest units of sound in words. *Hand* has four phonemes: /h/, /ă/, /n/, and /d/. Choice A has three phonemes: /sh/, /ē/, and /t/. Choice C also has three phonemes: /r/, /ī/, and /t/. Choice D has two phonemes: /s/ and /ē/.

52. C: Silent reading fluency can be monitored over time by giving the Test of Silent Contextual Reading Fluency (TSCRF) four times a year. A similar assessment tool is the Test of Silent Word Reading Fluency (TOSWRF), in which words of increasing complexity are given as a single, undifferentiated, and unpunctuated strand. As with the TSCRF, three minutes are given for the student to separate each word from the next.
Itwillcannotschoolbecomeagendaconsistentphilosophysuperfluous is an example of such a strand.

53. C: When students make text-to-self connections, they make connections between the texts and their own personal experiences. This student connects Alicia's experiences adjusting to a new situation to her own adjustment when moving to a new school. Choice A demonstrates a text-to-text connection, when students make connections between two or more different texts they have read. Choice B demonstrates a text-to-world connection, when students make connections between texts and events that have happened in the real world, but not to themselves personally. Choice D represents a student's reaction to the book rather than a connection between two or more things.

54. D: Prosody refers to reading with appropriate intonation, rhythm, and stress. Because Liz is reading in a monotone voice and not using appropriate phrasing, it would be beneficial for her teacher to focus on prosody during small-group instruction. Her accuracy rate is in the independent range, which demonstrates she has strong word recognition skills. Her high accuracy rate also suggests she is already reading with automaticity.

55. A: The student is adjusting his language according to his current social situation. When speaking to a friend, he uses informal language. When presenting a report in front of the class and teacher, he switches to more formal language. Cultural context refers to the ways that messages are delivered and received based on differing cultural backgrounds and norms. Contextual clues are clues in a text that assist readers with determining the meanings of unknown words. Personal context refers to how communication is affected by an individual's age, gender, educational background, and other personal factors.

56. B: Choice B requires the highest level of thinking out of these options because it requires students to evaluate the author's craft. Comparing, contrasting, and inferring are in the comprehension level, which is lower. Identifying the setting is at the knowledge level of Bloom's taxonomy, which is the lowest level.

57. A: A story map outlines the main elements of the story, including the characters, setting, conflict, plot, and resolution. Recording these elements will assist the student in remembering and analyzing the story after it has been read. If the student has retention issues, he or she may not recall the story elements even after reading the story twice or listening to an audio version. A KWL chart can be used to activate prior knowledge and help the student reflect on what was learned, but it does not outline the story elements needed to analyze plot.

58. A: During interactive writing experiences, teachers and students work together to create writing pieces. Teachers and students share the writing utensils, with teachers guiding the students as they record their thoughts. In shared writing experiences, teachers record students' thoughts on paper. Students do not help with the writing. In independent writing, students utilize the strategies they have learned to complete writing pieces independently. Guided writing occurs when teachers work with small groups of strategically grouped students on targeted writing skills.

59. A: A key tenet of Marie Clay's theory is the understanding that children take different paths to becoming readers based on differences in prior knowledge and experiences. As a result, teachers must meet the needs of individual learners rather than using a one-size-fits-all approach to instruction. Choice B is incorrect because Clay's theory also explains the interrelationship between reading and writing. Choice C is incorrect because Clay's theory emphasizes the importance of individualized instruction based on students' unique needs and experiences. Choice D is incorrect because frequent observation and data collection are important components of individualized instruction, as they allow teachers to determine students' strengths and needs.

60. B: Verbal dyspraxia refers to confusing word or sentence order while speaking. Dyspraxic individuals do not process spoken language sequentially due to a neurological distortion. The dislocation of sounds within a word, such as vocalizing *lamp* instead of *palm*, is one indication of verbal dyspraxia.

61. C: Following the text with a pointer and pointing to each word with a finger both help with the concept of directionality. Directionality includes the understanding that you read from left to right, from top to bottom, and from the left page to the right page. Spacing refers to the understanding that you include spaces between words and between sentences. Book orientation refers to knowing how to hold and open a book correctly. Letter concepts include recognizing letters and knowing the difference between a letter and a word.

62. B: Children tend to confuse letters that are visually similar, such as *b* and *d*. Introducing them separately helps to prevent confusion between them. While there are differing theories on which order to use when introducing letters, generally alphabetical order is not the most effective. Letters are sometimes grouped for instruction by the difficulty of their sounds, their formation, or relevance to the students (such as introducing letters in their names first). Letters may be introduced in small groups to allow students to practice them in context, and both letter sounds and letter names are important for students to learn.

63. C: She should locate the vowels, then locate familiar word parts. Syllables are organized around vowels. In order to determine the syllables, this student should begin by locating the vowels. It's possible to have a syllable that is a single vowel (*a/gain*). It isn't possible to have a syllable that is a single consonant. Once the word has been broken into its component syllables the reader is able to study the syllables to find ones that are familiar and might give her a clue as to the word's meaning, such as certain prefixes or suffixes.

64. A: The child will feel more confident because the story is already familiar, so this strategy is useful. She will also feel that the lesson is a conversation of sorts, and that she is communicating successfully. She will be motivated to learn the English words because they are meaningful and highly charged. As a newly arrived immigrant, the child feels overwhelmed. Presenting her with a book of folk tales from her country tells her that she needn't lose her culture in order to function in this one. It also comforts her by reminding her that her past and present are linked. Allowing her to speak in Korean helps her express herself without fear of judgment or failure. Presenting her with an English vocabulary that is meaningful ensures that she will eagerly embrace these words, her first words in her new language.

65. D: The teacher is considering the cultural load the student is facing. Cultural load is concerned with how the relationship between language and culture can help or hinder learning. By using the Korean folk tale, the teacher offered the child the opportunity to learn new words in a context that was culturally familiar. By demonstrating respect for her student's culture, she helped lighten the cultural load.

66. B: In a cloze test, a reader is given a text with certain words blocked out. The reader must be able to determine probable missing words based on contextual clues. In order to supply these words, the reader must already know them.

67. C: CVC words, which contain a consonant, a short vowel, and another consonant, are typically taught before the other listed spelling patterns. These words are easy to decode for beginning readers. Long vowel sounds, such as those in choices A and B, are typically taught after short vowel sounds. Additionally, consonant blends and digraphs, as found in choice D, are also typically taught after CVC words.

68. B: The student's responses include random strings of letters that do not correlate with the sounds in the spoken words. Additionally, she has represented the /c/ sound at the beginning of each word differently in her responses. Understanding that letters make predictable sounds is part of the alphabetic principle. Her three-letter responses indicate that she has some phonological awareness skills. She knows there are three sounds in each word, but she is not aware of which letters are used to represent each sound. Teaching phonics generalizations will be more helpful after the student has developed an awareness of the alphabetic principle and consistently matches letters to their sounds.

69. B: Closed syllables are those that end with a consonant. *At, dog, spit, duck,* and *pluck* are all examples of closed syllables.

70. B: The word *manuscript* has the Latin root *manu,* meaning *hand,* and the Latin root *script,* meaning *write.* By recognizing these roots, a reader can determine that the word *manuscript* means something written by hand. *Trees* does not contain any Greek or Latin roots that could be identified to determine the word meaning. *Butterfly* is a compound word, but the *butter* component does not assist with the meaning of the compound word. Although *ceiling* has the inflectional ending *-ing,* it is unlikely to assist students with identifying the meaning of the word when added to *ceil.*

71. C: Phonological awareness and phonemic awareness are distinct terms. Phonological awareness is a broader term that refers to the ability to identify and manipulate sounds in spoken words. Phonemic awareness is one component of phonological awareness involving the ability to identify and manipulate sounds in spoken words at the phoneme level. Because phonemes are the smallest units of speech, phonemic awareness is an advanced component of phonological awareness. It typically develops after simpler skills, like rhyming and blending.

72. B: The keywords in choice B are used to signal how two or more items are the same and different, which is the purpose of compare-and-contrast texts. The keywords in choice A would likely be found in descriptive texts. The keywords in choice C would likely be found in cause-and-effect texts. The keywords in choice D would likely be found in sequential texts.

73. D: Suffixes appear at the end of words. Prefixes are attached to the beginning of words to change their meanings. *Un+happy, bi+monthly,* and *re+examine* are prefixes that, by definition, change the meanings of the words to which they are attached.

74. B: Scaffolding refers to any kind of special instruction designed to help students learn a new or challenging concept. There are countless forms of scaffolding techniques. The three techniques mentioned in the question prompt are all used to facilitate student understanding of a given text or a concept taught within the text. Scaffolding should not be confused with modeling strategies, which refer to the process of demonstrating how something should be done before a student tries it on his or her own.

75. C: Readers use the syntactic cueing system when they consider sentence structure and grammar to decode unknown words. Alex is substituting a word that sounds right in the sentence. If Alex were using the graphophonic cueing system, he would choose a word that is structurally similar to the existing word, such as a word that starts with the same sound. If Alex were using the semantic cueing system, he would use picture cues or prior knowledge to guess the word. The pragmatic cueing system refers to consideration of the purposes of reading in given situations.

76. C: Differentiation involves instructing students according to their individual strengths and needs as indicated by assessment data. Instruction should challenge students in their zones of proximal development to ensure that they learn new skills without becoming bored or frustrated. Choice C provides both groups of students with words at their appropriate levels of difficulty. Choice A involves simply giving extra words to highly proficient readers. If they have already mastered decoding CVC words, decoding many of them is likely to be boring and unchallenging. Similarly, if highly proficient readers have already mastered CVC words, writing them in sentences is likely to be less challenging or beneficial than learning to decode more complex words. While paired experiences can be beneficial in many situations, choice D does not provide more challenging words for the highly proficient readers, nor does it ensure that they will scaffold the struggling readers rather than decoding the words for them.

77. C: The most effective lesson would be brainstorming a list of verbs that mean ways of talking or ways of going, then adding them to the word wall along with some nouns that specify common topics. Second graders aren't developmentally ready for a thesaurus; most will believe that any words in a particular list are interchangeable. For example, a student who wrote *my little sister walks like a baby* might find the verbs *strut, sidle,* and *amble* in the thesaurus. None of these verbs would be an appropriate substitution. Supplementing a noun with an adjective often results in flat writing: *There's a tree in my yard* might become *There's a nice tree in my big yard.* Adjectives such as *pretty, fun, cute, funny,* and so forth don't add much in terms of meaning, but they are the adjectives younger writers reach for first. A more specific noun is both more meaningful and more interesting. *There's a weeping willow in my yard* is evocative.

78. B: Decodable texts use many words containing previously taught phonics skills, allowing readers to practice those skills in context while reading new books. They can be one component found in classrooms that use explicit phonics instruction. Choice A describes predictable books, which rely more on patterns in language rather than phonics skills, to assist readers with decoding. Because most words in decodable texts contain previously learned phonics skills, they do not often have content-related vocabulary words with more complex spelling patterns. Additionally, the focus is on using decodable words rather than on complex plot development, so they may not be appropriate for close reading activities.

79. C: Text features are one factor used to level books. They help determine how much support readers have in decoding and comprehending the text. For example, pictures are one text feature essential for early readers. Other text features, such as headings and labels, can assist readers with expository texts. Therefore, text features are considered when leveling books. Considering both the author's purpose and craft can help students comprehend texts, but they do not typically affect leveling. Interest level will vary from student to student and is also not typically considered when leveling books.

80. C: Homophones are words that are pronounced the same, but differ in meaning. For example, a bride wears a 2-caret ring, but a horse eats a carrot.

81. B: Pointing to each word as it is read aloud will help students understand the relationship between the printed and spoken word. They will begin to understand that the meaning of the story is contained in the text. Showing students where to begin reading on each page and how to complete a return sweep will help them track the text appropriately. Asking students what they see in the pictures encourages the use of the semantic cueing system.

82. C: Word sorts assist students with comparing and contrasting features of words. While completing the sort, students must analyze each word to determine and categorize its vowel sound and determine how each word is similar to and different from other words in the set. Segmenting words using Elkonin boxes helps students break words into individual phonemes, but it doesn't assist with comparing and contrasting. Tracing words may help students practice short vowel spelling patterns, but it doesn't assist with comparing and contrasting either. Including words with short vowel sounds on the weekly spelling list will mainly assist with learning spelling patterns.

83. A: Proficiency with oral language enhances students' phonemic awareness and increases vocabulary. Understanding that words are scripted with specific letters representing specific sounds is essential to decoding a text. Students cannot effectively learn to read without the ability to decode. An enhanced vocabulary supports the act of reading; the larger an emergent reader's vocabulary, the more quickly he will learn to read. He will be able to decode more words, which he can organize into word families and use to decode unfamiliar words.

84. A: Generally, the sequence of instruction is as follows: explicit instruction, modeling, guided practice, independent practice and application, and generalization. The teacher has already completed the explicit instruction, modeling, and guided practice portion of the sequence. Therefore, independent practice and application would come next. Choice A best demonstrates this stage of instruction. Reteaching is only necessary if informal or formal assessments indicate that students did not learn the skill after the first attempt at instruction, which is not indicated in this example. Choice C represents the generalization stage, which typically comes after students have had independent practice with the skill. A formal assessment, such as a test, should also come after independent practice opportunities.

85. C: The words in this set can be grouped into two categories: academic vocabulary and content vocabulary. Academic vocabulary words are commonly used in school but are not specific to one subject area. For example, students may compare shapes in math, compare living things in science, and compare characters in reading. Content vocabulary refers to words related to one specific subject area. *Organism*, *cell*, and *habitat* are typically used in science.

86. C: A morpheme is the smallest unit of language with meaning, and a morpheme cannot be broken down any further without losing that meaning. *Dogs* has two morphemes: *dog* and the *s*, which indicates that the word is plural. Choice A has three morphemes: *de, frost,* and *ing*. Choice B also has three morphemes: *re, align,* and *ed*. Choice D has one morpheme: *tip*.

87. C: Orthographic processing refers to recognizing letter patterns that make up words or word parts. For example, a student may see the word *sight* and immediately recognize the *ight* pattern. The ability to separate spoken words into component sounds is a part of phonological awareness. Alphabetic principle is the understanding that each letter makes a predictable sound. Receptive language involves understanding spoken words.

88. C: Although teachers may supply the possible options, students are typically given choices about the books they read for literature circles. This helps maintain interest and engagement throughout the process. Students participate in literature circles in small groups, and there are usually multiple books being read and discussed throughout a classroom. Students are encouraged to lead the discussions and introduce questions and topics for analysis. Additionally, groups may change frequently as students finish books and move on to new texts.

89. A: The focus of this activity is on comparing the meanings of the words before and after the suffix *less* is added. Students should recognize that the newly formed words mean *without* (base word) and be able to apply this knowledge to figure out the meanings of other words containing the same suffix. While students may also learn to spell and decode words containing *less* as a result of this activity, the primary focus is on the words' meanings. Choice D is incorrect because *less* is a suffix. Prefixes are letters or groups of letters added to the beginnings of words.

90. B: This book contains elements of fantasy due to the time travel, and it contains elements of historical fiction with the characters' participation in the American Revolution. Choice A is incorrect because it is not a story passed down over time, so it is not a folktale. Additionally, while some portions of the story may seem realistic, the time traveling element makes it more fantasy than realistic fiction. Choice C is incorrect because the story doesn't focus on a moral or contain talking animals. Choice D is incorrect because it is not a folktale.

Constructed Response

Sample Constructed Response #1

INSTRUCTIONS

Review the sample below and identify at least one of the student's strengths and at least one of the student's weaknesses in reading fluency. Provide a recommendation for how to target the student's needs in future instruction relying on your knowledge of language and reading comprehension, including phonics, word structure, context-clues, and vocabulary acquisition.

SCENARIO

Ally, a third-grade student, reads an excerpt from the Tortoise and the Hare. Ally was primed on the words "Hare" and "Tortoise" prior to reading the passage. After reading the passage aloud, a short quiz assessed her comprehension of what she had just read. Ally normally scores well on reading retention, but struggled to remember particular details about what she had just read. Below is the notation of Ally's oral reading performance. Ally's reading was highly accurate, but very slow and included pauses throughout. Ally's reading performance did not include much verbal inflection to indicate the sentence type and breaks in her speech were relatively pervasive.

SAMPLE TEXT

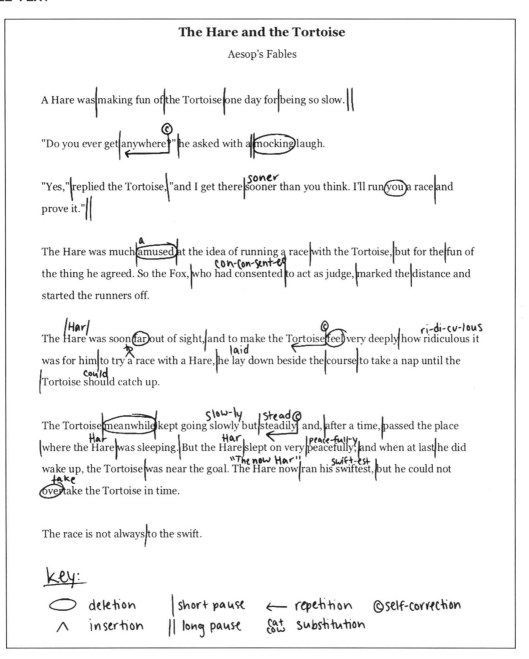

The Hare and the Tortoise

Aesop's Fables

A Hare was making fun of the Tortoise one day for being so slow.

"Do you ever get anywhere?" he asked with a mocking laugh.

"Yes," replied the Tortoise, "and I get there sooner than you think. I'll run you a race and prove it."

The Hare was much amused at the idea of running a race with the Tortoise, but for the fun of the thing he agreed. So the Fox, who had consented to act as judge, marked the distance and started the runners off.

The Hare was soon far out of sight, and to make the Tortoise feel very deeply how ridiculous it was for him to try a race with a Hare, he lay down beside the course to take a nap until the Tortoise should catch up.

The Tortoise meanwhile kept going slowly but steadily and, after a time, passed the place where the Hare was sleeping. But the Hare slept on very peacefully; and when at last he did wake up, the Tortoise was near the goal. The Hare now ran his swiftest, but he could not overtake the Tortoise in time.

The race is not always to the swift.

key:

⬭ deletion | short pause   ← repetition   Ⓒself-correction

∧ insertion || long pause   cat/cow substitution

SAMPLE STRONG RESPONSE

Ally's oral reading performance sample showed few errors with actual phonic performance. She was capable of sounding out many longer words with relative success. The words she had the most difficulty with were words that she was less familiar with the spelling of, such as "Hare." Additionally, she would periodically skip multi-syllabic words that she struggled with. Ally seemed to have the most difficulty with maintaining the pace of her reading, which detracts from her actual reading fluency as she would frequently pause between roughly every three and four syllables. She seemed to have particularly long pauses before more difficult words and at the end of a line, where she would need to find the beginning of a new line. The segmentation of Ally's reading makes comprehension and expression difficult, as she is not reading the passage with natural inflections as it would be read by a more experienced reader. With Ally's high accuracy and lower reading speed in mind, one general recommendation would be to focus on facilitating opportunities for Ally to improve the areas hindering her overall fluency in reading. Fluency is functionally made up of accuracy, speed, expression, and comprehension. Ally's expression and comprehension are likely negatively impacted by her frequent pauses when reading. This pattern of pausing to ensure accuracy in pronunciation is likely a problem that will self-resolve with general practice, but targeting her speed in decoding complex words and improving her fluidity in reading sight words is likely to be more effective.

In response, a teacher can employ targeted practice by simply providing Ally with more opportunity to practice reading aloud. Ally will benefit from practicing reading aloud with passages high in sight words that do not require her to stop to decode larger chunks. If Ally continues to pace herself slowly so she does not make any mistakes, the teacher can tell Ally explicitly that the activity is about speed and not about making no mistakes. The teacher can also permit Ally to repeat a sentence that she struggled with to break down the tendency to pause when reading. This should help her practice reading more fluidly with room for proper stress and intonation in her speech with fewer unnatural pauses.

Ally can also benefit from reading more challenging passages, intentionally helping her encounter more difficult, multi-syllabic words. By learning larger vocabulary words and encountering them naturally in passages, she should have ample opportunity to practice sounding out difficult words faster. With one-on-one reading instruction, the teacher can effectively help Ally challenge herself with these new words by asking her to re-read the whole sentence if she does try to skip a difficult word.

In summary, Ally needs targeted practice to help her increase her overall reading fluency. She is strong in her accuracy, but needs to practice reducing her pauses in reading and become more comfortable with encountering larger words in reading practice.

Sample Constructed Response #2

INSTRUCTIONS

Review the following briefing of a student's writing sample. Identify one type of grammatical deficit student's sample, citing specific examples of the deficiency. Provide one instructional strategy that can help the student achieve in the area of difficulty. Provide sufficient theoretical or research-based support for the proposed instructional strategy, explaining why it is appropriate and targeted to the particular needs of the student.

SCENARIO

Adrian recently immigrated to America and is being placed in general 6th grade classes as he scored well on an English placement test. He spoke English in his home country as a school language and still struggles with certain common grammatical forms. Adrian occasionally has points taken off on some of his assignments due to these grammatical errors.

SAMPLE OF THE STUDENT'S JOURNALING ASSIGNMENT

Write about one of your favorite activities you get to do at school this year. Describe what has been the best part and the most difficult part about that activity. Think about the future and describe how you hope your activity will develop by 8th grade and by 12th grade.

January 27

This year I got to join the cross country team and run outside. The best part about the running is that I get to go out into the sun every day and be with friend on the team. Since this is my first year doing this running, I'm not fast and have a hard time finish the run when it is a longer one. The hard part is having to keep going after I'm tired already. We usually run 2 to 3 mile before we stop, but at first, I could only run 1 mile. My teammate encouraged me and helped me get better at running, and I am glad they have become my friend. When my dad picks me from school, he can usually tell how much fun I had with my group of friend. He is glad I want to stay on the team and practices running with me on the weekend. My hope for the future is that I can run in a 5k race by 8th grade and place in my age group. I hope to keep to push my limits and eventually run a half-marathon before I graduate high school and can go on to run in college.

SAMPLE STRONG RESPONSE

Adrian's journal entry had several grammar deficiencies, but one of the most frequent areas that Adrian could improve on is his omission of the plural -s to words such as "friends" and "miles." It is possible that Adrian's primary language does not use morphemes to indicate if a word is plural or not, so he may be experiencing primary language interference. One primary goal in helping Adrian address this grammar issue is to help him raise his own awareness of the grammatical form through direct teaching and then help Adrian employ the correct grammar form independently over time.

Krashen's monitor hypothesis asserts that in second language acquisition, a learner can only refine their language production by self-monitoring their output and working to correct their own mistakes. This requires that Adrian is aware of the correct grammar form as well as having the time and attention to focus on correcting his own grammar. With Krashen's theory in mind, the teacher should first try to assess if Adrian is able to successfully identify the correct grammar form on a targeted formative assessment without any prior instruction. Regardless of whether or not Adrian does successfully add plural -s indicators to plural words, he may need explicit instruction or

157

reinforcement of the concept to make sure he understands it fully. If he is able to succeed on the initial assessment, he may just not be putting the effort into monitoring his own speech and needs to be coached.

A good way to start Adrian off on self-monitoring is to begin a targeted correction program. The teacher can discretely remind Adrian when he has made an error in omitting the plural -s. If this is to be effective and inclusive, the teacher needs to limit corrections to times that Adrian won't be put on display in front of the class. As Adrian improves, the teacher should make the cueing more subtle and only ask Adrian to repeat himself, implying that he can make a correction to what he said. Although directly helping Adrian monitor his own grammar is helpful, Adrian is more likely to encounter success if he is able to monitor and correct his grammar in non-school environments.

Sample Constructed Response #3

Read the following scenario and provide an analysis of the teaching method, taking into account the class's assessment results. Provide at least two critiques of the instruction methodology and identify targeted recommendations on how to improve the teacher's instructional practices in areas of student deficits. Be sure to support your recommendations with your knowledge of language acquisition and reading development.

SCENARIO

Mrs. Johnson is reading a challenging fictional passage to her 2nd grade class with new vocabulary words used throughout. She uses a projector to allow the students to follow along as she reads the text. Periodically through the text, Mrs. Johnson switches to recall questions about the plot and characters of the story. She usually waits until about a third of the class has their hands raised before asking a student to provide the answer to the question. The classroom is alphabetically arranged and is set up in groups of four for a project in another subject. The teacher reads the story aloud to the class and is generally able to mediate classroom disruptions.

ASSESSMENT RESULTS

Mrs. Johnson provides an individual assessment to the students to determine if they learned the key vocabulary words and remember the plot and characters of the story. The assessment format was fill-in-the-blank, with an answer bank provided for the vocabulary portion. She found that students' scores showed a fairly normal distribution of scores regarding the vocabulary words, but that there was a steep divide in the results regarding comprehension of the plot and recognition of the characters. Some students performed as expected and were able to recognize the plot with confidence, whereas other students left questions blank or clearly guessed at the questions.

SAMPLE STRONG RESPONSE

Mrs. Johnson's class demonstrates an increased need for improved classroom organization, improved access to the materials during the instruction process, and better implementation of formative assessment during the instruction. Firstly, the divide in the students' assessment results is most likely indicative of distractions during the reading process. Students who were unable to focus on the story while it is being read aloud would inevitably have no knowledge with which to answer the fill-in-the-blank questions. Having the students move to an area circled around the teacher, rather than in groups of four, would be more helpful in gaining the student's attention and minimizing distractions throughout the reading portion of class.

A second factor is that this scenario allowed little time for students to re-read the passage for themselves. The use of a shared text via projector, rather than individual reference materials, is a natural impedance to a student's ability to read the text at their own pace. Displaying a text while reading it aloud can be a helpful way to provide scaffolding to some students, but many students at this age need to be able to re-read the text to remember important plot points.

Mrs. Johnson admirably employed the use of formative assessment throughout the reading-aloud portion of the class, but rather than only waiting for a portion of student hands to be raised, she should allow an appropriate amount of time for the students to review the text by verbally specifying when she will expect an answer ('I'll check back in with you for an answer in a minute and a half'). This time allotment should allow for the students to re-read the portion of the passage in question and think before responding. Then, rather than selecting students only based on who has raised their hand, she should employ a method to choose students who do not commonly answer to assess comprehension on a whole-class level rather than focusing on specific individuals.

159

In summary, Mrs. Johnson's class should be rearranged with a better setup for supporting students' attention during the reading process, along with employing assessment strategies with the whole class in mind. The students should also be given a copy of the passage and enough time to read it at their own pace.

How to Overcome Test Anxiety

Just the thought of taking a test is enough to make most people a little nervous. A test is an important event that can have a long-term impact on your future, so it's important to take it seriously and it's natural to feel anxious about performing well. But just because anxiety is normal, that doesn't mean that it's helpful in test taking, or that you should simply accept it as part of your life. Anxiety can have a variety of effects. These effects can be mild, like making you feel slightly nervous, or severe, like blocking your ability to focus or remember even a simple detail.

If you experience test anxiety—whether severe or mild—it's important to know how to beat it. To discover this, first you need to understand what causes test anxiety.

Causes of Test Anxiety

While we often think of anxiety as an uncontrollable emotional state, it can actually be caused by simple, practical things. One of the most common causes of test anxiety is that a person does not feel adequately prepared for their test. This feeling can be the result of many different issues such as poor study habits or lack of organization, but the most common culprit is time management. Starting to study too late, failing to organize your study time to cover all of the material, or being distracted while you study will mean that you're not well prepared for the test. This may lead to cramming the night before, which will cause you to be physically and mentally exhausted for the test. Poor time management also contributes to feelings of stress, fear, and hopelessness as you realize you are not well prepared but don't know what to do about it.

Other times, test anxiety is not related to your preparation for the test but comes from unresolved fear. This may be a past failure on a test, or poor performance on tests in general. It may come from comparing yourself to others who seem to be performing better or from the stress of living up to expectations. Anxiety may be driven by fears of the future—how failure on this test would affect your educational and career goals. These fears are often completely irrational, but they can still negatively impact your test performance.

Elements of Test Anxiety

As mentioned earlier, test anxiety is considered to be an emotional state, but it has physical and mental components as well. Sometimes you may not even realize that you are suffering from test anxiety until you notice the physical symptoms. These can include trembling hands, rapid heartbeat, sweating, nausea, and tense muscles. Extreme anxiety may lead to fainting or vomiting. Obviously, any of these symptoms can have a negative impact on testing. It is important to recognize them as soon as they begin to occur so that you can address the problem before it damages your performance.

The mental components of test anxiety include trouble focusing and inability to remember learned information. During a test, your mind is on high alert, which can help you recall information and stay focused for an extended period of time. However, anxiety interferes with your mind's natural processes, causing you to blank out, even on the questions you know well. The strain of testing during anxiety makes it difficult to stay focused, especially on a test that may take several hours. Extreme anxiety can take a huge mental toll, making it difficult not only to recall test information but even to understand the test questions or pull your thoughts together.

Effects of Test Anxiety

Test anxiety is like a disease—if left untreated, it will get progressively worse. Anxiety leads to poor performance, and this reinforces the feelings of fear and failure, which in turn lead to poor performances on subsequent tests. It can grow from a mild nervousness to a crippling condition. If allowed to progress, test anxiety can have a big impact on your schooling, and consequently on your future.

Test anxiety can spread to other parts of your life. Anxiety on tests can become anxiety in any stressful situation, and blanking on a test can turn into panicking in a job situation. But fortunately, you don't have to let anxiety rule your testing and determine your grades. There are a number of relatively simple steps you can take to move past anxiety and function normally on a test and in the rest of life.

Physical Steps for Beating Test Anxiety

While test anxiety is a serious problem, the good news is that it can be overcome. It doesn't have to control your ability to think and remember information. While it may take time, you can begin taking steps today to beat anxiety.

Just as your first hint that you may be struggling with anxiety comes from the physical symptoms, the first step to treating it is also physical. Rest is crucial for having a clear, strong mind. If you are tired, it is much easier to give in to anxiety. But if you establish good sleep habits, your body and mind will be ready to perform optimally, without the strain of exhaustion. Additionally, sleeping well helps you to retain information better, so you're more likely to recall the answers when you see the test questions.

Getting good sleep means more than going to bed on time. It's important to allow your brain time to relax. Take study breaks from time to time so it doesn't get overworked, and don't study right before bed. Take time to rest your mind before trying to rest your body, or you may find it difficult to fall asleep.

Along with sleep, other aspects of physical health are important in preparing for a test. Good nutrition is vital for good brain function. Sugary foods and drinks may give a burst of energy but this burst is followed by a crash, both physically and emotionally. Instead, fuel your body with protein and vitamin-rich foods.

Also, drink plenty of water. Dehydration can lead to headaches and exhaustion, especially if your brain is already under stress from the rigors of the test. Particularly if your test is a long one, drink water during the breaks. And if possible, take an energy-boosting snack to eat between sections.

Along with sleep and diet, a third important part of physical health is exercise. Maintaining a steady workout schedule is helpful, but even taking 5-minute study breaks to walk can help get your blood pumping faster and clear your head. Exercise also releases endorphins, which contribute to a positive feeling and can help combat test anxiety.

When you nurture your physical health, you are also contributing to your mental health. If your body is healthy, your mind is much more likely to be healthy as well. So take time to rest, nourish your body with healthy food and water, and get moving as much as possible. Taking these physical steps will make you stronger and more able to take the mental steps necessary to overcome test anxiety.

Mental Steps for Beating Test Anxiety

Working on the mental side of test anxiety can be more challenging, but as with the physical side, there are clear steps you can take to overcome it. As mentioned earlier, test anxiety often stems from lack of preparation, so the obvious solution is to prepare for the test. Effective studying may be the most important weapon you have for beating test anxiety, but you can and should employ several other mental tools to combat fear.

First, boost your confidence by reminding yourself of past success—tests or projects that you aced. If you're putting as much effort into preparing for this test as you did for those, there's no reason you should expect to fail here. Work hard to prepare; then trust your preparation.

Second, surround yourself with encouraging people. It can be helpful to find a study group, but be sure that the people you're around will encourage a positive attitude. If you spend time with others who are anxious or cynical, this will only contribute to your own anxiety. Look for others who are motivated to study hard from a desire to succeed, not from a fear of failure.

Third, reward yourself. A test is physically and mentally tiring, even without anxiety, and it can be helpful to have something to look forward to. Plan an activity following the test, regardless of the outcome, such as going to a movie or getting ice cream.

When you are taking the test, if you find yourself beginning to feel anxious, remind yourself that you know the material. Visualize successfully completing the test. Then take a few deep, relaxing breaths and return to it. Work through the questions carefully but with confidence, knowing that you are capable of succeeding.

Developing a healthy mental approach to test taking will also aid in other areas of life. Test anxiety affects more than just the actual test—it can be damaging to your mental health and even contribute to depression. It's important to beat test anxiety before it becomes a problem for more than testing.

Study Strategy

Being prepared for the test is necessary to combat anxiety, but what does being prepared look like? You may study for hours on end and still not feel prepared. What you need is a strategy for test prep. The next few pages outline our recommended steps to help you plan out and conquer the challenge of preparation.

STEP 1: SCOPE OUT THE TEST

Learn everything you can about the format (multiple choice, essay, etc.) and what will be on the test. Gather any study materials, course outlines, or sample exams that may be available. Not only will this help you to prepare, but knowing what to expect can help to alleviate test anxiety.

STEP 2: MAP OUT THE MATERIAL

Look through the textbook or study guide and make note of how many chapters or sections it has. Then divide these over the time you have. For example, if a book has 15 chapters and you have five days to study, you need to cover three chapters each day. Even better, if you have the time, leave an extra day at the end for overall review after you have gone through the material in depth.

If time is limited, you may need to prioritize the material. Look through it and make note of which sections you think you already have a good grasp on, and which need review. While you are studying, skim quickly through the familiar sections and take more time on the challenging parts.

Write out your plan so you don't get lost as you go. Having a written plan also helps you feel more in control of the study, so anxiety is less likely to arise from feeling overwhelmed at the amount to cover.

STEP 3: GATHER YOUR TOOLS

Decide what study method works best for you. Do you prefer to highlight in the book as you study and then go back over the highlighted portions? Or do you type out notes of the important information? Or is it helpful to make flashcards that you can carry with you? Assemble the pens, index cards, highlighters, post-it notes, and any other materials you may need so you won't be distracted by getting up to find things while you study.

If you're having a hard time retaining the information or organizing your notes, experiment with different methods. For example, try color-coding by subject with colored pens, highlighters, or post-it notes. If you learn better by hearing, try recording yourself reading your notes so you can listen while in the car, working out, or simply sitting at your desk. Ask a friend to quiz you from your flashcards, or try teaching someone the material to solidify it in your mind.

STEP 4: CREATE YOUR ENVIRONMENT

It's important to avoid distractions while you study. This includes both the obvious distractions like visitors and the subtle distractions like an uncomfortable chair (or a too-comfortable couch that makes you want to fall asleep). Set up the best study environment possible: good lighting and a comfortable work area. If background music helps you focus, you may want to turn it on, but otherwise keep the room quiet. If you are using a computer to take notes, be sure you don't have any other windows open, especially applications like social media, games, or anything else that could distract you. Silence your phone and turn off notifications. Be sure to keep water close by so you stay hydrated while you study (but avoid unhealthy drinks and snacks).

Also, take into account the best time of day to study. Are you freshest first thing in the morning? Try to set aside some time then to work through the material. Is your mind clearer in the afternoon or evening? Schedule your study session then. Another method is to study at the same time of day that you will take the test, so that your brain gets used to working on the material at that time and will be ready to focus at test time.

STEP 5: STUDY!

Once you have done all the study preparation, it's time to settle into the actual studying. Sit down, take a few moments to settle your mind so you can focus, and begin to follow your study plan. Don't give in to distractions or let yourself procrastinate. This is your time to prepare so you'll be ready to fearlessly approach the test. Make the most of the time and stay focused.

Of course, you don't want to burn out. If you study too long you may find that you're not retaining the information very well. Take regular study breaks. For example, taking five minutes out of every hour to walk briskly, breathing deeply and swinging your arms, can help your mind stay fresh.

As you get to the end of each chapter or section, it's a good idea to do a quick review. Remind yourself of what you learned and work on any difficult parts. When you feel that you've mastered the material, move on to the next part. At the end of your study session, briefly skim through your notes again.

But while review is helpful, cramming last minute is NOT. If at all possible, work ahead so that you won't need to fit all your study into the last day. Cramming overloads your brain with more information than it can process and retain, and your tired mind may struggle to recall even

164

previously learned information when it is overwhelmed with last-minute study. Also, the urgent nature of cramming and the stress placed on your brain contribute to anxiety. You'll be more likely to go to the test feeling unprepared and having trouble thinking clearly.

So don't cram, and don't stay up late before the test, even just to review your notes at a leisurely pace. Your brain needs rest more than it needs to go over the information again. In fact, plan to finish your studies by noon or early afternoon the day before the test. Give your brain the rest of the day to relax or focus on other things, and get a good night's sleep. Then you will be fresh for the test and better able to recall what you've studied.

STEP 6: TAKE A PRACTICE TEST

Many courses offer sample tests, either online or in the study materials. This is an excellent resource to check whether you have mastered the material, as well as to prepare for the test format and environment.

Check the test format ahead of time: the number of questions, the type (multiple choice, free response, etc.), and the time limit. Then create a plan for working through them. For example, if you have 30 minutes to take a 60-question test, your limit is 30 seconds per question. Spend less time on the questions you know well so that you can take more time on the difficult ones.

If you have time to take several practice tests, take the first one open book, with no time limit. Work through the questions at your own pace and make sure you fully understand them. Gradually work up to taking a test under test conditions: sit at a desk with all study materials put away and set a timer. Pace yourself to make sure you finish the test with time to spare and go back to check your answers if you have time.

After each test, check your answers. On the questions you missed, be sure you understand why you missed them. Did you misread the question (tests can use tricky wording)? Did you forget the information? Or was it something you hadn't learned? Go back and study any shaky areas that the practice tests reveal.

Taking these tests not only helps with your grade, but also aids in combating test anxiety. If you're already used to the test conditions, you're less likely to worry about it, and working through tests until you're scoring well gives you a confidence boost. Go through the practice tests until you feel comfortable, and then you can go into the test knowing that you're ready for it.

Test Tips

On test day, you should be confident, knowing that you've prepared well and are ready to answer the questions. But aside from preparation, there are several test day strategies you can employ to maximize your performance.

First, as stated before, get a good night's sleep the night before the test (and for several nights before that, if possible). Go into the test with a fresh, alert mind rather than staying up late to study.

Try not to change too much about your normal routine on the day of the test. It's important to eat a nutritious breakfast, but if you normally don't eat breakfast at all, consider eating just a protein bar. If you're a coffee drinker, go ahead and have your normal coffee. Just make sure you time it so that the caffeine doesn't wear off right in the middle of your test. Avoid sugary beverages, and drink enough water to stay hydrated but not so much that you need a restroom break 10 minutes into the test. If your test isn't first thing in the morning, consider going for a walk or doing a light workout before the test to get your blood flowing.

Allow yourself enough time to get ready, and leave for the test with plenty of time to spare so you won't have the anxiety of scrambling to arrive in time. Another reason to be early is to select a good seat. It's helpful to sit away from doors and windows, which can be distracting. Find a good seat, get out your supplies, and settle your mind before the test begins.

When the test begins, start by going over the instructions carefully, even if you already know what to expect. Make sure you avoid any careless mistakes by following the directions.

Then begin working through the questions, pacing yourself as you've practiced. If you're not sure on an answer, don't spend too much time on it, and don't let it shake your confidence. Either skip it and come back later, or eliminate as many wrong answers as possible and guess among the remaining ones. Don't dwell on these questions as you continue—put them out of your mind and focus on what lies ahead.

Be sure to read all of the answer choices, even if you're sure the first one is the right answer. Sometimes you'll find a better one if you keep reading. But don't second-guess yourself if you do immediately know the answer. Your gut instinct is usually right. Don't let test anxiety rob you of the information you know.

If you have time at the end of the test (and if the test format allows), go back and review your answers. Be cautious about changing any, since your first instinct tends to be correct, but make sure you didn't misread any of the questions or accidentally mark the wrong answer choice. Look over any you skipped and make an educated guess.

At the end, leave the test feeling confident. You've done your best, so don't waste time worrying about your performance or wishing you could change anything. Instead, celebrate the successful completion of this test. And finally, use this test to learn how to deal with anxiety even better next time.

Review Video: Test Anxiety
Visit mometrix.com/academy and enter code: 100340

Important Qualification

Not all anxiety is created equal. If your test anxiety is causing major issues in your life beyond the classroom or testing center, or if you are experiencing troubling physical symptoms related to your anxiety, it may be a sign of a serious physiological or psychological condition. If this sounds like your situation, we strongly encourage you to seek professional help.

Additional Bonus Material

Due to our efforts to try to keep this book to a manageable length, we've created a link that will give you access to all of your additional bonus material:

mometrix.com/bonus948/texesscitread